HMS EAGLET

The Story of the Royal Naval Reserves On Merseyside

Bob Evans

Eaglet

First Published 2003 by Countyvise Limited, 14 Appin Road, Birkenhead, Wirral CH41 9HH in conjunction with the author R. A. Evans

British Library Cataloguing in Publication Data.
A catalogue record for this book is available from the British Library.

ISBN 1 901231 380

CONTENTS

Picture on Cover:
Tramp was held on the ship's books as an AB and qualified for rations. He was just a stray found in Eaglet's shed, but then lived in the luxury of life on board. We voted him to be the best looking matelot in the ship.

LOOK OUT AT SEA

Watching, watching, ever watching,
Combing every fleck of sea.
Counting wave tops, always searching
Judging hour's eternity.

Constant pitching, rolling, dipping,
Seldom poised on even keel.
Chilling winds bring salt tears dripping
Glasses frozen to the feel.

Blistering eyelids scarcely waver
Scanning near and groping far
Looking for the hostile raider
Minutes dragging to the hour.

Hours seem short with pleasured comfort
Minutes long with trying strain
Sweeping for the threatening danger
Weeping seas to sweep again.

(Found in the 'Ditty Box' magazine dated 1942.
Written by Lieutenant-Commander M. Horday, RNVR.)

This book is dedicated to the memory of friends, both past and present and to the companionship we shared.

'And all I ask is a merry yarn from a laughing fellow rover,
And a quiet sleep and a sweet dream when the long trick's over.'

Sea Fever ... John Masefield

FOREWORD

It is very fitting that, in this Centenary Year of the Royal Naval Reserve, Canon Bob Evans has chosen to tell the story of HMS EAGLET and the outstanding contribution made by members of the Reserves during the first hundred years. With his extensive experience of maritime affairs in the Liverpool area and his long attachment to the RNR, there could be no better man for the task. Having had the privilege of knowing Bob for many years, I have always revelled in the wit and warmth of his uplifting company whenever we have met. A natural raconteur, he also possesses that rare gift of being able to transpose his sparkling sense of humour onto the written page as readers of his previous books will readily attest. This volume is no different and, as ever, represents many long hours of painstaking research. I am delighted and honoured to have been asked to write the Foreword.

My own first recollection of HMS EAGLET and the RNR on Merseyside stems from the 1960s when I was at school 'across the water' at King William's College, Isle of Man. The RN Section of the Combined Cadet Force, of which I was a member, enjoyed occasional visits from the staff of HMS EAGLET to add some much-needed realism to its training. On one such occasion, I believe I gave Roy Humphreys Jones, a subsequent Commanding Officer, something of a shock when, in reply to his rather weary (because it usually attracted a negative response) question of whether any of us were considering a Naval career, I replied that I was. Thereafter, he gave me the greatest possible encouragement and always showed a close interest in my career whenever our paths crossed in later years.

Since those days I have come to know Merseyside and HMS EAGLET even better, both through a number of visits by submarines in which I have served and also by regular attendance, with members of my family, at the annual commemoration of the Battle of the Atlantic. Liverpool was not just a Base Port for my grandfather, Captain F. J. Walker CB DSO***, during those difficult days of the Second World War, but also a home for him, my grandmother and their children. The vital role of HMS EAGLET during the war years is chronicled elegantly within by the author, and my family forged many enduring friendships from that time.

During my 36 years in the Royal Navy, I have had the frequent pleasure and benefit of working with the men and women of the Royal Naval Reserve. I believe it is fair to say that, without their selfless, loyal and highly professional service alongside their RN counterparts, the United Kingdom's ability to participate successfully in recent periods of conflict, such as the Falklands and two Gulf Wars, might have been somewhat different. Today, in the face of some significant manpower shortfalls, the Royal Navy depends heavily on RNR personnel to fill a number of important posts both ashore and at sea. Indeed I have several Reservists on my own staff, who prove daily that they are easily the equal of their Regular colleagues. I have nothing but the most profound respect for the Royal Naval Reserve and am so pleased that Bob Evans has now added another key, interlocking piece to the jigsaw of this country's proud maritime history.

Captain P. J. Walker, Royal Navy
Captain Faslane Flotilla
August 2003

PREFACE

The request that this book be written came from the Sea Urchins - the Liverpool Royal Naval Reserve Officers Club - and I delighted that they sponsored the work. Naturally, all profits will be given to nautical charities. The purpose was clear. This book marks the Centenary of the Royal Naval Reserves in Liverpool. The Royal Naval Voluntary Reserve on Merseyside was founded in March 1904 and based in HMS Eagle, as she was first named. In the past there have been a number of attempts at the formidable task of writing the history with little to show for the efforts involved, apart from lists of dates and five large boxes of undated newspaper cuttings and a clutter of nothing very much. However, it was sufficient to prime the pump for my research.

Happily, I had written a brief outline of the Eaglet Story in my book The Training Ships of Liverpool. This has helped. However, history is much more than dates. It is the life story of those who have preceded us and, possibly to our surprise, it is also the saga of our own lives. We are part of the history! My request for help was akin to drawing a tooth, but once started, full sets of molars appeared. Inevitably, most anecdotes were repetitious and much editing was needed.

Where possible tales are acknowledged in the script, but this leaves so much material without ownership ... and much has been cannibalised. The majority of newspaper cuttings existed with no visible date or name of the paper, but obviously the majority of the material must be attributed to the Liverpool Post or Echo as the main local source. Where possible, that presumption has been acknowledged.

The staff of the Liverpool Central Libraries Record Office and Local History Office not only allowed me to withdraw material, but were ever cheerfully helpful. Again, it is almost impossible to indicate the source of many snippets of information.

Photographs were a far bigger headache. The vast majority had no dates, no names and no source of ownership. They were rather varied in quality, but some are precious and could not be omitted. I am greatly indebted to an old friend, Neville Willasey, RNVR, former Picture Editor of the Liverpool Post and Echo, both for his advice and research, and to Colin Hunt, their Chief Librarian, without whom many photographs would have not been produced. Sadly space has restricted the usage of many excellent photographs. Happily most of the material that I have collected will be deposited in our archives and placed in the Central Libraries Local History Department.

Much of the material in this book has technical overtones specific to the Royal Navy. No RNR Padre would claim such expertise! So I am much indebted to another old friend, Commander Harry Harley, RN, who has made a threefold contribution ... he read and revised the script, he helped research and correct the naval content and he was talked into making his own personal contribution to the Eaglet Story.

It is no surprise that the current Regular and Reserve Staff of our Royal Naval Headquarters have afforded time and complete entry into any archival memorabilia. Without their support and enthusiasm for the project, during a very stressful period for the Royal Navy, it would have been impossible to complete the book.

I am grateful to Captain Patrick Walker, RN, the Captain of the Faslane Flotilla, not only for his encouragement and interest over the years, but for the immense friendship that he has shown in Merseyside's nautical affairs. He was a natural choice to write the Foreword.

All the members of my family over the years have proved themselves to be excellent critics and proof readers, skilled computer photographic exponents, willing printing machinists, food and wine providers and, above all, superb and tolerant listeners to the endless, single-minded enthusiasm of the author for his subject.

Jean and John Emmerson of Countyvise Limited are not only responsible for the printing and publishing, they have always given friendship, laughter and encouragement. However, any blemishes, mistakes, misjudgements and omissions can only be attributed to me ... with apologies.

This book is about friendships in good times and not so good times, it is about companionship that stretches across the centuries and, most' importantly, it is about pride and loyalty and commitment.

This is the story of the Royal Naval Reserves on Merseyside.

Bob Evans
The tail end of 2003
Liverpool

ADMIRAL
Leaps tall buildings at a single bound.
Is more powerful than a locomotive.
Is faster than a speeding bullet.
Walks on water.
    GIVES POLICY TO GOD

CHIEF PETTY OFFICER
Lifts buildings and walks under then.
Kicks locomotives off the tracks.
Catches speeding bullets in his teeth and eats them
Freezes water with a single glance
HE IS GOD

HISTORY OF MERSEY DIVISION

1903   Formation of the Royal Naval Volunteer Reserve.

1904   Mersey Division established under the command of the Earl of Lathom in HMS EAGLE and a year later in the Customs House, Liverpool.

1911   Headquarters moved to HMS EAGLE, a 74 gun frigate, commissioned in 1804. The strength of the Division was now six companies of 100 officers and men, four at Liverpool, two outlying companies at Birkenhead and Southport.

1914   World War I - Sussex, Mersey and Clyde Divisions formed into Howe Battalion of the Second Brigade of the RN Division for military, not naval service. The RN Division won undying fame at Gallipoli, Vimy Ridge, Passchendaele and Cambrai.

1922   Mersey Division reformed under the command of Captain W. Maples, RNVR. HMS EAGLE had been renamed HMS EAGLET to enable the RN to commission an aircraft carrier.

1926   The wooden walled HMS EAGLET replaced by a First World War sloop, HMS SIR BEVIS and renamed HMS EAGLET.

1939   HMS WALLACE, a V and W Class Destroyer, attached to the Division to train gun crews.

1939   World War II - 1,000 Officers and men of the Division mobilised for service with the Royal Navy, of whom 120 lost their lives in the conflict. HMS EAGLET commissioned as Base Ship Liverpool wearing the flag of the Commanders-in-Chief Western Approaches, Admiral Sir Percy Noble and Admiral Sir Max Horton; the latter is buried in Liverpool Cathedral.

1946   The Division reformed under Commander, later Captain E N Wood, DSC, VRD, RNR.

1947   MMS1045 attached to the Division as Sea Training Tender and named HMS MERSEY.

1952   RNVR wavy stripes replaced by straight stripes with 'R' in curl.
WRNVR formed.

1953   Golden Jubilee of the RNVR.

1954   HMS AMERTON, Coastal Minesweeper, replaced MMS 1045 as the Division's Sea Tender and renamed HMS MERSEY.

1955   HMS DROXFORD, seaward defence boat, attached to the Division and renamed HMS DEE..

1958   RNVR amalgamated into a new, unified Royal Naval Reserve.

1959   Centenary of the old RNR.
HMS AMERTON replaced by HMS POLLINGTON and renamed HMS MERSEY.

1965   HMS MERSEY with RNR Ship's company made operational visit to West Indies.

1972   HMS EAGLET moved to new shore Headquarters at Princes Dock.
Official opening by Vice Admiral Sir Gilbert Stephenson (The Terror of Tobermory).

1975   HMS MERSEY renamed HMS POLLINGTON and returned to RN service.

1976   HMS CRICHTON repositioned from South Wales Division at the advent of hull sharing post Mitchell report.

1977   HMS HODGESTON repositioned from Severn Division.

1978   HMS CROFTON repositioned from Solent Division.

1981   Division converted to mine hunting and HMS BRERETON repositioned from Tyne Division.

1984   HMS STRIKER (Tracker Class) commissioned and attached to the Division.

1985   HMS STRIKER repositioned to Liverpool University RN Unit.
HMS BRERETON returned to RN Service.

1986   HMS BITER (P2000 Class) commissioned as Sea Tender to the Division.
HMS RIBBLE (Fleet Minesweeper) commissioned as Sea Tender to the Division.

1990   HMS BITER returned to RN Service with Manchester and Salford University Unit.

1991   HMS RIBBLE taken into preservation at Portsmouth.
HMS HUMBER transferred from London Division.

1993   Freedom of Entry into the City of Liverpool was conferred upon HMS EAGLET on 2nd May.
Fiftieth Anniversary of the Battle of Atlantic.

1994   HMS EAGLET re-categorised as a Reserve Training Centre.

1998   The New Headquarter Building opened in October by HRH the Duke of Edinburgh.

2003   The Centenary of the formation of the RNVR.

2004   The Centenary of the formation of Mersey Division RNVR.

"It is on the Navy, under the good providence of God, that our wealth and peace depend."

Charles II (1660 - 1685)

THE SHIPS

Old HMS EAGLET ... ex HMS EAGLE

1800   August Laid down at Northfleet ... HMS EAGLE ... launched 1804.

1859   August Royal Naval Reserve (Merchant Navy) formed.

1862   June 29th Arrived in Liverpool under tow from Spithead to become RNR Headquarters in Queens Dock in place of HMS HASTINGS.

1873   August 5th Liverpool Corps of Royal Naval Artillery Volunteers formed.

1892   March 31st RNAV disbanded.

1904   January 1st Mersey Division RNVR formed.

1904   March 8th First RNVR drill in HMS EAGLE.

1904   HMS EAGLE moved to Salthouse Dock.

1905   RNR returned to HMS EAGLE. RNVR moved to Customs House (prior to this RNR had trained in seagoing cruises).

1911   RNVR returned to HMS EAGLE.

1914   ... 1918 Served as Flagship for SNO Liverpool.

1918   June 8th Renamed HMS EAGLET on launching of new carrier HMS EAGLE.

1921   Mersey Division RNVR reformed.

1926   September 2nd Last drill in HMS EAGLET. Classes marched to new HMS EAGLET.
September 29th Guns removed by floating crane in Salthouse Dock.

1927   February 16th Towed from Liverpool.

1927   April 19th Destroyed by fire at Mostyn.

New HMS EAGLET ... ex HMS SIR BEVIS IRWELL

1918   May 17th Launched from yard of Barclay Curle & Co. as HMS SIR BEVIS.

1920   February 20th Paid off.

1923   September Went to Manchester as HMS IRWELL,
        Headquarters of Manchester Sub-Division, which was
        formed in 1922.

1926   August 25th Returned to Liverpool to relieve old HMS
        EAGLET.

1926   September 2nd Renamed HMS EAGLET. First drill on
        board.

1941   Became Flagship of Admiral Sir Percy Noble C in C
        Western Approaches.

1946   March 1st Mersey Division RNVR reformed.

1958   January 31st RNVR disbanded. Reformed as RNR
        together with old RNR.

1971   March Towed to Garston (Liverpool) breakers yard.

HMS IRWELL ex GOOLE

1918   Built at Goole, but never commissioned. Laid up in
        Gareloch.

1926   September Berthed alongside old HMS EAGLET in
        Salthouse Dock.

1926   September 2nd Renamed HMS IRWELL.

1926   September 4th Went to Manchester.

1931   Manchester Sub-Division disbanded. HMS IRWELL
        towed to Birkenhead.

1932   May 1st Opened as drill ship in Birkenhead.

1939 ... 1945 Served as Depot Ship for minesweepers in
        Wallasey.

1956   Modernised as training ship in Morpeth Dock.

1956   February 16th Towed from Morpeth Dock, Wallasey to
        Salthouse Dock, Liverpool and berthed on HMS
        EAGLET.
        HMS IRWELL was used for radar instruction and social
        events, but was really not needed. In the early sixties she
        was towed to the breakers yard at Garston.

GLOSSARY

AA	Anti-Aircraft
ACR	Admiral Commanding Reserves
ADC	Aide de Camp
AMC	Armed Merchant Cruiser
ASW	Anti-Submarine Warfare
AWNIS	Allied World Wide Navigational Information
BUFFER	Senior Seaman
CINCWA	Commander in Chief Western Approaches
CINCNH	Commander in Chief Naval Home Command
COXSWAN	Senior Pilot and Naval Regulator (MP)
CMS	Coastal Minesweeper
CPO	Chief Petty Officer
CTC	Communication Training Centre
DEMS	Defensively Equipped Merchant Ships
FOIC	Flag Officer in Charge
FTRS	Full Time Reserve Service
GI	Gunnery Instructor
LMEA	Leading Mechanical Engine Room Artificer
	Lieutenant (E) Engineer Officer (S) Supply
	Officer (X) Executive Officer
LL	Low Level
LMS	Loop Magnetic Sweep
LURNU	Liverpool University Royal Naval Unit
MEM	Mechanical Engineer Marine
MCM	Mine Counter Measures
MMS	Motor Mine Sweepers (Mickey Mouse)
MTB	Motor Torpedo Boat
MW	Mine Warfare
NAAFI	Navy, Army and Air Force Institute
NCAGS	Naval Co-operation and Guidance for Shipping
(NCS)	
NCS	Naval Control of Shipping

NORNE	Naval Officer Northern England Region
OOW	Officer of the Watch
PUSSER	Supply Officer
Pusser	Anything naval
RD	Reserve Decoration
RMR	Royal Marine Reserve
RMFVR	Royal Marine Forces Volunteer Reserve
RNAV	Royal Naval Artillery Volunteers
RNCV	Royal Naval Coast Volunteers
RND	Royal Naval Division
RFA	Royal Fleet Auxiliary
RFCA	Reserve Forces and Cadet Associations
RNAS	Royal Naval Air Service
RNR	Royal Naval Reserve
RNVR	Royal Naval Volunteer Reserve
RNXS	Royal Naval Auxiliary Service
RNV(S)R	Royal Naval Volunteer (Supplementary) Reserve
RNV(W)R	Royal Naval Volunteer (Wireless) Reserve
RTC	Reserve Training Centre
STC	Sea Training Centre
TAS	Training Anti-Submarine
V and W	First War destroyers with names starting with these letters.
VRD	Volunteer Reserve Decoration
VD	Volunteer Decoration
WRNVR	Women's Royal Naval Volunteer Reserve
WRNR	Women's Royal Naval Reserve

MARSALA

Chapter One

THE OLD EAGLE
THE MERCHANT NAVY RNR

My contact as a Padre has involved over forty years of work and contact with HMS Eaglet and this has resulted in lasting friendships with the men and women of the RNR. It is one of the finest 'clubs' in the world ... and I was proud to become Eaglet's Chaplain in 1966.

But let us go back to the beginning.

HMS Eagle, as she was originally called, a wooden walled Frigate, was built at Northfleet on the Thames and was launched in February 1804. She was to see a remarkable 123 years of service before a fire destroyed her remains in 1927. For 64 of her later years she was the home base for Naval Reservists at Liverpool. In 1918 the Admiralty reclaimed the name Eagle for a newly converted aircraft carrier and the original bearer of that name assumed the title of HMS Eaglet.

Until the middle 19th century the ships of the Royal Navy were classified by Rate. Eagle was a Third Rate. This system had originally been based upon the rates of pay to which captains of warships had been entitled according to the sizes of the vessels that they commanded. In course of time, this system came to refer to the number of guns that these vessels carried. A First Rate mounted between 100 and 120 guns, the Rate decreasing with the number of guns mounted, until the lowest Rated ships were the Sixth Rate frigates of 20 to 28 guns. Most vessels of the day, like H.M.S. Eagle, were seventy-four gun ships, ideal for the work of patrolling and relatively easy to handle.

The 1954 RNVR Jubilee Review (price two shillings) contained a fascinating article. 'From time immemorial Naval Volunteer Seamen have served in the King's ships under many titles and varying conditions of service. A report of a Naval Committee of 1891 vouches for the existence of Naval Volunteers as far back as the days of Edward the Confessor (1041 - 46). In 1049 mention was made of the inclusion of 42 of 'peoples' ships' with 'the King's ships'. The 'people's ships' were manned by the Lithsmen of London. In the eleventh century the Lithsmen and Buscarls developed into the Corporations of the Cinque and London Portsmen: these were in fact the RNVR of the Middle Ages.

'In the fifteenth and sixteenth centuries many Royal ships, and others for exploration and trade, were manned by 'volunteers'. There were several 'Voluntary Gentlemen' serving as officers with Drake in The Golden Hind. Sir Richard Grenville of The Revenge was perhaps the most famous of the early RNVR officers. The first suggestion, however, of Naval Volunteers as a distinct force was made by Captain John Cochrane, RN, in November 1794, when he offered to raise a Brigade of Naval Volunteers in the Port of London, to be divided into three regiments of 1,000 men each.

'Early in 1798 the question of raising a Naval Volunteer Force was suggested by Captain Home Riggs Popham, RN. On March 14th 1798, the King in Council approved of a memorial from my Lords of the Admiralty proposing the formation of a

'Corps of Sea Fencibles' from the inhabitants of coastal towns, ports, etc., under officers of His Majesty's Navy assisted by 'inferior officers'. On 24th July 1801 Lord Nelson used the Sea Fencibles as part of his command.'

The Sea Fencibles were disbanded in 1810 ... they numbered at that time 61 Captains, 245 Lieutenants and 23,455 men. Nothing happened until on 14th February 1853 it was decided to create a Coast Militia to be called the Royal Navy Coast Volunteers. They were appointed for a year at a time and could be used 'afloat' at no more than 100 leagues from the coast (a league was about three miles). However, they actually served in the Crimean War as the RNCV. This Force was allowed to fall into disuse and along came the Royal Naval Artillery Volunteer Force Act, passed on the 3rd April 1873. This new Force was for Coastal Defence', but also included knowledge of mines, etc. The uniform for the officers was to be similar to the Royal Navy, but the gold stripes were to be wavy. By February 1878 the Liverpool Brigade (founded in 1874) comprised 506 men (including those at the batteries at Bangor, Caernarfon and Southport). The London Brigade, at its own expense, volunteered for service in South Africa for the Zulu War of 1878 - 79. The Brigade was attached to HMS Active's Naval Brigade and hit the headlines. However, the RNAV was disbanded in April 1892.

The creation of the RNVR was largely the result of public interest and demand. Public meetings were organised all over the country and they led on January 15th 1902 to the setting up of a Naval Reserve Committee by the Admiralty. The result was the 'Naval Forces Act,' passed on 30th June 1903 to establish a Force to be called 'The Royal Naval Volunteer Reserve'.

But let us return to Eagle.

In February 1800, the contract for the construction of a seventy-four-gun ship was awarded to Thomas Pitcher, a shipbuilder at Northfleet in Kent. Four years and three days after the placing of the order, His Majesty's Eagle was launched into the Thames on the 27th February 1804.

In those days a ship was manned by volunteers, the pressed men, the quotamen etc., and, as with her armament, so the number of men in the ship's company was fixed by Establishment. Eagle carried some 600 men. Her officers were the captain and five lieutenants, a master and his mate and a lieutenant of marines with his detachment consisting of about ninety-six scarlet-coated rank and file. The non-military officers were the surgeon and his assistant, the chaplain and the purser - these gentlemen carried no rank. Her seamen ratings numbered some 556 men and thirty boys exclusive of officers' servants and 'widows' men'. The latter were non-existent and in theory amounted to one per cent of the actual crew. The books of Eagle carried about six 'widows' men' as her share of these mythical sailors, whose pay and allowances, by very old naval custom, provided a fund from which pensions were paid to the widows of officers. These fictitious 'widows' men' continued to be borne on the books of HM ships until about 1830 and their rate of pay was that of an able seaman. Nelson's blind eye was put to good use and saved much bureaucracy.

Fitted for sea at Woolwich Dockyard, Eagle was commissioned for service in the Channel Fleet. The first entry in her log is dated 16th March 1804. The next day, according to the official notes, she 'hoisted the flag of Rear-Admiral Thornborough, who came aboard with his retinue'. The first commander of HMS Eagle was Captain David Colby, RN.

Eagle was part of the blockading squadron and life aboard in the Channel was damp, cold and miserable. The weather was always bad and visibility down to half a mile most days. The next year it was the same chore off Spain, but the French made a dash for the West Indies and Eagle joined in the general chase. Nothing of note happened.

After Trafalgar in 1805, with Captain Charles Rowley in command, she sailed for the Mediterranean in the November and accomplished the surrender of the French Garrison at Capri. Next came an expedition to Walcheren and Eagle was employed as a troop-ship, conveying men and horses and guns across the North Sea.

In 1810 she was employed at Cadiz, on the Mediterranean Station, and in the Gulf of Venice until 1814, after which she returned to Chatham and was paid off. Then she was laid up until 1844. During that time she was cut down to a frigate and treated as a Fourth Rate of 50-guns.

Re-commissioned at Chatham, she served off the South East Coast of South America, the West Indies and on the Mediterranean Station. Eagle returned to England in February 1848, and was paid off at Devonport where she remained in reserve until 1856. Then she was fitted for Coast Guard Service and was stationed at Falmouth until 1858 before moving to Milford Haven. Finally she returned to Portsmouth and there she was paid off.

She was next fitted as a training ship, and stationed in Southampton Water in November 1860, where she remained until March 1862, when she again returned to Portsmouth to be paid off once more. Finally, she was to serve as RNR drill ship at the Port of Liverpool, where she arrived in June 1862.

During her service afloat, the Eagle wore an admiral's flag three times. She was flagship at the Texel in 1804, again on the South East Coast of America Station in 1844 and yet again seventy years later when she became flagship in Liverpool between 1914 and 1919. She was never involved in action, but gave sterling service to the Royal Navy.

Old Eagle with the Custom House in background.

The Fleet Reserve was instituted in 1852 and continuous service in the Navy in the following year. Obviously it was finally realised that there would be a dearth of trained seamen in the Navy for some years, and particularly in time of war. Permanent service was a new idea.

In 1853 the Naval Volunteer Act provided for the recall of naval pensioners and for the retention in the Navy in times of emergency of men who had completed their engagements. This power was exercised in the next century during the Korea and Suez periods. The Royal Naval Reserve (Volunteer) Act was passed in 1859 and authorised a Reserve of trained merchant seamen. It was anxiety about the growing strength of the German Navy that led to the Naval Forces Act of 1903, which instituted the Royal Naval Volunteer Reserve, for the first time a Reserve of civilian volunteers. Such was the interest in this Reserve that some of its Headquarters were built from private funds.

Recruitment of merchant seamen into the Royal Naval Reserve commenced in 1861 and officers in the merchant service were first offered commissions in the following year. Times change and today there are no merchant ratings in the RNR, although the officers remain. To train these newcomers in the ways of the Navy, three drill-ships were established - in London, North Shields and Liverpool. So commenced the long association of Her Majesty's Ship Eagle, the Naval Volunteers and the Port of Liverpool. The first Liverpool drill-ship was the old warship Hastings that had been District Ship of the Liverpool Coast Guard District, but she did not remain long here and departed for Queenstown upon the arrival of her successor, Eagle in 1862.

To understand the character of those early members of the RNR we must look at the men involved. Such a man was George Cawley. His career has been sketched by Captain Harry Hignett, FNI, Vice-President of the Liverpool Nautical Research

Society. The article appeared in the March edition of Seaways, 1987.

'George Cawley was born on July 4th 1839. He began his career at sea in 1853 as a ship's boy, the lowest form of life, on the most humble of coasting vessels at the age of 14, rising to become one of the few Commanders, RNR, of his day. His father, a Bristol cabinet-maker, was able to send him to the local nautical academy for two years at the age of 12. His second voyage was as cook! There followed trips in various vessels until in January 1867 he passed as second mate in Bristol.

'Needing a wider sea experience he came to Liverpool to sail in Champion of the Seas, a crack ocean vessel, claimed by some to have made one of the fastest passages ever to Australia, including one period of 24 hours at an average speed of 17 knots! On arrival home in 1861 he joined the Royal Naval Volunteers, later that year named the RNR, as a deck rating - initially there were no commissioned ranks.

'Passing the 'only mate' examination on January 22 1862, he sailed on the Margaret as mate from Bristol. The ship was stranded on the Canadian coast and declared a total loss. Involvement with the American Civil War delayed his return home. Eventually, having done more trips out of Liverpool, he sat his 'first mate' ticket in 1863. In time he obtained his master's 'full' certificate. Many voyages followed with hair raising adventures and earning extra income from the sale of freight; he married a Bristol girl. When he finally left the Richard Rylands, another East Indiaman, having been in command for two years, he reported to the RNR base in Liverpool, HMS Eagle, where he was commissioned Sub-Lieutenant, RNR.

'During the summer of 1878, Cawley came to Liverpool to speak to a new shipping agent that was starting a new shipping line. This visit resulted in his appointment as master of the Clan

Alpine on the maiden voyage, the first of Messrs Cayser Irvine's fleet, sailing from Liverpool to Bombay. His last voyage was in 1880.

'In 1883 a number of pilots based around the Bristol Channel began to work towards the formation of an Association of United Kingdom Pilots. George Cawley became the president of UKPA for some twenty years. He was a remarkable man.

'He was always interested in promoting matters allied to the prosperity of the British Merchant Marine and the RNR. He was promoted Lieutenant, RNR, in 1874 and spent much of his leisure time in HMS Daedalus, the RNR base. Promoted Commander in 1894, he was placed on the retired list in 1895.

'In 1910 Commander George Cawley died after being one of the first to be awarded the newly-instituted Reserve Decoration.'

Captain Harry Hignett has written another article that concerns us in Liverpool. It was published in the November edition 1985 in Seaways.

It tells of the career of Captain C.H.E. Judkins, who was a senior master of the Cunard Line from 1842 to 1871 and was also the first to be designated Commodore of the Cunard Fleet. Born in Chester in 1809, he married in 1837 and lived on Wirral. The McIver Brothers first maiden crossing to Canada began on 4th July 1839, the ship being the Britannia. There were four ships, Acacia, Britannia, Caledonia and Columbia. The chief officer on the maiden voyage of Acacia in the August was Judkins. He stepped down in rank to make the voyage, but took over Britannia in the October.

'An outcry for better management of ships induced the British Government to introduce a system of certification for shipmaster in 1845 and in the following year brought in voluntary examinations for officers. These were to be conducted by local marine boards, but at Liverpool the Pilotage Committee (reluctantly) took on the task.

'Candidates were invited to apply for examination in one of three categories: only mate, mate, and master. And, additionally, candidates for master who attained a high standard in nautical astronomy, astronomical navigation and surveying were awarded a master's certificate 1st Class Extra. The certificates were numbered and distributed to the several examination centres. For this reason the order of numbering does not accord with the order of issue; the first certificate issued was on the Northeast coast, but its number was in the 200s.

'Charles Judkins entered the examination at Liverpool without even taking a voyage off. He was successful and on 14th November 1846 received certificate No. 153 as Master 1st Class Extra.'

Judkins was a remarkable man. During the second voyage of the Persia (she carried 150 passengers and 1,050 tons of cargo with a crew of 440!) he regained the Atlantic speed record for Britain with an eastward passage of 13.47 knots. For a couple of years Judkins and Persia lorded their superiority on the Atlantic.

'He could be awkward at sea. For instance, he is said to have been staring over the bridge rails in fog when a woman passenger called up to him: "Tell me, Captain, is it always as foggy as this on the Grand Banks?" To which Judkins is said to have replied: "How the devil should I know? I don't live here!" On another occasion, in a similar situation he was asked: "Why are you going so fast in fog?" At which Judkins snapped: "The quicker you go through it, the quicker you are out of it!"

'In 1861 the Government began recruiting into what

initially was to be known as the Royal Naval Volunteers; merchant seamen who would provide crews in the event of war ... and avoid the use of the hated press-gangs.

'Many ship's officers joined the RNV, taking lower deck ranks to do so, for there was no entry into commissioned status. In 1862 it was decided to change the name of the RNV to Royal Naval Reserve, a title that had previously been applied only to former RN officers. Merchant Navy Officers were invited to apply for commissions in the RNR. Two types of commission were available: active and honorary. The holders of the latter were not expected to train for active service; it was merely that they could command naval vessels in times of emergency and be subjected to naval discipline.

'The first RNR commission was that of Honourable Lieutenant, which was granted on 22nd February 1862 to C.H.E. Judkins and bore the seniority of 17th November 1846, the date of Judkin's master's certificate. There were other commissions granted later with dates giving superiority over Judkins, but against Judkins' name in the Board of Trade records of service is the cipher RNV 0001 (there was in the beginning some confusion as to the name of the new service).'

Judkins actually sailed as master on the maiden voyages of seven top-class passenger vessels. From 1839 he had only sailed in paddle-steamers. In 1868 a screw-driven steamer took the westbound record using only three-quarters of the paddle steamer fuel. It was to be the end of paddle-steamers.

Judkins retired in 1870, shortly after giving evidence to the Parliamentary Select Committee on Pilotage, and became a nautical consultant in Liverpool. He was involved with many Liverpool seamen's charities and was a member of the governors of the training ship HMS Conway.

Captain Hignett concluded his article: 'On his death in

1878 he was buried with full naval honours. His estate took a couple of years to value, but in 1880 it was assessed at over £40,000. Not bad for a young man coming from nowhere; and with 500 crossings of the Atlantic I think he earned it.'

The story of HMS Eagle has been written by John Smart and Edward Jones and was presented as a paper, on the 13th November 1958, to the Liverpool Nautical Research Society. I was privileged to be the President of that illustrious Society for a number of years and have received permission to recall some details from that paper and much of this chapter is the result of that research.

'The drill-ship Eagle arrived from Spithead in tow of HM paddle sloop Geyser at 4.40 a.m. on Sunday, June 29th 1862. In the excitement of reporting the fraternal conflict between Confederates and Federals, Monday's paper overlooked any mention of her arrival, but a few days later she took up her berth in the north east corner of the old Queen's Dock. In those days the layout of the docks in that area differed considerably from that which now prevails. Entrance was by means of the Queen's Basin leading into Queen's Dock. King's Dock, much smaller than the present dock, was entered by a short passage on the north side of the Basin. Despite her having been in Liverpool for over sixty years, very little information is available with regard to the ship or her berths. One supposes that being such a familiar feature of the dockland of her day she was taken very much for granted.

'The Royal Naval Reserve continued to drill aboard her until 1911, her Captain carried the rank of a Commander, RN. Between 1862 and 1908 this appointment was held in succession by nineteen officers, and she had the honour of claiming that, of all the RNR centres in operation in 1898, those of Liverpool and Stornoway had trained a number of men far in excess of any others in the country.

'The Royal Naval Volunteer Reserve is seen to be descended from the Royal Naval Artillery Volunteers. Hitherto, such volunteers as had been available were professional seamen, but the RNAV opened enlistment to young civilians who were interested in matters naval. The Liverpool Corps of the RNAV was formed in 1873 with headquarters in HMS Eagle. Each Corps was composed of two or three batteries, each consisting of a Sub-Lieutenant, a Chief Petty Officer, 1st and 2nd class Petty Officers and from fifty to seventy gunners. The combined Liverpool and Southport Corps united to form the Liverpool Brigade in 1876. A brigade comprised from four to six batteries with an establishment of about 450 men.

'The volunteer gunners were intensely enthusiastic and at its zenith the Brigade had units in Liverpool, Southport, Bangor, Caernarfon and Birkenhead. By this time Eagle had changed berth from Queen's to King's Dock and in the 1880's lay at what is now the berth of the Booth Steam Ship Company at North 2 King's Dock. Unfortunately, as had happened with the Sea Fencibles (men recruited for the defence of UK only and dating back to Nelson's time) and again with the Royal Naval Coast Volunteers (started in 1853), official encouragement was lacking. The guns were vintage pieces, the gear scanty and there was little or no provision for sea training. In effect the gunners were soldiers dressed as seamen. An interesting feature of the uniform was that the blue jean collars had waved tapes, the officers' silver stripes were waved and both these features were revived in later years upon the formation of the RNVR. The waved lace, in gold instead of silver, continued to distinguish RNVR officers until recently replaced by the regular pattern, but can still be seen upon the sleeves of officers of the Sea Cadet Corps.

'In 1892 the Admiralty who, in truth to tell, had never cared for anything less than the genuine article, saw fit to disband these eager young men and today an In Memoriam notice preserved aboard HMS Eagle proclaims that the RNAV 'Died of Neglect' '.

The Board of Admiralty was not as ready as the War Office to accept volunteers and to direct their enthusiasm into useful channels. One suspects that the formation of the RNVR was accepted sceptically by authority and not with the enthusiasm it deserved. However, time to the present day has proved the value of the Royal Naval Voluntary Reserve and the enduring worth of volunteers.

John Masefeld was a cadet on board HMS Conway, 1891 to 1894. He wrote his book entitled 'HMS Conway' in 1933. His account of his time in Conway was written in 1944. That book was called 'New Chum' and in it he recalled his first encounter with Eagle.

'There just ahead was Eagle, with Dick at her gangway. Dick hailed us and told us to come on board. We went up, feeling ourselves in luck. Below, she seemed like a ship of another world. Above, she was boxed in with a roomy superstructure, in which sea cannon were mounted. Naval reservists lived on board whilst doing their drills; and drills were in progress as we entered. Dick had a relative on board, a Lieutenant, who welcomed us all and showed us the ship.

'I was often aboard her later; but I cannot forget the thrill of that first time. The modern Navy was divided into guns' crews about us. A Lieutenant, taking the drill, was directing the guns upon parts of the ships near-by. He was calling 'Port Battery,

upon the bow, Starboard Battery, upon the beam. Carry on.'
Then some numbers hove upon wheels, and other numbers
hauled upon side tackles, and the cannon swung on to their
targets. Our host told us to come on down; he showed us a hatch;
and in an instant, I was away from the modern Navy aboard the
Hispaniola, going below into the eighteenth century.

'The hatchway rail was coach whipped with new white
line, a miracle of plaiting; then, we were on what had once been
her main deck; and strange as the main deck was, it was
commonplace to her lower deck. Captain Flint might have died
on the lower deck; it belonged to men with pigtails, who drank
rum from pannikins. It was so low and so dark that it made us all
stoop instinctively. It was the deck Israel Hands had been gunner
on, and at one or other of those ports, Old Pew had lost his dead

lights. To myself, all fresh from 'Treasure Island', the sight of that old ship was an entrancement of romance. I could have stayed there all day.'

As a small boy in 1890, Joseph Pierce was taken on board by his father, who was carrying out reconstruction work. In 1954 he wrote: 'If I remember right, there were extensive repairs to her hull, new decks and deck roofing, and, I think, new masts and rigging and resetting of her heavy guns. My father and I were both graciously entertained aboard the Eagle by Commander Willis.

'Well do I remember the low, timber-panelled ceilings of his state-cabins and the gleam of the burnished guns. In my father's office there hung the Drawing Board on which the subsidiary drawings, relating to the reconditioning of the ship, were displayed. This 'relic' is now the Notice Board of the Hoylake Historical Society.'

The 'Liverpolitan' in May 1937 gave a fitting tribute to the old Eagle. It is a justified comment of every year that the old ship was in service and on those who served in her.

'To the uninitiated a visit on board is both a revelation and an inspiration - a revelation in that it seems almost a miracle how so many departments, each with a vast amount of necessary equipment, could be housed in a vessel of such size and - inspiration through observing the conscientious way in which all tackle their respective jobs. Truly a wonderful organisation manned by men whose work is inspired by the traditions of our Navy.'

That was the background story to the opening of our Centenary history, which starts in 1904.

GIN AND 'IT'

Chapter Two

1904 - 1914
THE RNVR IS CREATED

When the Admiralty sanctioned the formation of the Royal Naval Volunteers in 1903 with a Division allocated to the Mersey, it would appear that the first step was to approach certain ship-owners and merchants for co-operation. The Force was officially designated, The Royal Naval Volunteer Reserve.

Sir Edward Grey's committee on Naval Reserves first mooted the idea in 1902 and the report stressed the absolute necessity for Reserves. A Bill was introduced by the Government to carry out the proposition and by the end of the session it became law. A permanent Committee with Mr. Chadwyck-Healey, KC, in the chair began its sittings in the Admiralty, and in August 1903 the official regulations and civil and administrative rules for the government of the Force were issued.

The Admiralty scheme was framed upon the principle of securing as much flexibility from oppressive and hard and fast rules likely to interfere with civil engagements as possible. A minimum standard of efficiency was laid down as essential with the ultimate aim to improve on such standards. Much was to be left to the discretion of the Commanding Officers. The scheme was particularly aimed to promote signalmen, telegraphists, electricians and armourers.

Divisions were quickly formed; in London under the

command of the Hon. Rupert Guinness, CMG, where between 800 and 900 men were enrolled including a company from Brighton and Hove, and on the Clyde under the command of the Marquis of Graham over 600 men joined and numbers were ever increasing.

In the London Division the Buzzard of 1,140 tons was being fitted in Sheerness. It was to have the most modern kinds of ordinance available. All Naval Reserve and Drill ships and Batteries were to be put into use. Until the Buzzard was ready to take up station on the Thames, the London volunteers had full use of President in the West India Docks. The Fishmongers Company provided the use of their Hall for the purpose of recruiting.

In Liverpool, discussions were protracted and it was not until the end of 1903 that progress was made. HMS Eagle, which had been berthed in King's Dock since 1862 as a RNR Drill ship, was moved to the north side of the Salthouse Dock and refitted ready for the instruction of the Force.

The Royal Naval Reserve (officers and men serving in the Mercantile Marine) had continued to use Eagle as a drill-ship for forty-one years, but they were forced to leave her in 1903 to make way for the newly formed Reserve. In that year was introduced a more realistic scheme of training in sea-going cruisers, but this only lasted for two years and in 1905 the RNR returned to the Eagle and this had compelled the RNVR to move to the Custom House.

The Liverpool Mercury reported the events of Monday, 15th February 1904. Mr. Robert Gladstone in Liverpool Town Hall moved: "that this meeting is of the opinion that the movement for the establishment of a Mersey Division RNVR is deserving of the fullest support and encouragement of the citizens of Liverpool, and cordially welcomes the appointment of the Earl of Lathom as Commanding Officer. "Liverpool people," he said, "have always been in the forefront of any movement connected with the defence of the country." While he could not remember the old days of privateering, he could remember the great movement in 1849 when this country was considered to be in imminent danger of invasion by the French. In a very few weeks 120,000 men came forward to enrol themselves as volunteers and among them was a very large number of Liverpool men. Times had changed. "It is quite impossible to leave the preparation of defences to the last moment. If our Fleet was overpowered and our ports blockaded, and we could get no food, we should have to surrender."

We are told, but cannot confirm, that the records show that the distinction of being the first member of the Mersey Division falls to one Thomas Williams, whose date of enrolment is shown as 1st January 1904. This is probably hearsay.

The next name on the records (but probably the first) was that of the first Commanding Officer, the Rt. Hon. the Earl of Lathom, who was gazetted as a Lieutenant on 9th January 1904 and made a Commander on 7th March 1904.

The Liverpool Mercury reported that: 'By May of 1904, the Earl of Lathom has grown a beard, which has so completely changed him that very few of his most intimate friends have been able to recognise him. Whether he will ever have such a magnificent beard as his late father, only time will tell.' The paper continued: 'The Countess of Lathom, who was Lady Wilma Pleydell-Bouveries, daughter of the fifth Earl of Radnor, is a tall handsome woman, and, like her mother, very musical'

Most of the Officers were enrolled on 3rd February 1904 but the general recruiting did not commence until the 18th February. On this day and the 23rd February hundreds of men arrived in Eagle to enrol.

The first drills under the supervision of Captain Ian McKenzie Fraser, DSO, RN, (Ret), were held on 8th March 1904 when CPO GI F.B. Mayne, RN, took all recruits as one large squad. Towards the end of the month three companies (Nos. 1, 2 and 3) were organised with one Lieutenant, one Sub-Lieutenant, two or three Petty Officers, four Leading Seamen and one CPO for each Company.

The Liverpool Mercury on 14th May 1904 carried this article. 'Mersey Naval Volunteers are making substantial headway, and soon their cutters manned by Naval Bluejackets will be a familiar and picturesque addition to the river panorama. A Liverpool Exchange Company is in course of formation, under the command of Lieutenant Kenion and quiet efforts are being put forth to raise a special Birkenhead Company. What is wanted on the Birkenhead side is a citizen with a view to the establishment of a semi-independent command on that side of the river. Among the numerous boating and yachting men resident in the borough surely a strong company can be raised.'

On the 21st May 1904 the London Gazette contained the following: 'Admiralty May 18th Royal Naval Volunteer Reserves. The under-mentioned appointments have been made viz:-The Rt. Hon. Right Rev. John Charles Ryle, DD, Bishop of Liverpool, to be Honorary Chaplain.'

'Daily Express ... 24th May 1904

Curious Blunder

'Admiralty appoints a dead Bishop as Chaplain

'The Admiralty has made the extraordinary blunder of appointing a dead man to an Honorary post at Liverpool. There is a dignified announcement in the London Gazette that the Admiralty has been pleased to appoint Dr. John Charles Ryle, Bishop of Liverpool, as Hon. Chaplain of the newly formed Mersey Brigade of the RNVR.

'Dr. Ryle, however, died on June 10th 1900 and the present Bishop of Liverpool is Dr. Chevasse, as the King knows, if the Admiralty does not, for he has just addressed a letter to this dignitary.'

There was a wide choice of articles covering this blunder!

After such a great response of recruits, not only from Liverpool but from Birkenhead and as far afield as Southport and Caernarfon, the Admiralty sanctioned the formation of a Company at Southport (No. 4) and Caernarfon (No. 5). So many applications were received from Birkenhead, that an additional Company (No. 6) was formed in the Town.

Many were still clamouring to join the RNVR and towards the end of 1904 a further Company (No. 7) was allocated to Liverpool. By this time all the companies were brought to full strength, 100 men in each, so the Force was at full complement by the end of 1904.

The Manchester Guardian carried a paragraph on 1st February 1904 reporting that the Caernarfon Corps of the Royal Naval Voluntary Reserve was to be resuscitated. Lord Lathom had written to Mr. Charles A. Jones, who was the prime mover in the matter, recommending that he be commissioned in the Mersey Division and be placed third in seniority. There had been a Corps of the Naval Artillery Volunteers in the town but it had been disbanded some decades earlier.

There was progress in the newly formed Southport Company. In May it was reported that numbers had reached 40 and that the men had been measured for uniform.

The first function of note for the Mersey Division was a guard of honour to King Edward VII when he laid the foundation stone of the Anglican Cathedral in July 1904.

During the summer of 1904 the senior ratings were allowed to volunteer for a gunnery course in HMS Grafton and it would appear that most of them from the Division never missed the opportunity of serving in the Fleet.

The social side was not neglected, but it was mostly confined to Company Hot Pot Suppers during the winter months; this carried on the tradition of the RNAV.

No. 3 Company held a Hot-Pot Supper at 7 o'clock at the Alexandra Hotel in Dale Street on Tuesday 13th December 1904. The menu was as follows: Hot-Pot, Pickles, Cheese with Wines, Beer and Ginger-Pop. Nine members of the company were on the list of singers, Seaman Buttery was detailed off 'to make a noise on the piano' and Seaman Russell was 'to astonish us with recitations'.

It is recorded that the RNVR No.1 Company, Mersey Division held a Hot Pot with Pickles, Celery and Cheese at the Alexandra Hotel, Dale Street on Tuesday, 31st January 1905 at 7 p.m. New members 'rendered' songs and a lantern show, entitled 'A Life in the Navy', illustrated by Limelight Views, was presented and 'edited' by Seaman Mangel. A special song was written for the evening and duly rendered.

'Here's to the Naval Volunteers,
The gallant RNV's,
Who hold themselves in readiness
To sail the stormy seas
To go and fight the Russians
To sink the Baltic Fleet
'Til then we'll drill in Salthouse Dock
In our working kit so neat.'

The year 1905 saw changes in training. In June a cutter and a whaler were sent to Merseyside for each Company. Those for the Liverpool and Birkenhead Companies were moored at the rear of the Birkenhead Ferry landing stage, sailing and rowing practice being carried out on the river, whilst those for the Southport Company were moored on the marine lake. There is no record of a regatta in 1905.

Also in June 1905 seamen were granted the opportunity of training afloat and those who volunteered were divided amongst battleships and two cruisers of the Reserve Fleet. From this time onwards, training with the Fleet during the summer months was an established feature of the Force and many members of the Mersey Division grasped this privilege to find out at first hand what life was like in the Navy.

Towards the end of the year it was decided to disband No. 5 (Caernarfon) Company through lack of recruits. Only 42 men had enrolled during the first two years. This Company was later transferred to Birkenhead, adopting the designation of No. 5 Company.

Another vital change made during the year 1905 at the time was thought to be detrimental to the Mersey Division. The Division left Eagle and was transferred to the Custom House. The Royal Naval Reserve (Merchant Navy) took over the ship.

So the RNVR became 'dry-land' sailors. The new headquarters was established on the top floor North East corner of the massive building, which was to be destroyed in the blitz of 1941. After climbing 150 steps, a turn to port and there was a long corridor. Instruction rooms for gunnery, anchor work, the canteen, etc. were situated on the starboard side with the Wardroom and Officers' Quarters on the port side. After what seemed an interminable walk, a short passage opened on the right. This housed the ship's office and at the end opened out on to the main deck. The Quarterdeck was situated just inside the door so every rating went in at the double.

There were annual recruiting drives. One account states that the men marched with fixed bayonets. But as this privilege would only be accorded to Units that had received the freedom of the city, that memory is questionable. The route on that particular occasion was South Castle Street, Lord Street, Church Street and along Lime Street, passing the saluting base at St George's Plateau, William Brown Street, Dale Street and thence to Headquarters in the Custom House.

The Liverpool Courier in March 1909 contained a strange article of some interest. The writer stated that as he had an appointment elsewhere he sent his son to deputise for him. The occasion was the hotpot and prize distribution in the Custom House, Canning Place. This is the remarkable report of the son.

'Jack's the lad for work, Jack's the lad for play, and Jack's the lad for saying just what he means in blunt Anglo-Saxon. Listen and ye shall hear. "Let us show people that we are not like the Territorials; that we do not want and do not need the newspapers to encourage us to join His Majesty's Service." Glad to hear it, Lieutenant Maples, and yet, somehow, it seems to the writer (he judges solely from your own words) that there is something rotten in the state of Denmark, and a little judicious advertising in the public Press would not do overmuch harm. Addressing his men on Saturday, after using the words quoted above, Lieutenant Maples said that some of the doings of the company were "disgusting" and "rotten". Moreover, the company was only half the strength it ought to be. Certainly, he added, they had won one or two prizes, and had been second once or twice, but they would have to do a lot better if they wanted to please him. In 1907 their total strength was seventy-nine, last year it was eighty-six, but out of eighty-six there were some who were absolutely of no use to the company. If these men couldn't or wouldn't 'buck up', the sooner they cleared out the better for all concerned. Lieutenant Maples concluded his blunt little speech by an appeal to his men to bring in some good recruits, as the company stood in sore need of them.'

Apparently another feature of that particular annual 'hot-pot -smoker' was a 'machine gun' speech of CPO Daw who told the members that though they had made themselves efficient by attending 24 drills, they were more keen on becoming efficient on the billiard table. Other companies had 50 men at Altcar, against their 25; and in the order of merit for general efficiency No. 1 Company was at the bottom, where they had never been before. He complimented the men upon their performance in the boat-pulling competition, and said that although they had won the field gun contest, they did several things that they should not have done. The cause of No. 1 Company's deterioration was the presence of so many "scallywags" in the company; but some of them had already gone and others would shortly follow.

The final words in the rather overlong article on the hot-pot stated a little more happily: 'An excellent list of artistes contributed to the success of the evening, of whom Mr. Harry Collins's banjo solos and the legerdemain of Professor Cobbett were the most popular.'

The spaciousness of the deck in the Custom House can be appreciated when the full strength of the four Liverpool Companies could easily be on parade at the same time. Visual signalling, knots and splices, small arms drill, compass and helm with steering model and sheer legs drill were all carried out on the same deck to the accompaniment of the crack of Morris tube rifle fire from the miniature range which was situated just off one corner.

Mr. McKenna, the First Lord of the Admiralty, as reported in the Liverpool Echo on 24th March 1909, applauded the formation of a new company of volunteers at the works of Messrs. Cammell Laird and Co., Birkenhead.

'Last evening No.6 Company (Birkenhead) paraded under its Commanding Officer (Lieutenant W.J. Lias). The Company was closely inspected by the Officer Commanding the Division, Commander the Earl of Lathom. He then turned to the recruits of the new company, which will be known as No. 5, and who, to the number of forty or fifty, were drawn up under the command of Lieutenant Stafford and congratulated them upon beginning their Volunteer career under such happy auspices.'

It was noted that Cammell Laird had a spacious drill hall and that the works had given the new company every encouragement

The Liverpool Echo on 8th May 1909 reported a visit by Lord Charles Beresford from Knowsley to the Southport Company. Present at the inspection were Lord Lathom and Sir George Pilkington, who was the Honorary Lieutenant. The speech of Lord Charles ended with these words: "We have an old adage, in the service with which I have been connected for 50 years, which says that one volunteer is worth six pressed men.

The time may come when the national service ideas which are sound may be necessary for this country, but as long as we maintain the volunteer principle the better it will be for the nation and for the Empire." Concluding, he remarked upon the smartness of the men, and said their appearance was a credit to themselves, their officers, and to the Mersey Division. Someone cried out at the close of the speech, "Get into Parliament, Charlie, and give them a broadside." To this the Lord Beresford replied, "That fellow must be an old mate of mine."

A handsome challenge cup was presented at the Annual Cutter Rowing Race in July 1909 by the Old Brigade (RNAV). The Mercury reported: 'There is nothing stops the way of a boat so much as the weight of the crew's bodies hurrying unevenly forward, and if to one cause more than to another Lieutenant Maple's lads owe their victory, it is that they got hold of the water at the very beginning of the stroke, never let the boat run away from them, pulled in perfect unison, and finished clean.'

Sometime during the year the Division was invited to Lathom House (the Commanding Officer's estate) at Burscough, where field exercises and divisional drill were carried out, refreshments being supplied by Lord Lathom.

A letter written in 1954 recalls the memories of the Southport Company. It is written in pencil, fading badly, and signed by T. Bond. 'There were numerous parades and dances and smoking concerts and boundary marches and gunnery practice, North of the Pier, firing at targets in the sea. Also a cutter and whaler kept anchored for weekend training. We paid many visits to Liverpool and Birkenhead for parades and route marches. We paraded also at Knowsley Park for King Edward's Review. Also an inspection in front of Southport Town Hall by

George VI and Queen Mary. The Territorial Army robbed us of members because many liked the change of uniform. So the Company became under strength and transferred to join Birkenhead Company. I don't remember doing any drills after that. We attended the naval funeral of Lord Lathom. There are not many of the old Company left.'

The Liverpool RNVR was inspected in August 1909 at the drill hall in the Custom House, Canning Street. The number on parade consisted of 7 permanent staff, 1 Bugle-Major, 12 Chief and Petty Officers, 9 Leading Seamen, 224 Able Seamen, 42 Ordinary Seamen, and 2 Buglers, making a total, with probationers, of 335. Twenty-seven seamen were at sea doing their training, and 39 were absent, with permission owing to business, sickness and other causes, and 7 were absent without permission, the strength of the headquarter companies being 375 officers and men, without counting 30 probationers. The total strength of the Division, including permanent staff and 59 probationers, was 688.

Lord Lathom died on board the Cunard liner Caronia in March 1910 The doctors had ordered him to take a sea trip to Egypt. Some months earlier an accidental shooting had just missed his eye, damaging his eyelid and badly affecting his hearing. The newspaper reports on the 17th March were lavish in praise of his stature in Liverpool and in particular of the founding of the RNVR.

The title of 'the Wavy Navy' was earned by the distinction from that of the Royal Navy in various details of the officer's and men's uniforms. The distinguishing rings on the sleeves of the officers' jackets were very narrow and there was a

distinct wave in them. The buttons on the jackets were embossed
with the letters RNV. The three white tapes on the seamen's
collars were also waved, the cap band bearing the letters RNV
with an anchor and a crown worked into the letter N.

The original gunnery, torpedo and tradesmen's badges were also
slightly different. 'A seaman who has completed the requisite
number of drills, 40 in the first year, 24 in the second and
subsequent years with attendance at the Annual Inspection,
thereby qualifies for the efficiency grant made to the Division by
the Admiralty, and is permitted to wear a distinguishing badge
consisting of a small gold wavy chevron on the right sleeve just
above the wrist for the first year with a second chevron for the
second. Subsequent years are denoted by a gold star worn above
alternative chevrons for each additional year of efficiency.' This
practise was eventually dropped.

A letter written in 1954 by CPO R.H. Lloyd, RN, contained this recollection of those early days of the RNVR. 'The Social side of the Division was of great importance, there being an Annual Hot-Pot Supper and Prize Distribution. I can well remember the Captain's traditional grace of "Stand up. Thank God. Sit down!" given in a booming voice, full of authority!

'The Annual Ball was also well attended. The Field Gun's Crew Event (ex-'The Chasm') was taken around to various Agricultural Shows as a social event and for recruiting. The Show authorities paid for the spectacle and this money was distributed to the teams.

'Occasionally there were night schemes between the RNVR and TA Units, involving landing parties on our part, followed by an 'attack', much enjoyed by all concerned.

'Not one of us had prior knowledge of the Royal Naval Division; indeed it was expected that we should join the Fleet in an emergency. I joined the Royal Navy in 1913, but believe that in fact that all Reservists, medically fit, were drafted into the Royal Naval Division.'

The Southport Post and the Mercury reported this story on 9th March 1911. 'For the first time since assuming command of the Mersey Division Royal Naval Volunteers Reserve Sir Richard Williams-Bulkeley, Bart, presided over the annual prize distribution and dance, which took place in St George's Hall last evening.

'Commander Sir Richard Williams-Bulkeley addressing the men of the Division - who presented a smart and sailor-like appearance - referred sympathetically to the death during the year of his predecessor in command, Lord Lathom. He announced with satisfaction that Lord Derby had been appointed honorary commander of the division (hear, hear). His Lordship, he said, unfortunately was not in the best of health; otherwise he would, no doubt, have been present that evening.'

The speech was very long and reported in full. At last there came an announcement of importance to the Division.

'Before long the Division would be changing its headquarters. They were, he was glad to say, getting off the shore - not a very long way off, for he believed that the actual distance was eight feet (laughter) - but still they would be off the shore, and that would make a deal of difference. He (the commander) intended to make the life of the men on board as much ship-like as possible. That would no doubt be attractive to the men, and he hoped that the attendance at drill and the general application to the work of the Division would continue to improve.'

That speech continued endlessly - at least another two pages!

On 31st March 1911, the RNR vacated Eagle and she was turned over to the RNVR for their sole use. Back home again! The Division comprised seven companies of 100 officers and men, four at Liverpool, two outlying companies at Birkenhead and one in Southport. They were not however to enjoy possession of Eagle for very long.

The Liverpool Daily Post reported the inspection of the Division on 24th October 1913. Admiral A.M. Farquhar, CVO, Commanding Coastguards and Naval Reserves, was the Inspecting Officer. 'On arrival at the quay the Guard of Honour under Lieutenant Cappel saluted the Admiral, who inspected the Guard and afterwards proceeded on board where the Boatswains Mates performed the ceremony of 'Piping the Side'. Meanwhile the four companies comprising the HQ Division were formed up in two ranks on the decks under Lieutenant W. Maples, the Senior

Officer. The officers were presented to Admiral Farquhar by Sir Richard Williams-Bulkeley, Commander of the Mersey Division. Then the Admiral made a very minute inspection of other ranks and ratings. He conversed freely as to their length of service and the trades they followed.

'The Mersey Division, for the first time in its history is at full war strength made up as follows: 716 ranks and ratings including 35 probationers and 11 permanent staff - 727. Out of this number there are 600 efficient and during the next four months it is confidently anticipated the above number will be increased by 70.

'There are 109 ranks and ratings of the HQ Companies alone, who had each put in upwards of 100 drills and these men were given a post of honour on the upper deck by Commander Instructor R. Leach'

During his speech the Admiral stated: "It is very creditable to find so many men taking such a keen interest in the work, and even more creditable to find so many men taking advantage of the opportunity of going to sea in HM Ships. After all that was the crux of the matter. I believe an ounce of practice at sea is worth a ton of drill on shore. Although the work possible in HMS Eagle is better than in an ordinary drill shed, it does not give the men much idea of a modern battleship."

Within a year of that visit the ship's company would wonder whether the Admiral had done his homework! There were to be no ships for the RNVR!

And the events of 1914 were to bring the old Eagle back into active service.

BEER

Chapter Three

1914 - 1922
THE ROYAL NAVAL DIVISION AT WAR

International events were moving to a gigantic climax, the results of which were to embroil even the centenarian Eagle. Shortly after the outbreak of war she was once again on active service, although in a stationary capacity. Captain H. H. Stileman was appointed to her as Senior Officer, Liverpool, and upon the 2nd of November 1914, he received his flag. Thus once again, and for the third time in her long and somewhat chequered career, she became a flagship. This duty she performed for the duration of the war.

Edward Jones continued his thoughts as he recalled his own observations on HMS Eagle during his time aboard during the First World War. 'On the lower deck, in the orlop, were the cells, very dark and small and not at all inviting. In the early hours of a cold February morning the alarm was raised. A prisoner had escaped from his cell. The guards were called out and stationed at all exits, but upon examination it was found that he had gone out by removing the bars from the port in the cell and dropped into the dock with the aid of his blanket and dare not let go. The water was perishing cold and it was freezing hard. He was told to come on board but with chattering teeth he answered, "I c-c-can't, there's no foothold. I can't hold on much longer." He was unable to obtain a foothold owing to the turn of the bilge and a rope was lowered to him, but he was so cold that he dare not let go of the blanket to tie the rope around his waist. He shouted, "I can't come up", then a vast voice from out of the darkness shouted, "Come up, or I shoot". Eventually a dinghy was lowered and he was picked up more dead than alive, a very sorry man.

'In one of the breast-hooks or stringers on the port side was cut:
Built by Sir Wm. Rule at Northfleet in 1804, 74 guns, 1723 tons. This particular beam was fifteen inches square and it was amazing how the frames and diagonals were fitted together in the forepeak. Above the quarterdeck was the figurehead, but unfortunately it was in a dark place and could easily be missed. I believe that the ship's wheel was aboard somewhere but I never saw this. The handrails of the companionway leading down to the wardroom were covered with coach whipping complete with turk's head and stopper knots, a beautiful piece of work.

'The old boatswain was always pleased to get someone interested and give a few lessons in passing the ball to and fro. Very interesting, but very tedious. He was quite a character, that old bosun. When he piped, 'Everyone aft!', he would stand at the top of the midship companion and say: "Come on, my dears, come along, my dears. Come along, gentlemen, come on you scallywags, come on, you lazy louts", and many other terms of endearment followed if we were slow enough to hear them.

'In the wardroom on the sideboard stood a beautiful model of a seventy-four in bronze, complete with guns, anchors, cables, masts, yards and all the details. It stood on a four-wheeled carriage and I admired it many times. I wonder what became of it?'

Eagle continued as the base ship in Liverpool throughout the war, as accommodation for ratings in transit. During this time there was little if any contact with the RNVR.

At the start of the First World War a battleship, called the Almirante Cochran, was being built by Armstrong, Whitworth and Co. Ltd. for the Chilean Navy. Work had stopped and she lay idle on her slip until 1917, when the vessel was bought by the British Government. She was redesigned as an aircraft carrier and it was proposed that she be called Eagle. When the carrier was launched on the 8th June 1918, our old friend in Liverpool, Eagle, was renamed Eaglet.

When the war had started in 1914, some RNVR Ratings had been drafted for sea service, but by far the majority was mustered into Naval Brigades and, for some obscure reason, were turned into soldiers! There was obvious disappointment that they were not drafted to ships. Nothing had been known previously about the existence of the Royal Naval Division and for the RNVR it was a bombshell. However they were content that they would all remain together as a unit. The casualty list would prove to be very heavy by the end of the conflict.

It was Winston Churchill, the First Lord of the Admiralty, who decided that the RNVR was to be formed into two four-battalion brigades, which together with a third brigade of regular Royal Marines, would make up a Royal Naval Division for the land defence of threatened harbours and fleet bases on the Continent.

The Commanding Officer of the Mersey Division, Commander Sir Richard Williams Bulkeley, RNR, was promoted to Commodore and became the first and only Commanding

Officer of HMS Victory VI, the requisitioned Crystal Palace.
There they prepared to take the first intake of volunteer recruits.

So there we were, a merry crew,
The Crystal Palace Army;
Butchers, bakers,
Pattern makers,
Grocers, tailors,
Dressed as sailors,
Good old Palace Army.

The Royal Naval Division was mobilised on the 1st
August 1914 and sent to Deal. Here the RNVR were given
intense training in order to fit them out as land soldiers. Out of
the Mersey Division no more than fifty ratings were drafted for
the Fleet - mainly signalmen, engineers, plumbers and fitters. No
officers joined the Fleet

As the RND was the first contingent of troops, other than
the old 'Contemptibles', to see active service during the war we
should look more closely at the events of those early days. The
British Government realised the importance of halting the
German advance on Antwerp with all its military stores and also
wished to lessen the pressure on the Belgians who were
retreating.

The 1st and 2nd Brigades sailed from Dover on the 5th
October and arrived at Dunkirk. These Brigades contained the
Nelson, the Howe (Sussex, Clyde and Mersey Divisions), the
Hood and the Anson Divisions and they arrived at Antwerp in the
early morning of the 6th October.

Antwerp was defended by a double ring of forts, the
outer of which was the real defence of the city. The Germans had
already broken through the outer ring when the Brigade of Royal
Marines relieved the tired Belgian troops on the night of 3rd and
4th. By the 6th the position was critical.

ROYAL NAVAL DIVISION

HANDYMEN TO FIGHT ON LAND & SEA

1ST BRIGADE

BATTALIONS:

"BENBOW"
"COLLINGWOOD"
"HAWKE"
"DRAKE"

RECRUITS WANTED

2ND BRIGADE

BATTALIONS:

"HOWE"
"HOOD"
"ANSON"
"NELSON"

RECRUITS WANTED

VACANCIES FOR RECRUITS BETWEEN THE AGES OF **18** AND **38**
CHEST MEASUREMENT, 34 · HEIGHT, 5 FT, 3½ IN.
PAYMENT from 1/3 per day. FAMILY ALLOWANCES

Besides serving in the above Battalions and for the Transport
and Engineer Sections attached,

MEN WANTED

who are suitable for Training as Wireless Operators, Signalmen
and other Service with the Fleet.
Apply to The Recruiting Office, 112 Strand, London, W.C.

J. MILES & Cº Lᵀᴰ Printers, 68/70 Wardour Street, London, W.

When the two Naval Brigades arrived, they were ordered to aid the Royal Marines, who had fallen back to the second inner line of defence. The Brigades dug in and at midnight on the 7th October the German bombardment began.

Much of the town was on fire and the water supply had failed. The Belgian army fell back in the evening under very difficult conditions. Many bridges were destroyed; the roads were crowded with thousands of refugees with their cattle and possessions on handcarts and barrows. The straggling mob made it almost impossible for the troops to retain formation. The result was confusion.

Unfortunately the 1st Brigade did not receive the order to retire in good time and many men were lost. Eventually they were to march some thirty miles that night ... a splendid performance.

The Commander-in-Chief, Field-Marshal Viscount French wrote: 'I have to state that from a comprehensive review of all the circumstances, the Force of Marines and Naval Brigades which assisted in the defence of Antwerp was handled by General Paris with great skill and boldness.

'Although the results did not include the actual saving of the fortress, the action of the Force under General Paris certainly delayed the enemy for a considerable time and assisted the Belgian Army to be withdrawn in a condition to enable it to reorganise and refit and regain its value as a fighting Force. The destruction of war material and ammunition - which but for the intervention of this Force, would have proved of great value to the enemy - was thus able to be carried out.'

On their return to Britain the first Lord of the Admiralty sent the following message: 'The First Lord welcomes the Royal

Naval Division home on its return from active service. Officers and men of all ranks and ratings have acquitted themselves admirably, and have thoroughly justified the confidence reposed in them. The loss of a portion of the 1st Brigade through a mistake in no way reflects upon the quality or character of the Division.

'The Brigade of Royal Marines, throughout the operations, sustained fully, by their firmness, discipline and courage, the traditions of the Corps. It is necessary to say more than this. The Naval Brigades bore themselves admirably under the artillery fire of the enemy; and it is to be regretted that no opportunities of closer contact with his infantry was afforded them.

'The despatch of the Naval Brigades to Antwerp has interrupted for a time the progress of their instruction and training. They were chosen because the need for them was urgent and bitter; because mobile troops could not be spared for fortress duties; because they were nearest and could be embarked the quickest; and because their training although incomplete, was as far advanced as that of a large portion, not only of the Forces defending Antwerp, but of the enemy Forces attacking.

'The Naval Division was sent to Antwerp not as an isolated incident, but as part of a large operation for the relief of the city. Other and more powerful considerations prevented this from being carried through. The defence of the inner lines of Antwerp could have been maintained for some days; and the Naval Division only withdrew when ordered to do so in obedience to the general strategic situation, and not on account of any attack or pressure of the enemy. The prolongation of the defence, due to the arrival of the Division, enabled the ships in the harbour to be rendered useless, and many steps of importance to be taken.

'It is too early yet to judge what effect the delaying, even for five or six days, of at least 60,000 Germans before Antwerp may have had upon the fortunes of the general battle to the southward. It was certainly powerful and helpful. Apart from the military experiences, which have been invaluable, the Division has been the witness of the ruthlessness of the German foe towards a small and innocent State. These facts should inspire all ranks to fit themselves in the shortest possible time for further service in the field, not merely as a fortress, but as mobile units.

'The Belgian people will never forget that the men of the Royal Navy and Royal Marines were with them in their darkest hour of misery, as, please God, they may also be with them when Belgium is restored to her own by the armies of the Allies.'

A postcard from France tells a story in another way!
'Dear Mother,
Just a few lines hoping you and all are quite well. I am alright myself only I am about fed up with Continental touring, especially when you have got to do it on foot. I have not had my clothes off for a week since last Saturday and have been fighting in the trenches South of Antwerp night and day. We kept them out alright till last night when they started shelling the city and paraffin tanks and it became too hot for us. So we had to beat it quick. We have boarded a train where I am writing this on the way to Ostend and I think we shall be sent home because all our clothes, etc. are burnt rags as they were all stored in a mill which caught fire when we were shelled.
Love to all from
Walter.'

Second Officer Ann White, Mersey Division (1955 - 70) recalls memories of her father. "In those days even a lowly sub sported a cocked hat, frock coat, etc., and what didn't go by the board in 1914 - 18 went after 1945. He was involved with the Division at Birkenhead and when war broke out he went to France and like all of them he wore khaki. I've seen photographs of him in khaki, breeches and boots, but with two rings on his sleeve, plus the executive curl in army braid. I remember him saying that they all insisted on wearing Navy caps and cap badges, but had to stick on a khaki cap cover.

"He was fortunate as the particular unit he was in never got very involved with fighting. The whole front was collapsing and the Commanding Officer of his lot decided to march across country to Antwerp and hope to get there before the Hun. This they did and were able to get back to England. I gather they marched until they could barely stand up and father's clearest memory was of Eric Elgood (later Captain of the Eaglet) who was his immediate senior, urging or beating his men on, over and through hedges and ditches with his walking stick, wearing carpet slippers, his feet were so sore! Now, Eric Elgood was, when I knew him in the 1930s, so immaculate that the thought of him in carpet slippers is unbelievable, but papa said it was true."

After Antwerp many came back to Britain for further training and were then sent to Egypt. This led to their involvement in Gallipoli. This was an attempt in 1915 to seize the Turkish Dardanelles Strait with the aim of taking Turkey out of the war and relieving the pressure on Russia. A Fleet action failed in the February. This encounter was followed by the shore landings in April. All forces were finally withdrawn at the turn of the year after a complete failure to break the stalemate and a loss of 250,000 men.

Here is the tale in greater detail.

In January 1915, the Marine Brigade left England for the Near East. At the end of February they were followed by the Drake and Nelson Battalions of the 1st Naval Brigade, and the Hood, Howe and Anson Battalions of the 2nd Naval Brigade who went direct to Mudros harbour in the island of Lemnos, arriving on the 12th March. Already on the 4th March, detachments from the Marine Brigade had been landed under cover of the Fleet at the two forts guarding the entrance to the Dardanalles - Seddel-bahr on the European side and Kum Kale on the Asiatic side.

The attempt to force a passage by the Fleet through the Dardanelles failed and the Naval Battalions were returned to Port Said and to Alexandria. By the 23rd April they all assembled again at Mudros and the landings at Gallipoli commenced.

Life for the RNVR in the Gallipoli Campaign is well illustrated by an article in the magazine, 'The Incubator', which was produced by the 63rd Royal Naval Division on behalf of the 2nd Reserve Battalion, RNVR.

'The Landings

'The landings at S and Y beaches were planned to take place at dawn on April 25th and those at V, W and X beaches at 5.30 the same morning.

'The Anson Battalion left Mudros with the 29th Division on the evening of April 23rd and arrived at Tenedos the following morning. They were transferred to warships and fleet sweepers in which they were to approach the shore. On the morning fixed for the landing they arrived before dawn at their rendezvous, off the southern end of the peninsula. At 5 a.m. it was sufficiently light for the ships to open fire and a violent bombardment of the enemy's defences began. The troops were then transferred to the small boats in which they were towed ashore.

'Except for shells fired from the Asiatic side of the

Straits, the guns of the Fleet remained unanswered. Detachments of the Anson Battalion were detailed to land at V, W and X beaches as working parties for the assaulting troops. At all the beaches the Turks allowed the boats to come right inshore before they opened fire. At V beach below the village and fort of Seddel-bahr, the Dublin Fusiliers were towed in small boats, whilst the Munster Fusiliers, two Companies of the Hampshire Regiment and a party of the Anson Battalion under Sub-Lieutenant Tisdall, were in the collier River Clyde. Commander Unwin, RN, was in command of the collier and men of the Hood Battalion acted as stokers.

'As the small boats reached the shore the River Clyde was beached and simultaneously a tornado of fire swept over the beach, the small boats and the collier.

'Many of the Dublin Fusiliers and the seamen who manned the boat were shot down; but a few managed to reach a low ridge of sand which ran across the beach and afforded some cover from the enemy's fire.

'Meanwhile the men aboard the River Clyde were attempting to place lighters in position between her bows and the shore, in order to form a bridge by means of which the troops, who were concealed aboard the collier could reach the beach.

'Our first Victoria Cross

'Whilst watching the operations from the collier, Sub-Lieutenant A. W. St. C. Tisdall saw a number of wounded Dublin Fusiliers and seamen lying on the beach and struggling in the shallow water. On his own initiative, and at the risk of almost certain death, he dived into the sea and with the assistance of three men of his platoon managed to push a small boat ashore. With great courage and determination he succeeded in bringing back to the River Clyde five boatloads of these helpless men. The gallant action was seen by those on board, but the heroes of the exploit were as yet unidentified. It was not until some time afterwards that Commander Unwin obtained the name of this heroic officer and his gallant helpers. For this act of valour Sub-Lieutenant Tisdall was awarded the Victoria Cross and the brave men who assisted him were also decorated. Unfortunately Sub-Lieutenant Tisdall was killed before the award was published. For twenty-four hours the survivors of the Dublins, Munsters and Hampshires held on to their precarious position on the beach; but on the morning of April 26th our troops attacked, captured the fort and village of Seddel-bahr, and established a position beyond the village.

'At W Beach

'At W Beach the landing was made by the Lancashire Fusiliers supported by the Worcesters and a working party from the Anson Battalion. This landing was quickly accomplished. By 9.30 a.m. a junction had been affected with the troops landing at X Beach, but touch could not be made that day with the troops who landed at V Beach. The right of the troops who landed at W Beach then rested on the edge of the cliff by Cape Helles lighthouse. At midnight the Turks counter-attacked heavily. The Anson detachment under Colonel Moorhouse reinforced the firing line. With the help of the guns of HMS Implacable this attack was beaten off; but for some time the position was very precarious. However, the next day, a junction was effected with the V Beach force.

'At X Beach

'At X beach the landing was made with little loss by the 1st Royal Fusiliers and a working party from the Anson Battalion. Working to the east they succeeded in joining up with the W Beach landing party.

'Skyros and - Rupert Brooke the Poet

'The remainder of the Royal Naval Division had been landed at Skyros, where they practised a divisional landing operation. It was here that death robbed the Division and England of Rupert Brooke, the poet. At the outbreak of the war Sub-Lieutenant Brooke took up arms in what he considered a just cause. He took part in the Antwerp expedition and later accompanied the Division to the East. But Rupert Brooke was not meant to be a soldier - he was cast in too fine a mould. Death followed an attack of sunstroke and he was laid to rest alone 'under the wide and starry sky'.

The Soldier
'If I should die, think only this of me:
That there's some corner of a foreign field
That is for ever England.'
Rupert Brooke 1887 - 1915

'Feint Landing in the Gulf of Xeros

'At 10 p.m. on April 24th all the Naval Battalions, with the exception of Anson, were taken north by sea, with the object of causing the Turks to think that a landing was intended on the western side of the peninsula, in the Gulf of Zeros. Only one man landed - Lieutenant Commander Freyberg of the Hood Battalion. In the early hours of April 25th this officer swam ashore taking with him a number of flares. These he lighted, and by shouting words of command and making as much noise as possible, he gave the Turks the impression that a landing was taking place. Afterwards he swam back to his ship. As a result of his adventure, a considerable force of the enemy was diverted for the time being from joining the Turkish forces in the main theatre of operations. For his gallant work, Lieutenant Commander

Freyberg was created a Companion of the Distinguished Service Order.

'At Y Beach

'At dawn on April 25th, the Plymouth Battalion of Royal Marines landed with the King's Own Scottish Borderers at Y Beach. Both Battalions at the first dash gained the heights above the landing place. Reserves of food, water and ammunition were hauled up to the top of the cliff and, in accordance with the plan of operations, an immediate endeavour was made to get in touch with the X Beach force; failing in this they dug in.'

Another publication for these nautical divisions was entitled 'The Mudhook'. It was published as the journal for the 63rd (R.N.) Division and incorporated another magazine called 'Dardanelles Dug-out Gossip' and was priced in France at half a franc. The sub-title of the 'Mudhook' was 'Per Wire - Per Tear 'Em'. The advertisements summed up the conditions and appeared in the Christmas Edition 1918

Desirable Dug-Out to let. Under fire nightly. Known to be nearly shell proof. Doorway needs digging out and a few other little repairs required. Low rent to suitable tenant.

Situations vacant. Unlimited number of Army Cooks wanted. Previous experience is a disqualification. Apply personally with specimen of bully beef.

Amorous. Glad to hear of your good time on leave. Our advice is to settle down now and concentrate on just two or three girls.

Gallipoli! Gallipoli!
With Thy joys and with Thy sorrows
Shall I forget Thee? Shall I forget Thee?
Never on this side of Time!

At home the First Sea Lord, Jackie Fisher, resigned and Churchill left the Government.

After Gallipoli large numbers at last served in HM Ships and by the end of the war only a handful remained fighting on land. Our Division's casualties in the Great War numbered 89 dead; their names were engraved on a plaque on Eaglet's drill deck, the timber having come from the old Eagle.

Humour always surfaces regardless of discomfort and human suffering. The 'Mudhook', the journal of the 63rd (RN) Division, contained this item in 1918.

'The Psalm of the Staff Officer
'An officer on the staff of our Division, who is unfortunate enough to have allocated to him the Ford car, was heard chanting the 23rd Psalm and it ran something like this:
'The Ford is my car; I shall not want another, he maketh me lie down in wet places.
It soileth my soul; it leadeth me into paths of ridicule for its name's sake.
Yea, it prepareth a breakdown for me in the presence of my enemies.
I fear much evil when it is with me; its rod and engine discomfort me.
It anointeth my face with oil; its tanks runneth over me.
Surely to goodness the darned thing won't follow me all the days of my life
Or I shall dwell in the house of the insane for ever.'

The driver of that car was evidently not addicted to the Psalms (having to take down and reassemble cars when other people are on Church Parade) and he could sing more blithely thus:

> *'A little spark, a little coil,*
> *A little gas, a little oil,*
> *A piece of tin and two francs-fifty of board;*
> *Glue them together and you've got a Ford.'*

This seems as good a time as any to include the Matelot's Prayer ... author unknown. It belongs to a much later date in this version, but must go back into the proverbial mists of time to ages long past.

> *'Our Father which art the Admiralty,*
> *Hallowed be thy name,*
> *Thy ships becalmed,*
> *Thy will be done*
> *As in the Queen's Rules and Regulations,*
> *And maybe in Heaven afterwards.*
> *Give us this day our daily tot,*
> *Instead of the 3d a day in lieu of,*
> *Lead us not into the ways of temperance,*
> *Forgive us our drunkenness*
> *For in that condition we serve you blindly.*
> *A tot to our power and glory,*
> *May it be reinstated or at least*
> *Remembered with the greatest affection,*
> *For ever and ever,*
> *Amen.'*

Sergeant Major: "What's your age?"
Fritz: "Dirty Zir! And Schmidt is dirty two."
Sergeant Major: "Yes! I know you both want a wash badly, but I want your age."

One black joke said it all:

Pal: "Well, Jock, had a good time on leave?"

Jock:"Aye, mon, it was fine to once again see a real decent
grave-yard."

> *They praise the British Army,*
> *And the sailors on the sea,*
> *But still they never mention*
> *The lads of the RND.*
>
> One of 'em

A radio broadcast in August 1956 by a W.G. Fry recalled his RNVR days in 1917. "As a RNVR recruit I'd received a very intensive course in naval signalling at the Crystal Palace (then known as HMS Victory VI) and at Devonport. This took six months and as I succeeded in passing out as a qualified signalman, I was available for drafting. My draft chit was waiting on my mess table at the beginning of May 1917, and I found that with other newly qualified signalmen I had to draw some additional kit. This to the amazement of all of us, consisted of a new suit of shoddy civilian clothes, a cloth cap, a coloured neckerchief, a broad-rimmed straw hat (in muslin cover), and a signalman's telescope.

"During the afternoon we were divided into two parties, and the party to which I was attached, perhaps a dozen signalmen, were put aboard a pinnace which eventually left Devonport and proceeded to Plymouth Sound. The only ship to be seen outside the breakwater was apparently a small merchant ship. Surely we were not being taken to that! But we were and I wasn't going to a warship after all, much to my disappointment.

"But that was my mistake. It was one of the famous 'mystery ships', the Q 35; the other party went to the Q 26.

"The first order on going aboard was to change into our civilian clothes and to stow our uniforms away out of sight. For a Royal Navy ship what an assortment we looked!

"We weighed anchor before long and it was shortly after that the captain had all available personnel mustered on the foredeck for a 'pep' talk. I don't remember much of it now, but I can recall his telling us that we could consider ourselves to be a lot of pirates, and that if a German submarine commander got hold of any of us we would probably be strung up to the periscope by the thumbs before diving.

"I'd read about 'mystery ships', but this wasn't a pleasant introduction to my first day at sea in the navy.

"However, we settled down and found the ship rather fascinating. There were all sorts of gadgets and ideas for deceiving the enemy submarine commanders and it had quite a good armament for its size.

"We soon discovered that we were extra crew taking passage, but we had to keep watches and do other useful work.

"We arrived at Gibraltar on 7th May 1917, and we remained there several Days for coaling. For security reasons we weren't allowed ashore. After each signalman had been given the name of the ship to which he had been allocated there was much speculation as to the type of ship it was going to be. We felt confident that we were going to destroyers ... my ship was Drake. So I felt a loss of dignity when, in due course, I was put aboard a small cargo-passenger ship.

"At the rendezvous next morning there was some confusion and it was indeed fortunate that the Straits had been kept pretty clear of enemy submarines. In later convoys the difficulty of getting all the ships into steaming formation was greatly reduced by giving each ship a number that was displayed by flag signal.

"The first convoy sailed, I think, in three very long line-astern columns of seven or eight ships in each column, with the two Q ships acting as escort. In subsequent convoys it was found safer to have (if possible) a broader front with fewer ships in line-astern.

"I never expected to serve at sea as the only signalman on a ship, but I found right away that I was responsible for visual communication on most of the ships in the convoys in which I sailed.

"It would be interesting to speculate as to how far the success of this visual communication had depended on the calm seas experienced on this first convoy's voyage from Gibraltar, as most of the signalmen had little experience of the sea!

"The important thing was that this fleet of small cargo ships arrived safely after quite an uneventful voyage. In the Channel, P Boats and trawlers joined the escorts for the protection of the convoy, and at Deal the signalmen were taken off at short notice, having no time to change from their shoddy civilian suits to uniform. The signalmen were then transported to London. Crossing London to Paddington station these ratings in 'civvies' were the subject of much amusement and speculation.

"We carried our straw hats in muslin bags and our signalmen's telescopes, and when we arrived at the barracks in Devonport, the Master at Arms, after he'd recovered from the initial shock, had much to say.

"It wasn't until some time later that I got to know that I had played a small part in the safe arrival of the first experimental convoy of merchant ships. This experiment proved that the smaller and slower merchant ships could steam in close formation, even at night without lights, and keep reasonable good station on their companions, making an attack by U-Boats a much more hazardous business for the submarine.

"Admiral Sims, then Chief of the U.S. Navy, said 'May 17th, the date when the convoy reached England, marked one of the great turning points of the war.' That critical voyage meant nothing less than that the Allies had found a way of defeating the German submarine."

This was yet another story of the contribution made by the Reserves in wartime.

Edward Jones read a paper on 13th November 1958 to the Liverpool Nautical Research Society recalling his service on board HMS Eagle during the war. "As a child I remember looking at the old vessel and saying to my father, "That's not a ship, that's a house. It has square windows and all ships have round ones." Seventeen years later I was on board and knew her better.

'On arrival we were told to go on board and to our surprise, at the top of the gangway, was a door with a knocker on it - the first ship we had seen with a knocker. We knocked, a whistle sounded and we were admitted. It was "Who are you? What do you want? What do you do? What is your rating? etc., etc. This ended with 'Stand over there".

'After half an hour we stood before the Commander, who again asked all the same questions. He said, "I don't know you men, who you are, what you do. In fact you can tell me to go to Hell if you like, but in the meantime I will put you in the hands of a CPO, who will take care of you until we find out more about you."

'Next morning, after prayers, requests, defaulters, etc., we heard: "Motor boat's crew, Fall in". This we did. The Commander took a look at us and said, "Today I know all about you men, who you are, what you are and what you do. You are borne on the books of HMS Eagle and today you cannot tell me to go to Hell. Carry on." That was my introduction to HMS Eagle.

'Life was seldom tedious aboard Eagle. A young boy was acting as messenger and was told to strike six bells. He did. Six in continuous succession. The effect was magical. Everything seemed to stop. Everyone looked at one another. What had happened? Then a voice roared out, "Who struck that Bell? NITWIT!"

Edward Jones was only on board twice after that, once to return the launch and stores, and again to be paid off on the 13th March 1919.

By that date in Liverpool the RNVR had almost ceased to exist.

HMS Eagle in King's Dock, Liverpool
during the 1890's.

WHISKY

Chapter Four

1922 - 1939
EAGLET PREPARES FOR WAR

By the end of the First World War with her new name, Eaglet, the old ship was in serious disrepair. Gone was the familiar white streak broken by her gun-ports and her black hull had been repainted in standard navy grey. What remained of her masts had at some time been cut down to the level of the roof ridge over the upper deck, and she looked more like Noah's Ark than ever.

On the return of peace Eaglet was paid off with no task to perform. However in 1921 it was decided to reform the Mersey Division of the RNVR with a strength of 400 men under the command of Commander William Maples, RNVR. The composition of the Division was by Companies, each 100 strong, of which numbers one, two, three and seven paraded in the ship at Salthouse Dock. Number four Company was located at Southport, number five mustered at Caernarfon and number six in Birkenhead. In 1922 the Southport Company was disbanded.

The Manchester Guardian in September 1922 reported that the attempt to start a 'sub-division' of the RNVR in Salford was under way. An old and dismantled chapel was found to serve as a drill hall. The account added that some 80 officers and men had enrolled and they were awaiting the arrival of a training ship.

This happened a year later when, in September 1923 the war-time sloop HMS Sir Bevis, now re-named Irwell, was berthed in Fairbrother Street Wharf, Salford. The local wits referred to her as HMS Neverbudge.

The Manchester Guardian, January 9th 1926, carried an article with a sad leader.

'A Gallant Wooden Ship of Nelson's Day.

HMS EAGLET FOR SALE.

The forthcoming sale is announced of HMS Eaglet, after a career glorious in her earlier days and useful up to the very end.'

There followed a description of the 'glory days' and then the article painted the picture as she really was, sitting in Salthouse Dock and falling apart.

'Outwardly she is now little more than a glorified houseboat, with a roof and a stove pipe sticking through it. But her hull is still sound, with a row of little latticed windows framed in white around the stern and a helmeted Viking for her figurehead.'

The article then takes a surprising turn, musing on the probability that the Eagle had been built in France and that she came to the British Fleet as a prize! But the final conclusion was that she really had been built by the British in Northfleet in 1804. A certain Mr. Hamilton Gibson, a consulting marine engineer in London, put forward another theory.

'Her round stern he ascribed to the drastic reconstruction undertaken by Sir Robert Seppings after his appointment as Surveyor to the Navy in 1813. Mr Gibson says that it was he who introduced the round stern, and that many square stern ships were afterwards converted.'

The rather strange article continued to ramble through the history of Eagle with an air of total disbelief and occupied far too many paragraphs with its contradictions.

A Farewell Dinner was held on 2nd June 1926 on board Eaglet for the purpose of bidding farewell and also to celebrate the third Annual Naval Services' Re-union. Commander Maples presided over the banquet and the guest of honour was Rear-Admiral Harry Stileman, KBE, RN who had been the Senior Naval Officer for the Port of Liverpool. The main deck of the ship had been transformed into a large dining hall and decorated with flags and hung with lights for the last time.

The Captain goes ashore
Captain Maples and CPO Storey, 1926.

In his speech Rear-Admiral Stileman recalled that he had commanded Eaglet for four years and eight months and that in her he had flown his Flag for the duration of the war. "I had received Eagle from the RNVR and an anxious commanding officer came to me, and said, "You have ripped the roof off, and whipped off the guns, and put them aboard other vessels. What will happen after the war? How am I to account for the loss of these things?" I replied, "I will give you a receipt." And I asked my secretary, "Write him a receipt, 'Received from Sir Charles Mannering one wooden frigate complete.'" In three months' time the commanding officer was back. "I've lost that receipt. Will you give me another one?" I told him, "No. You've had your receipt and you'll get no more from me!"

The Admiral continued. "One day we were fitting out

one of the White Star liners ... I think it was the Laurentic ... we were fitting 6 inch guns, when one man came to me about the oxyacetylene burners. The delegate stated, "You will have to engage 25 boilermakers for each machine." I told him, "Go over to that boilermaker's residence and take this letter, 'I hereby order and direct you to present yourself at the Senior Officer's office forthwith, and if you do not, it will be at your peril." The delegate arrived at the office and I read the King's proclamation of the 4th August to him, that loyal citizens were not to impede the fighting forces in time of war. The answer from the delegate was "That is the regulation. We have our committee in Newcastle." My answer was, "You are the principal man in Liverpool, and you are the man I shall try by court-martial." The delegate responded, "I'd better go and take the restrictions off." "Yes, before the night shift come off!" The work continued and there was no more trouble with that delegate."

The response at the dinner was made by Commodore C.A. Bartlett, CB, CBE, RD, RNR. He said that they all knew Admiral Stileman as 'The Liverpool Admiral'. He could not understand why on earth they gave the Eagle the name of Eaglet. They might just as well call their great grandfather a baby. He was talking as a Royal Naval Reserve officer. The Eagle had been a wonderful fighting ship in the Navy. The RNR and the RNVR had the use of the ship for the greater part of her life, 66 years out of 122, and the number of officers and men who went through her was really remarkable.

John Smart and Edward Jones (The Liverpool Nautical Research Society in Transactions, volume IX, published in April 1963, the twenty-fifth anniversary of the founding of the Society) continued their well-researched memoirs. 'By 1926 the old Eaglet, which had now been afloat for almost a century and a quarter, was deemed to be unfit for further service and was ordered to be paid off for disposal. It was originally intended to replace her by HMS Goole, a wartime minesweeper, but the Goole was too small for this duty and was transferred to Manchester. In August, 1926, all three drill-ships, the Irwell (the war-time sloop) on the west side and the Eaglet with the Goole alongside, lay in Salthouse Dock together for a short time, a unique occasion. Without going into too much detail regarding the change-over, the Irwell (ex HMS Sir Bevis) from Manchester became the present Eaglet and the Eaglet-designate, late the Goole, became the Irwell which we know today, and both ships now lie side by side on the west side of Salthouse Dock (1959).

'A farewell banquet had been held aboard the old veteran on the 2nd June and upon the evening of Thursday, the 2nd September 1926, the Division was mustered aft and at eight bells, as the notes of the Last Post echoed across the quiet dock, her ensign was slowly lowered for the last time and her service as one of the King's ships was ended. She had served under a Queen and five Kings in the 126 years that had elapsed since Sir William Rule designed her. Her ship's company marched away to the new ship and she was left, silent and deserted as she had been left so frequently before. Again the bugles rang out across the still waters, signalmen aboard the new Eaglet hoisted her ensign and the change over was completed.

'There had been a movement afoot to preserve the old ship as a floating maritime museum but, as with so many projects for the preservation of surviving links with our historic past, it was doomed to failure and the old ship was sold for demolition. The work commenced with the removal of her upper works as she lay in the dock, and the guns were removed by the Mersey Docks and Harbour Board's floating crane Samson. Work continued during the ensuing months and on the 16th February 1927, she was towed away to be broken up.

'Few saw her leave on that misty morning. Some workmen on the quay raised their caps in silent salute, the ship-keepers on board her successor watched her slowly move past and she left as she had arrived some sixty years before, slowly and quietly. Guided by tugs and almost unnoticed she disappeared into the morning mist and Liverpool never saw her again.'

Farewell Eaglet.

She was towed to a ship-breaking wharf at Mostyn, where she was beached preparatory to the difficult task of taking apart her aged timbers. On the 19th of April 1927 she caught fire as she lay at Mostyn Deeps on the Welsh side of the Dee and was burnt out. Many regarded the end as a 'Viking funeral' and a pleasing passing for the old warrior. Her epitaph is contained in a few pages of verse preserved aboard her successor.

'Now not a vestige of her remains,
The old ship has gone for good
To some special Valhalla for seventy-fours
And the ships which were built of wood.'

The old ship's magnificent figurehead, a bearded and helmeted warrior, her wheel and an original door and door frame still remain intact today in the shore-based Eaglet, the new Reserve Training Centre.

Lieutenant Glover, RN, Commander Hallet, RN, DSO, VD,
Commander Maples, RNVR, Lieutenant-Commander Elgood.
In background, the Head Ship Keeper, CPO Williams Storey, RN,

A plaque was unveiled by Captain W. Maples on the 28th March 1928 on the wall outside Ward 4 in the Royal Infirmary. A short service was conducted by the Division's chaplain, Reverend E.H. Carew. Ward 4 was specially chosen because over 600 men of the RND had been treated there.

The new Eaglet had been originally built as a Fleet Sweeping Vessel, a Sloop, and was first commissioned in 1918. She was one of a planned 24 ships (not all completed) and was dubbed 'The 24 Class'. The design of the ships did not provide a conventional stern with either a destroyer type square transom or a rounded cruiser stern. The stern was, in fact, identical in construction with the bow. When these ships were 'dazzle painted' it was hard to distinguish bow from stern! 'The 24 Class' had a displacement of 1320 tons, and a designed horsepower of 2500 giving a speed of 17 knots. They carried 260 tons of coal. The ships were armed with two 4-inch guns in single mountings fore and aft and had a ship's complement of 82.

In 1920 she underwent a full conversion to a RNVR Drill Ship. Her original name was Sir Bevis and then she became the Irwell. She was a sister ship to HMS Flying Fox, which was the Headquarters ship of the Severn Division RNVR.

With the closure of the outlying unit in Manchester, the Division's strength fell from 550 to 330. However this was only a temporary fall and was soon put to rights after HMS Irwell opened as a Drill Ship on the 1st May 1932 in Birkenhead.

Entering Eastham Locks
August 25th 1926.

An unnamed reporter wrote an account of Irwell's inland voyage. 'We left Manchester at 5 a.m. under a full moon. There were two tugs, one to pull and the other to keep us in order astern.

It was a voyage when we were never out of sight of the land. We seemed to scrape under bridges with cows and horses looking on. We have been going down in the world ever since we left Manchester. She will arrive at Salthouse tomorrow. This 1,300-ton ship looked rather queer coming down the canal, for between her masts she carries something that looks like a public meeting hall.'

The history of the Division is the story of thousands of individuals, each one adding a page or a paragraph or a line or two ... each one is important. Here is another memory written by Richard Rogers. 'I joined HMS Irwell at Morpeth Dock on 3rd October 1933, number MOX 1578 and served until I was mobilised in August 1939.

'We had a regatta every year against Eaglet when we pulled whalers and cutters from the four bridges at Wallasey to the Poulton bridge about a mile. We used to make it a day out as we had a band, dressed like marines, but they were civilians. The band played at Poulton bridge and all the wives and children were there with refreshments.

'We also competed against Eaglet in the field gun. This took place on Lever Brothers' Founder Day at Port Sunlight Oval and in front of a very big crowd.

'We used to do recruiting marches round Birkenhead with the band and the field gun, and attended some shows in Liverpool parks. We were guard of honour at the launch of Ark Royal in 1937, and guard at Rock Ferry Station in '33 or '34 when King George and Queen Mary left on the Royal train after the opening of the Mersey tunnel.

'We were also present at the Coronation of George VI in '37. We stayed overnight at Crystal Palace with other service men, and then marched at 6 a.m. behind the Marines' band to line part of Whitehall. We were alongside the Cenotaph, and had one break in about six hours to use the toilet, etc.

'In early 1939 we used to go to Eaglet two nights a week to train on twin 4-inch guns. There was an old 1917 V and W destroyer tied up alongside Eaglet, and she had been fitted out with two mountings of the 4-inch, LA HA. (Classes of WW1 Anti-aircraft destroyers, collectively known as V&W ... Low angle, High angle). She also had new range finders and TS (transmitting station), and besides two full crews for those from Irwell, there were crews from Eaglet.

'Our crew went to HMS Excellent, Whale Island, and trained again on the 4-inch. After about six weeks we moved to Pompey Barracks where we took over dockyard defence. In November '39 we commissioned HMS Vega at Devonport Dockyard ... she had been modernised with the twin 4-inch, etc. Our two officers were Lieutenant Woods, RNVR and Sub-Lieutenant Booth, RNVR from Irwell. We served in the Vega until November 1940 when we hit a mine and had to be towed to dock. In January 1941 the whole ship's company took over HMS Atherstone in Chatham Dockyard.

'Please excuse writing as my eyesight is none too good (cataracts).

Yours sincerely,
Richard Rogers.'

The Division in October 1936 received a Special Fleet Mention from the Commander-in-Chief Home Fleet with reference to Able Seaman William King, RNVR Mersey Division, who was serving for a year with the Royal Navy in HMS Nelson.

'1. Officers and men of the Fleet are informed of the following praiseworthy action of William King, Able Seaman, D/J.X.

146063, of HMS Sturdy on 5th March 1936.

'2. Following an aircraft crash on board HMS Furious, which caused the aircraft to fall over the side and the three occupants to fall into the sea, Able Seaman King was the first person in HMS Sturdy to appreciate that one of the occupants of the machine was in difficulties. He immediately dived off the forecastle of HMS Sturdy and swam with a lifebuoy to his assistance, then supporting him until a boat arrived.

'3. The initiative and pluck displayed by Able Seaman King on this occasion is most commendable.

March 1936

R.Backhouse.

Admiral C in C.'

The Commanding Officer of the RN Gunnery School at Chatham congratulated the Division for its contribution in the RN Unit at the Coronation on 12th May 1937 and similar thoughts were expressed by the Lord Mayor of Liverpool as the Division played a major role in the March Past.

Merchant Navy Defence courses started in Eaglet on 13th September 1937. Because there were many officers in the Merchant Navy with no war experience, the aim of the training was to familiarise them with the special duties that might be theirs in time of war. Steps were also being taken to supply defensive equipment for merchant vessels in time of war

The Defensively Equipped Merchant Service, better remembered as DEMS, was a wartime corps of the Royal Navy and Merchant Navy gunners, largely recruited and trained in Liverpool in Eaglet. Their task was to fight off the submarine and air menace from the decks of merchant ships in convoy. Over 2,600 of the men who passed through Eaglet's school fell in action.

Special note was made in the Liverpool Post, 25th October 1937, and reveals the opinions of the day.

'Plea for Retention of Armistice Day

Rector of Liverpool at Memorial Service

'The retention of Armistice Day remembrance was urged and those who advocate its abolition were condemned by the Reverend David Railton (Rector of Liverpool) at the Memorial Service held by former members of the Royal Naval Voluntary Reserve, Mersey Division, in HMS Eaglet, at Salthouse Dock, yesterday afternoon.

'Prior to the service the salute at the march past of present members of the RNVR was taken by the Lord Mayor of Liverpool (Alderman W. Denton), who was supported by the Lady Mayoress, the Mayor of Wallasey (Councillor G.L. Reakes) and the Mayoress (Mrs. F.H. Thornton), Captain E. Elgood, VD, of the Eaglet, Commander C.J.L. Bittleston, RN, and Surgeon-Captain L.S. Ashcroft, VD, RNVR.

'Unworthy the Name

'Mr. Railton said no Englishman was worthy of the name that advocated the abolition of Armistice Day. If men had not fought and died, none of the liberties that we cherished in this country would have been secured; the least they could do was to go down in reverence on their knees in memory of men of character who bore witness to their religion even in the midst of the horrors of war. Another significance behind the Armistice Day was that of an unboasted victory devoid of arrogance.

'The service, during which the two minutes silence was observed, was conducted by the Rev. E.H. Carew of Lymm, and the hymns were accompanied by the band of the RNVR.'

Two years later the country was at war.

The Times ran an article on October 11th 1938 under the heading 'The Misunderstood RNVR Must Be Supported By Civic Authorities'

'In an address given by Surgeon-Captain L.S. Ashcroft in Liverpool to the Boleader Club, he said that he had seen the RNVR confused with the Sea Scouts and with a Reformatory. (laughter) It was 5,000 or 6,000 strong and corresponded to the Navy exactly as the Territorials to the Regular Army. Mersey Division had two ships, HMS Eaglet on the Liverpool side and HMS Irwell in Birkenhead Docks. Mersey Division consisted of twelve instructors, petty officers and an officer instructor. These were regular Navy, the backbone of the Division, responsible for teaching and training; then they had their own officers, executive, accountancy, medical and dental. Actually we now have 118 officers with a recently increased number of 'snotties' - 24; so much so that we have had to create a gun-room for them. Otherwise the wardroom would be overrun with a seething mass of young people. He had eleven doctors, now being raised to 18 - roughly two for each Division, consisting of 100 men.'

On October 11th 1938 the Liverpool Evening Express included this statement: 'When the Fleet Order for mobilisation was given, officers and men of the Mersey Division RNVR were called up in batches as the occasion demanded, and within 48 hours a large number left Liverpool.'

On March 25th 1939 an appeal for RNVR recruits was made by Surgeon-Captain L.S. Ashcroft at the Gordon Smith Institute for Seamen. It was illustrated with a film of the Mersey Division at work and play. Certain Divisions, including Mersey Division, would soon have sloops fitted with the latest electronic devices. Heads of businesses were asked to look more kindly on the RNVR and give more facilities and more encouragement for their employees to serve.

HMS Wallace docked in Salthouse Dock, Liverpool, on Saturday 19th June 1939, brought from Devonport under the captaincy of Lieutenant-Commander R.C. Beckett, RN, the officer instructor attached to the Mersey Division. She occupied a permanent position alongside HMS Eaglet, as an additional unit for training the Mersey Division of the RNVR in high angle gunnery. A destroyer of 1,480 tons, Wallace had attained a speed of 32 knots on her trials and had up-to-date equipment for gunnery instruction.

Wallace was a V & W destroyer and gave great delight and satisfaction to the Division. She was fitted with twin 4-inch HA LA guns and the Admiralty gave a formal promise that every anti- aircraft unit trained would be given an immediate place in a seagoing destroyer on the outbreak of war. HMS Wallace lay alongside HMS Eaglet and in September 1939 was placed on a war footing with officers and men of the Division helping form a substantial part of her ship's company.

Wallace was built under the European War Emergency Programme as a flotilla leader. Laid down in 1917, she was launched in October 1918 and completed in February 1919.

In the adjacent Albert Dock were two minesweepers, HMS Hebe and HMS Seagull. They were there following the tragic sinking of the submarine Thetis in Liverpool Bay.

War was imminent.

STOUT

Chapter Five

1939 - 1945
THE SECOND WORLD WAR

On September 3rd 1939 the Division was 30 over strength, i.e. 1,030 - of this number two men failed to report (one on compassionate grounds). This was a remarkable achievement. Three failed to pass the doctor and twenty were drafted to HMS Royal Arthur in order to continue training. The remainder received immediate appointments.

Of this number 120 failed to return - 20 officers and 100 ratings. Many were to receive decorations for valour and bravery. A number of officers achieved command. The record of service is a proud one and the Division lost men in such sea epics as Rawalpindi, the Rajputana, and the tragic sinkings of the Hood, the Prince of Wales and the carriers Glorious and Courageous.

HMS Eaglet was officially commissioned in October 1939 as Base Ship Liverpool. The ship's captain, Captain Eric Elgood, was appointed in command and also as Maintenance Captain on the Staff of FOIC Liverpool.

When the Commander in Chief Western approaches established his base in Liverpool in February 1941, he (Admiral Sir Percy Noble) flew his flag in HMS Eaglet as did Admiral Sir Max Horton who succeeded Noble in 1942. The principle Staff Officers lived on board throughout the War as did about 150 ratings.

Eaglet was used extensively for the training of DEMS Ratings, both British and Allied, whilst HMS Irwell became the minesweeper base in Wallasey Dock, Birkenhead.

Perhaps one of the better ways of understanding the 'life' of a RNVR officer is to examine the service histories of the men involved. It will reveal the dedication and tenacity needed to succeed in the Reserves.

This script was hand-written by Lieutenant-Commander Dennis Robert Bennett-Jones and is not too easy to decipher. The training was long and demanding.

'The Service History of Dennis Robert Bennett-Jones. Born 15th September 1910. British subject by birth. Baptised into Church of England 1st November 1910.

Record of Service in Rossall School OTC. Joined September 1924, resigned August 1929, Rank Sergeant. Attended Annual Camp 1926, 1927, 1928 and 1929. Passed Certificate 'A' 1928. Musketry qualification .22 First Class, .303 First Class. Attended Army School of Physical Training Aldershot August 1927 and April 1929.

1930 June 12th   Appointed Probationary Midshipman RNVR
        and attached to Mersey Division, List 1.
1931 May 16th Appointed HMS Repulse additional for 28 days
        training as Probationary Midshipman RNVR.
1931 August 18th   Confirmed as Midshipman RNVR with
        seniority 12th June 1930.
1932 March 11th   Promoted to Acting Sub Lieutenant, RNVR.
1932 June 18th   Appointed HMS Renown additional for 14 days
        training as Acting Sub Lieutenant RNVR.
1933 May 3rd   Promoted Sub Lieutenant RNVR with seniority
        11th March 1933.

1933 May 20th   Appointed HMS Excellent additional for 7 days
Gunnery Course, and completed with 72%.

1933 May 27th   Appointed HMS Dryad additional for 7 days
Pilotage Course, and completed with 80%.

1934 May 27th   Mersey Division Official RNVR sailing parties
began and continued each year until 1939. My only
regret is that all ratings were not paid full subsistence, but
the balance went to Mersey Division Funds!

1934 September 15th Appointed HMS Halcyon additional for
disposal to HMS Skipjack for 14 days training.

1935 March 11th   Promoted to Lieutenant RNVR.

1935 August 31st   Appointed HMS Halcyon additional for
disposal to HMS Skipjack for 14 days training. NB. At
the end of the first week's training the RNVR Officers
were put ashore and the 1st Minesweeping Flotilla sailed
for the Mediterranean.

1936 September 5th   Appointed HMS Halcyon additional to
disposal to HMS Skipjack for 14 days training.

1936 October 23rd   In charge of Firing Party at Funeral of
Captain Maples.

1937 April 12th   In charge of the Guard of Honour when First
Lord of the Admiralty visited HMS Eaglet.

1937 May 12th   In charge of the Mersey Division Platoon lining
the Street in Whitehall for Coronation of his late Majesty
King George VI and awarded the Coronation Medal.

1937 July 24th   Regatta Officer Pulling Regatta, East Float,
Birkenhead.

1937 September 4th   Coxswain Mersey Division Officers'
Whaler at the Northern Pulling Regatta at the Tyne.

1937 September 19th   Appointed HMS Drake additional for 14
days training (First Part Qualifying 'G' Course) 86%

1938 March 20th   Appointed HMS Drake additional for 14 days training (Second Part Qualifying 'G' Course) 82% Total 83% First Class.

1938 May 19th   Second in Command Guard of Honour outside Town Hall, Liverpool, for his late Majesty King George VI. (Lt. Cdr. S Lynch in charge.)

1938 July 23rd   Regatta Officer, Pulling Regatta, East Float, Birkenhead.

1938 September 3rd   Coxswain Officers' Whaler, Mersey Division at the Northern Pulling Regatta at the Tyne.

1938 September 29th   Appointed HMS Pembroke additional for Port and Harbour Defence Invergordon. Crisis over and returned home 4th October 1938.

1938 October 30th   Appointed HMS Drake additional for 7 days Anti Gas Course.

1939 January 1st   First Lieutenant HMS Irwell, Birkenhead.

1939 March 19th   Appointed HMS Excellent additional for 14 days training (AA Course.)

1939 April 22nd   In charge of the RNVR Party at National Service Parade, Birkenhead.

1939 May 3rd   In charge of Guard of Honour for the Princess Royal at the launch of HMS Prince of Wales at Birkenhead.

1939 May 23rd   Attended Revue at St. James' Palace.

1939 August 13th   After we had sailed the late Lord Derby's Yacht Mersey to the Menai Straits, we also sailed her back to Rock Ferry; but when on this Sunday morning I reported her safe arrival to Captain Elgood by telephone, he seemed to think the yacht was being brought into a danger zone! Should have left her there!

Active National Service.

1939 August 25th   Appointed HMS Wallace as Lieutenant

RNVR (Duties: Correspondence Office, Forecastle
Officer, and at sea Terrestrial Navigation, and in action
Director Control) until 20th January 1940.

1940 January 22nd   Appointed HMS Excellent additional as
Lt. RNVR for AA Course, until 18th February 1940.

1940 February 19th   Appointed HMS Cairo as Lieutenant RNVR
(Duties: AA watch-keeping and look-out officer in
Spotting Top by day and on bridge by night) until 25th
April 1940.

1940 April 26th   Appointed HMS Southampton as Lieutenant
RNVR and to study their AA Gunnery Control, until 17th
May 1940. (I had to wait a few days in HMS Dunl??
Castle before joining HMS Southampton.)

1940 May 19th   Appointed HMS Excellent for course with Gun
Crews to go to HMS Alynbank on commissioning (until
9th June 1940). (While in Gunnery School, in Officers'
Team which ran twice round Whale Island and won!)

1940 June 9th   In command HM Transport Hebe II.   Wounded
while lying off St. Very-en-Caux ???? on night of 11th
June 1940 and wounded again on 12th June 1940 when
aground off the shore a little East.

1940 13th June   Taken Prisoner of War by German Army
together with many of the 51st Highland Division, the
132 Field Ambulance, and the French. (Gun shot wound
right leg and thigh, bad compound fracture tibia and
fibula according to later reports.)

Prisoner of War.

1940 13th June   Forges les Eaux for about a fortnight.
D'Erummout, Rouen, until February 1941.

1941   Freysa in Germany until August. Marburg/Lahn for about
three weeks during October. Obermansfeld from say

November to March 1942.

1942   Marburg/Lahn from March 1942 to October 1942.
Egendorf about 25th October 1942 to 11th November
1942. Kloster Heina November to August 1943.

1943   Lamsdorf August to October 1943.
(Souvenirs: Prisoner of War tally No. 14529 and
Bescheinigung dated 25 9 1942 stating that on 13 11
1941 at Obermansfield nach Artikel 70 Kr.-Gef. Hk v
1929 der Gemichter Artzekommission vorgestellt. Sein
Heimkehrberchtigung wurde bejaht), but the Germans
informed me I had to wait patiently until proper
arrangements were concluded for any repatriation. I also
have a letter from the American Embassy, Prisoner of
War Section, dated Berlin, November 28th 1941
informing me that my letter of the 1st instant regarding
X-rays had been received and my complaint had been
forwarded to the International Red Cross and the British
Government in accordance with my wishes.

1943 March 11th   Promoted Lieutenant-Commander RNVR.

1943 October   Repatriated via Sassnitz/Rugen to
Trelleborg/Sweden and thence to Gottenburg to the
Swedish American Line 'Drottinghholm' which did
paravane trials while awaiting the German Prisoners of
War from Great Britain. Eventually after a quiet trip we
arrived at Leith, Scotland on 25th October 1943. After a
good reception we went by train to Royal Victoria
Hospital, Netley, Southampton, for examination.

1944 February 26th   Medical Survey and found unfit for further
Active Naval Service.

1944 April 7th   Placed on Retired List (Article 246(a) RNVR
(Officers) Regulations).

1944 October   Reported at Admiralty, Whitehall, London S.W.1.

Campaign Stars, Medals and Awards.

The Distinguished Service Cross ... June 1940.

In the Supplement to the London Gazette, 2 August 1940, the citation was as follows:

"The KING has been graciously pleased to approve the following Awards for courage and resource in the withdrawal of troops from the neighbourhood of Le Havre:-

Lieutenant Dennis Robert Bennett-Jones, RNVR."

The 1939 - 45 and Atlantic Stars and 1939 - 45 War Medal.

Coronation Medal 1937.

Volunteer Reserve Decoration.

Civilian Qualification

Associate of the Institute of Chartered Shipbrokers. Passed their Intermediate Exam in December 1935 and Final Exam in May 1936.'

This is a remarkable record of service and needs no embroidery to endorse the total dedication needed to be a RNVR Officer.

The memories of Lieutenant-Commander Frank Jennings, VRD, RNR, are full of interest for us. 'My friends were joining up - mostly to TA Regiments - there being no RAAF on Merseyside. Who it was I forget, but someone said to me "Why not come along to Eaglet? I've got an appointment." I was nineteen and had no close naval connections, except an elderly relative - an Engineer Captain in Southsea. After applying I was summoned in 1937 to repair on board HMS Eaglet in Salthouse Dock to see Captain Eric Elgood - the 'Great Agrippa'.

'He occupied the 'Great Cabin' in the stern of Eaglet. Over coffee, one morning, he appraised me for a moment or two, asked what school I had attended - Liverpool College - what I did, and then said, "I know your father" and, apparently approving of the 'cut of my jib', "We'll be in touch - with your appointment, not commission." Then he added "Don't go to Gieves for your uniform and dirk, go to Vic Pennell in Cable Street, he'll fix you up - cheaper!" Big Mistake! Vic Pennell was a good tailor and he produced a good outfit, but the maroon patches on the monkey jacket were a shade too dark and the cap badge was a mite too narrow - and this was noticed, and I was conscious of it. Got a cap from Gieves in Castle Street.

'Eaglet then had a Wardroom and a Gunroom. There were, I recall, about twenty Midshipmen.

'There were two drill nights, on Tuesdays and Thursdays, always with Divisions and Prayers, and a 'Stand Easy' mid-time with beer and meat pies. We had the usual 'Dartmouth Type instructions - how to be Naval Officers'.

'Highlights were the two Annual Balls, held on Grand National Night and New Year's Eve, with Dance Programmes and Full Rig - bum freezers and tin trousers. It was the 'extra-mural' activities that were the great attraction.

'Eaglet had six 'dipping lug' cutters, and eight pulling whalers, in the dock alongside, for instruction and recreation. In summer months we sailed the whalers in the Mersey - mainly in the Sloyne to visit Conway and, less frequently, Indefatigable.

'A favourite trip was into the West Float at Birkenhead and to tie up alongside one of Erricson's square riggers - grain ships from the Aalund Islands in the Baltic, and Pamir, Passat and the Penang, which was sunk by a U-boat under full sail and full load. But the highlight was the Easter Sailing party to the Point of Ayr. A dangerous trip in cutters, attended by a wheezy motor boat. Cutters are rough sailors - 'lower and dip' to 'go about', avoiding twenty-knot Cunarders in the Rock Channel and being nearly driven on to the Revetment. Give way to sail!

'Eaglet officers were honorary members of the Royal Mersey Yacht Club at Rock Ferry. Lord Derby had presented a

Mersey One still afloat thanks to Sally Collings and shipwright George.

Mylne Class boat for the use of the RNVR, and much use was made of it. All the Mylne Class names began with the letter 'M' - Mark, Merrimac, Merlin and Mersey was painted in black enamel.

'1939 saw the serious sophistication of the arrival alongside of HMS Wallace, with modern 4-inch AA guns. We felt that this meant business.

'We were never paid, except when on 'sea training' when we got the 'rate', and I don't think that mess bills came to anything very much.

'I don't recall all the Gunroom names, but the Stowell twins, Richards, Fuller, Groom, Dagleish, and I, were called up in August '39 to join Repulse. And Marcus Graham, who latterly went blind and who, last year, was visited by the Admiral of the Fleet Sir Henry Leech and was belatedly presented with his VRD at St. Dunstan's in Brighton.

'Others will, no doubt, talk about the Wardroom, but who could forget Paymaster Captain Bunney, who owned the delightful West Arms at Llananmoor D.C.; and my particular old school pals - Sub-Lieutenant Ronnie Fryer-Smith, a solicitor, or Paymaster Sub-Lieutenant Gerry Unsworth.

'On mobilisation, the strength and diversity of the pre-war RNVR manifested itself. The Division was scattered over the entire Navy - general training allowed this. A vital and enjoyable feature was the compulsory Sea Training. I did two periods of a fortnight, one in Iron Duke in July 1938, and another two weeks in Royal Oak on Spring Fleet exercises in March 1939, war routine.

'Captain Elgood usually had a couple of words when he knew what ship you were joining. His words to me, prior to Iron Duke, "Remember, sit far apart from the next person at breakfast and don't talk, and remember the Naval code of speech - don't address anyone unless you are in the same room or can see them!"

'Iron Duke's midshipmen ate in the Wardroom and remembering this advice, at first breakfast I sat far apart from the others sitting behind their (ironed) morning papers. Timidly, I asked the nearest officer "Sir, would you kindly pass the salt?" Growled from behind the newspaper "Young man, what do you think the bloody servants are for!" '

Time passed and Frank was to marry Barbara who had joined the Wrens as a MT driver in 1940. One frozen morning on overnight duty in London Docks in 1941 she was called by the Duty rating, "Wakey-wakey, Jenny, there's as 'ow there's a priority dispatch to be got to 'arwich. Here's a cuppa!" The car, being a Hillman Ten, would not have passed the current MOT ... no headlights, no fog lights, no heater, no power brakes, no synchromesh, and, worse, synthetic tyres. There was a whirlwind romance and marriage in 1943. Frank's story continues.

'When I was appointed Base Gunnery Officer at HMS Irwell, Birkenhead, in 1943, after service in Repulse and Valiant, Barbara applied for transfer to Liverpool. She served in HMS Eaglet, based on the Liver Building, with the MT Garage at Linnet Lane.

'The cream of the Western Approaches Wrens were employed both in the Headquarters of Admiral Sir Max Horton at Derby House, and those with great intellect at Captain Robert's A/S Tactical School. The 'Wrennery' was at the Rathbone House in Greenbank Lane.

'We were honoured in February 1945 by a visit from Their Majesties, The King and Queen, who both inspected the Royal Guard, which, as 'G', I commanded. The King was most incisive - wanting assurance that the Guard was composed of sea-going personnel and not Base wallahs. He was pleased to hear that most had just returned from escorting a 'QP' from Murmansk.

'I was demobilised in 1945. I don't recall how Eaglet reverted back to a RNVR drill ship, but there was certainly no activity and I received no communication. A group of half a dozen of us - Tom Horsfall, Gerry Unsworth, Ronnie-Fryer Smith, William Kershaw, Tony Dalzell and I approached the Ship Keeper, the indomitable Sawberg, and we opened up the Wardroom and the partially stocked bar. With Sawberg cooking alfresco meals - many whale steaks - we met weekly for lunch.

'The new Commanding Officer was Captain Norman Wood, DSC. Slowly my old friends drifted away and I resigned before we lost our Wavy Stripes and RNVR designation.'

It had been good to converse with Frank Jennings and to 'swing the lamp'.

Commander D.A. Rayner, DSC and Bar, VRD, RN, is one of ours. The author of the Official History of 'The War at Sea 1939 - 1945', Captain S.W. Roskill, DSC, RN, wrote this of him. 'I know of no other officer, let alone one of the Royal Naval Volunteer Reserve, who served continuously for more than five years in command of escort vessels; nor of any other who graduated from a trawler at the very beginning to a corvette, then to a small destroyer, to several larger destroyers or groups of destroyers, and finally to command of a group of the new and greatly improved war-built escort vessels.' Rayner with modesty told his remarkable story in 'Escort. The Battle of the Atlantic', published by William Kimber, London in 1955. The preparation for his career is firmly part of the Eaglet story.

'Within a month of leaving school I was knocking at the door of the Captain's cabin in HMS Eaglet.

'Sadly the establishment was full, but he went back every month from March to June 1925. By this time Captain Maples was beginning to recognise him. Most of the applicants were recommended by other officers and there were far too many of them. Finally in July he was 'in'. This started twenty-four years with the RNVR.

'Throughout the RNVR it had been generally supposed that Gunnery was the branch in which it was worthwhile to specialise. This had come about not only because the gun was so obviously the weapon of the Navy, but because it was the easiest weapon in which to train in a drill ship. In Eaglet we had an excellent gun battery fitted with all the manually operated guns from big 6-inch to the 4-inch breech loading and quick firing guns. These were controlled by a director tower that was coupled to an ingenious device for teaching officers the principles of gunnery control.

'To be confirmed in the rank of Lieutenant it was necessary not only to pass an examination, but also to undergo a qualifying course in some specialist branch, such as Gunnery, Navigation, Signals or Torpedo. 97 per cent qualified in Gunnery. I was the exception.

'Early in 1932 I had asked Captain E. Elgood for permission to take a specialist Navigator's course. He explained to me that I was a bloody fool and that if I wanted to spend the whole of the next war correcting charts I was going the right way to do so. I have never worked so hard in all my life. I passed with the percentages of 94 and 98 in the two papers. The ACR wrote a complimentary letter to Captain Elgood and thus spiked the Captain's guns.'

In 1936 the anti-submarine school in Portland trained officers to act as Unit Commanders in the fleet of trawlers. For each group of five trawlers there was to be one trained Group Commander and two Unit Commanders. The Group Commander was to be a retired RN officer and the Unit Commanders were from the navigation specialists in the Reserves.

'Once again this seemed too good to be true and I went to see Elgood. Again he told me I was crazy. To this I replied that I wanted to get command of an anti-submarine vessel. "You'll never get command, Rayner - the Navy won't give RNVRs command of a ship, no matter how long the war lasts." He tried hard, but could not shake my resolution. In 1937 I took the first part of the course. I was to have completed this in the autumn of 1938, but the Munich Crisis intervened.

'I received a telegram ordering me to report to Naval Officer in Charge, Kirkwall. All the other officers of the Mersey Division were going off to join the Fleet or to man ships of the Reserve Fleet. The only difference between their telegrams and mine was that mine instructed me to join 'with all despatch' whereas theirs only carried the words 'forthwith'. 'Forthwith' in naval language means without wasting time. 'With all despatch' means get there whatever happens'.

That journey proved to be horrendous and should be studied as an example of how not to organise a transport system. However, he did eventually arrive in Kirkwall, but not before Chamberlain had returned from Munich with his piece of paper. Later Rayner discovered that he had been destined to establish a contraband control base and was full of gloom at the thought.

Back in Eaglet, Captain Elgood proceeded to point out just what a fool he had been and was! Rayner had been the only officer who had not had an interesting appointment. He carried on with his anti-submarine training.

'It was a busy winter for us in the RNVR. The Admiralty had given approval to increase the strength of the Division above the eleven hundred we were allowed. Our numbers rose steadily until we had sixteen hundred men, and sometimes as many as four hundred drilling on a single night. At the last minute to sweep the yachtsmen into the fold, the Admiralty created the

Supplementary Reserve, or RNVSR. Many of them took a fortnight's holiday with the Fleet and an attempt was made to teach them navigation and gunnery in the drill ship on nights when the RNVR was not using her. Elgood seized on me and placed me in charge of their navigational instruction, so that I often went to the ship three nights a week. When mobilisation came Captain Elgood had the satisfaction of sending off more than forty officers and sixteen hundred trained men from Merseyside.'

So began Rayner's war. Four days before the declaration he was at Lowestoft 'for disposal' as a Unit Commander of anti-submarine trawlers. He chose a Devon trawler skipper, Skipper Lang, and they took over a 900 ton vessel, Loch Tulla. Lang appeared not to trust any navigational aid.

"Thick weather or clear Skipper?" I'd ask.

"Oh thick Sir, with a mizzle of rain. Did you notice how red was the rust on the buoy we passed a while back - blood red it was. 'Twill be thick as the Earl o' Hell's riding boots tonight."

Some time later Loch Tulla had been compass swinging in the Mersey and was returning to Birkenhead Docks. No pilot was on offer and Rayner thought that he was well versed with the necessary knowledge. 'We took towards the dock with reasonable speed and round the corner we found a brick wall barring our path. The Harbour Board had decided to close this particular passage between one dock and the next. We came to a grinding stop, and Loch Tulla was ten feet shorter than she had been a moment before!'

Four days later the Board of Enquiry in the Liver Building seemed puzzled as to whether Rayner or Lang had been in charge and came to no conclusion. Rayner called to see Captain Elgood.

'He was pleased to see me. "Rayner, I have always told

you, but you never listen. The Navy cannot give command to an RNVR officer. Your experience today proves what I've always said."

"Oh well, it's too late to change now, and you know, Sir, I wouldn't anyway."

"You always were a bloody fool," he said as he shook my hand. They were the last words I ever heard Elgood speak.

'Much to my surprise I found myself included in the first honours list of the war, but had no idea for what reason the DSC had been given me. I would like to have thought it was for our action south of Flamborough Head on our way north, and perhaps at the time I did think so.

'I took Loch Tulla to Aberdeen and then went to attend the first investiture of the war in Buckingham Palace. I was the only RNVR there, and so the last naval officer in the line. When it came to my turn His Majesty said conversationally, "I'm so pleased to see one of you here today." I was so surprised that I muffed my going astern and turn to starboard, so that the very senior Army officer who was behind me had to do a quick shuffle to avoid a collision.'

There was to be another award of the DSC and much adventure. That book is a good read ... and he was one of ours!

No person in this country realised that when U-30 torpedoed the Liverpool to Canada-bound liner Athenia, on the first day of the war, she fired the opening shots of the Battle of the Atlantic. Liverpool became the nerve-centre of the vital, grim fight that took a hideous toll in lives, ships and cargoes.

It was not until March 6th 1941 that Churchill declared '...we must assume that the Battle of the Atlantic has begun'. Here in Merseyside we already knew that. The people had been battered for 19 months by the Luftwaffe. Hitler declared

Liverpool his primary target in the Battle of the Atlantic. It was not revealed at the time that the port was under siege and I suspect that to this very day it has passed unnoticed.

During the week ended May 7th 1941, when Liverpool was reeling from seven consecutive nights of heavy bombing, in the infamous 'May Blitz', 43,000 tons of shipping was lost in the North West Approaches. The total loss from March to May was 1,691,499, involving 412 ships. Churchill said a little later '... the issue hung in balance'.

Another rather different, but excellent book entitled 'The Sea Chaplains' by the Reverend Gordon Taylor, a wartime chaplain himself and the RNR chaplain of the London Division until 1970, includes a section of especial interest to Merseysiders.

'In September 1939 the Royal Navy began its blockade of Germany in Northern waters by using the older cruisers to cover the exits to the Atlantic, the Denmark Strait and the Faeroe Islands Passage. In the October the ships were augmented by the first of the liners which had been converted into Armed Merchant Cruisers (AMCs).

'In February 1940 twenty AMCs sailed on the Northern Patrol, four were with the Halifax Escort Force and twelve were in the Mediterranean.

'A chaplain for the AMCs. was appointed in August 1940 in order to minister to the men who had the arduous work of the Northern Patrol, and he was a particularly good choice. He was the Reverend Eric Evans, RNVR, then Vicar of Crossens, near Southport, Lancashire, who for five years before the war had been the Senior Chaplain of the Mersey Mission to Seamen, and who therefore knew well many of the merchant service officers and men who were serving under the T124 (or T124X) Agreement. Such to a large degree were the ships' companies of the AMCs, though their captains and commanders were generally Royal Navy officers who had been brought back from fairly recent retirement and a considerable proportion of the seamen were also from the Royal Navy.

'Evans made his first patrol in the former Bibby liner Cheshire, and followed this with others in the former P&O Chitral, the former Anchor liners Cilicia and Circassia, and the Wolfe, which was the former Canadian Pacific Montcalm as renamed. He remembers spending Christmas 1940 in northern waters. From early in 1941 he worked from the base at Halifax (Seaborn) on a roving commission with the AMCs of the Western Patrol, before returning to Britain in the former Cunarder Alaunia.

'As Evans' ships in the North Atlantic reduced in number, his suitability for work in such ships was again recognised by his appointment in October 1941 to the base-ship which was anchored permanently at Freetown, Sierra Leone, the very old former Union Castle liner Edinburgh Castle, for sea-going duty with the AMCs, operating in the South Atlantic in the South American Division.

'He joined the former Union Castle liner Carnarvon Castle and stayed in her at the captain's request until March 1942 when he took passage to Cape Town to join, first the former Furness Withy liner Queen of Bermuda and the former Royal Mail Alcantara. After almost three years in AMCs, he returned home to Britain and in due course joined the cruiser Bermuda, which became engaged in Russian convoy work. He ended his service on the staff of the Admiral at Bombay. Few clergy who joined the Navy as Temporary Chaplains, RNVR, can have seen more sea-time then Eric Evans. After all his voyaging he returned to parochial life in West Lancashire, and saw many arduous years as Rector of North Meols and Archdeacon of

Warrington. He died on 25th of December 1977.'

When I arrived on Merseyside in 1961 and took charge of the Mersey Mission to Seamen, Eric Evans was a member of the Committee. He never talked to me about his wartime adventures, but proved to be a mine of information and a loyal friend.

One well retired RNR officer, shyly anonymous, has written his memories for me of his time in the RNVR. When war broke out he was Third Officer of the Ellerman Hall Line, received a chit in Liverpool and via Scrabster ended up in 'Tin Willy', HMS Iron Duke. The next day there was some high level bombing, followed at sundown by a very low level attack. In the New Year of 1940 he joined HMS Worcestershire (ex-Bibby Line) in Beardmores Basin, Glasgow. Junior officers, RNVR Subs and Midshipmen were promptly sent off to the Clyde RNVR Depot and were given a couple of days learning how to load 6-inch guns on the dummy loader. There were many memories, but none better than what is described as 'gun control'.

'The gun control was from the former 'monkey island' where a small hand operated range finder and 'control position' had been added. From here the range and spotting data and corrections were passed down by a voice pipe to the 'transmitting station' (a converted inside cabin), which was equipped with a Vickers Range Clock and a Dumerique Clock operated by two of the RNVR Subbies. Both instruments having been set up with the data sent down from the control position ... range, estimated course with reference to line of sight (most confusing to the unenlightened), bearing on the bow ... the resulting range and deflection settings were transmitted to the guns by telephone and set on the gun sights by the sight setters. The trainer and layer of each gun sat on a seat each side of the gun and looked through the telescope attached to the sights. When the fire gong sounded, the guns were fired by the layer when the cross wires of his sights were on. The layer and trainer kept their cross wires on the target with their hand wheels, taking care of the ship's roll ... it all depended upon how good these gentlemen were.'

There were, of course, problems! 'The forward gun in Worcestershire was found to be too stiff to be trained unaided (one assumes that they pushed it by hand!) and the after gun when the stops were released waved gently from side to side in sync with the roll of the ship.' There was much more, but we must be thankful that they survived.

Eaglet was very much the centre for training the men who served in the DEMS (Defensively Equipped Merchant Ships). Here are some memories.

Edmund Drew, now a retired Liverpool Pilot, put pen to paper. He was in his second year in HMS Conway.

'On the 31st May 1943 I wrote to DEMS in HMS Eaglet. On the 2nd June I had a reply ... within two days! ... ordering me to report to HMS Eaglet on 30th August at 0900. I attended as instructed in Salthouse Dock (I was home for my birthday on holiday) and was met by a (to me) very old and grizzled CPO. There were about twenty others there, MN, some old and some young, but in civilian clothes. I was the only one in uniform.

'After a while we were all ticked off on the CPO's list and then we all walked with him to Canning Dock where the Dome was. The building is still there; it has Grecian type columns and is next door to the Maritime Museum. Inside was a domed ceiling that was painted white and on which were projected films of aircraft crossing from different angles and also diving directly down upon us. All this took place with the appropriate engine noise. The dive-bomber was a Stuka and the scream filled the building. There was a mock gun position and each of us in turn had a 'go' with the gun. The instructor could tell us where our shots were going in relation to the aircraft. I think it was all done with lights. We were constantly told to aim well ahead by using the rings of the sights. This went on all morning and after lunch we went back to Eaglet. We were put into a sort of classroom and shown how to dismantle a Lewis anti-aircraft gun and also a Hotchkiss machine gun. We were also taught the basics of loading and firing.

'The next morning we were met by the same CPO and were shepherded on to a single-decker bus. Off we went to the ranges at Altcar, between Liverpool and Southport. Here we started with clay pigeon shooting, using tracer shotgun cartridges. We all had about ten shots each and urged to shoot well ahead of the clay.

'Next we were taken to the small gun emplacements to fire the Hotchkiss and Lewis guns. A biplane ... one wonders what the pilot had done to deserve such a task ... from nearby Woodvale was towing a red drogue about 150 feet astern for us to fire at it! We could see where our shots were going by the tracer. It was great fun.

'Back in Eaglet, we were given our DEMS Certificates.'

Thank you, Edmund Drew. Another old friend, Sid Davies, tops up that tale.

'In August 1943 I was sent to a gunnery course in Liverpool prior to going to sea with Brocklebanks as a deck apprentice. The Eaglet was a bizarre looking wooden hulk in Salthouse Dock with what looked like a village hall placed on top of it. Gnarled RN CPOs introduced a motley crowd of MN types to the intricacies of gunnery. Models were used to explain the art of shelling where range and deflection were adjusted to straddle and eventually hit a moving target. Browning and Lewis guns were displayed and we were taught (to quote one Petty Officer) how to 'dismantle and then mantle them together again'!

'On Ainsdale sands we were taught how to fire real guns. "Do not, I repeat, do not fire at the aircraft. "We were told that the RAF in Woodvale considered the task of target towing to be a suicide mission with one plane having been shot down. In addition to MN personnel there were naval ratings firing 'Chicago Pianos', as Pom-poms were known. The racket of these and Oerlikons and other hardware was exciting.

'At the end we were given certificates and I was ever so proud at 17 years of age to have one which said, 'This officer is capable of taking charge of the armament of a Defensively Equipped Merchant Ship'. It was stretching it a bit!

'The extra sixpence a day for being sight-setter on a 4.7 inch gun was a most useful addition to my £3. 10s a month wage when I got to sea.'

Sometimes memories are brushed down and given an airing. Happily as the years passed, I joined the 'old and bold' on many festive occasions, when anecdotes were spun out to amuse and little was made of the suffering and hardship of wartime at sea. Eaglet was a great meeting place for 'swinging the lamp' and telling the tale with humour.

Memories often increase the size of the waves, yet some memories need no embellishment. The announcement in November 1959 that HMS Starling was to go into the Reserve preparatory to being sold for demolition took Liverpool's memories back fifteen years. An article appeared in the Journal of Commerce.

Perhaps the most impressive naval occasion on Merseyside was in 1944 when the Starling under the command of the late Captain F.J. Walker, RN, CB, DSO*** led the Second Support Group back into port after a period of action in the Western Approaches during which six German U-Boats were sunk.

'Each ship in turn was cheered in - a distinction seldom accorded under modern conditions of warfare - and with such an assembly that the noise was almost overwhelming'

It was an inspiring event recalled by one of the protagonists, Commander D.E.G. Wemyss, DSO, DSC, who as Commander of HMS Wild Goose, was one of Captain Walker's team. After describing in his book 'Walker's Groups in the Western Approaches' how the Second Support Group sank the six U-boats during a trip in which one of the Group, the Woodpecker was lost, Captain Wemyss continued the story.

'Meanwhile the rest of us, the Starling, Wild Goose, Magpie and Wren, were informed by Sir Max Horton (then Commander-in-Chief, Western Approaches) that on our return home to Liverpool he intended that we should be cheered into harbour. And what a welcome they gave us! We steamed up the channel into the Mersey in line ahead and turned left in succession to enter the lock leading into Gladstone Dock, and there was the crowd.

'Rows and rows of our comrades from the escort ships were there together with the captain and ship's company of the battleship King George V, which was in dock nearby, masses of Wrens (who were making as much noise as all the rest put together), merchant sailors, crews from Allied ships and dock workers.

'To lead the cheer party stood Captain G.N. Brewer on a dais, himself not long returned from a career of violence at sea that included one of the longest and most savage battles fought round a convoy in the course of the whole war. He was now in command of our base; he had strung up a hoist of flags which read: 'Johnny Walker Still Going Strong', and he conducted the cheers that greeted each of us as we took our turn to berth.

October 1998, Prince Phillip unveils the Walker Memorial at Pier Head.

'My ship was flying her banner for the first time and looked a credit to her First Lieutenant (Lieutenant W.P. Chipman, RCNVR) and his wash and brush up party. My personal impressions of the proceedings, however, were over-shadowed by the anxiety of having in the midst of all the hubbub, to con the ship to her berth in the lock without hitting either the quay or HMS Starling where the Boss was receiving his wife and daughter.

'Later when we were all berthed in the dock and had landed our prisoners, Sir Max Horton came to welcome us, bringing with him the First Lord, Mr. A.V. Alexander (now Viscount Alexander of Hillsborough), who was on a visit to Liverpool and who made us a rousing speech.

'The proceedings came to an end with that ever popular wind up to a day of emotional strain, a splicing of the Main Brace, which needless to say was duly noted on our banner, and then the lucky ones among us went on a few days leave.'

One lady recalls her brothers who were in the Division at the start of the war. "Many of their friends were lost at sea aboard HMS Royal Oak and HMS Hood. During the war the river was an unforgettable sight to see the destroyers forming up and the troopships leaving Liverpool Landing Stage to join the convoys and very proudly sailing out to the Bar.

"I also remember an Irish boat getting a direct hit in the river near to Egremont, and dead cattle on the shore the next day and a boy that was one of our neighbours drowned on it. Also the boat that was sunk between Liverpool and Seacombe and you could hear the shouts and cries from the men on board. I also remember a German airman getting pulled out of the river dead; least said the better after the terrible air raids we had had."

Whilst it was not revealed the following episode must be placed firmly in Eaglet, although the source of the information is not known. It was a press release.

'Service in Flagship
Broadcast to Allied Forces
'From the chapel of one of his Majesty's ships in a North-West port - the ship which carries the flag of the Commander-in-

Chief, Western Approaches (Admiral Sir Max Horton) - a service, in which representatives of the British, United States and Canadian Forces took part, was broadcast yesterday morning to the Allied Expeditionary Forces in North-West Europe.

'Impressive in its homely yet dignified simplicity, the service was the more moving for those attending it because they were told that it would be heard right up to the battle line of the present offensive, wherever the Forces had radio sets. The service was interdenominational as well as international in character, for the chaplains who shared it were the Rev. C.H.R. Cocup, Senior Naval chaplain of the port, who is Anglican; Major Stuart M. Rohre, Senior Chaplain U.S.A., a Presbyterian; and Squadron Leader the Rev. E.L. Curry, Royal Canadian Air Force, a Congregationalist.

'Decorated Chapel

'The chapel looked beautiful with its decorations of flowers and plants. The Stars and Stripes and the Canadian

National Flag with the maple leaf hung side by side on the cross-beam above the altar which bears as an inscription the words of Samuel Pepys forming the opening sentences of the preamble of the Naval Articles of War: 'It is upon the Navy under the providence of God that the safety, honour and welfare of this realm do chiefly depend.' Draping the wall behind the altar were the Union Jack and the White Ensign. Prominent on the wall at the opposite end of the chapel is the text in scroll form, 'Fear God, Honour the King'

'On the Air
'Flashing of a small red light having signalled that the ship was "on the air" the hymn 'Glorious Things of Thee are Spoken' was sung.'

And there the flimsy stopped as the other pages are adrift, but those who knew or know Eaglet will be aware that there was no chapel. That service was on the drill deck and those inscriptions are there to this day.

How the Battle of the Atlantic was finally won is now a matter of history, fading into memories, yet we forget at our peril.

Si vis pacem, para bellum.

If you desire peace, be prepared to fight for it. Our Lord did not say, "Blessed are the peaceful" but "Blessed are the peacemakers". Peace often comes at a cost.

GIN AND ANGOSTURA

Chapter Six

1946 - 1958
THE RNVR RECOVERS

In 1946 the Division was reconstituted under Acting Commander E.N. Wood, VRD, RNR. Recruiting was steady and slowly picked up momentum, but received a real boost when in 1947 a sea training tender, MMS 1045, was attached and named HMS Mersey. HMS Irwell was also available for training in Birkenhead.

The first night's instruction in November 1946 was memorable because there was only one instructor! He was Chief Petty Officer Bell and was to become the Ship Keeper. He had first instructed in the Division on the 13th October 1929. On March 10th 1948 the 100th rating was engaged and the numbers grew. Quickly the Division was to become the second largest in the country.

At first, recruitment was confined to men not liable for conscription under the Military Service Acts. Ex-servicemen, particularly seafarers, were certainly welcomed and all ratings that had served in the Division previously were asked to rejoin to aid with the instruction of the new recruits.

The guns that had helped drive the German pocket battleship Graf Spee to her inglorious scuttling at Monte Video, and later in the Mediterranean had sunk two and crippled a third of Mussolini's fast destroyer fleet were brought to Liverpool. They were from HMS Ajax and were installed alongside Eaglet

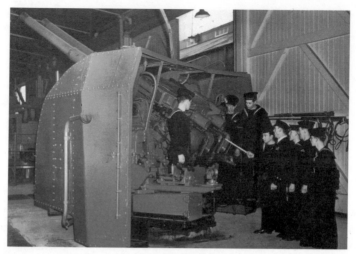

Ajax's twin 4in turret.

in Salthouse Dock. The armament comprised two 4-inch power operated guns, twin Bofors with remote power operation and control of modern standard, two single power-operated Bofors, and two single Oerlikons with gyro sights.

With the advent of National Service after the War, the only way for a seventeen-year old recruit to enter the Royal Navy was by joining the RNVR and this enabled Eaglet to play a vital role. The minimum training requirements were eighty drills a year of an hour each. This was achieved with a minimum of two hours a week for forty weeks, although they were encouraged to do more if possible.

Captain H. Grattan, who was the DEMS officer in Eaglet, planned to install a memorial plaque to fallen DEMS men. He stated in October 1947 that the surplus of canteen funds could cover the cost. The Defensively Equipped Merchant Service was a wartime corps of Royal Navy and Merchant Navy gunners who fought off the submarine and air menace from the decks of merchant ships in convoy. The training base had been in HMS Eaglet and over 2,600 of the men who had passed through the school had been killed at sea.

Their Lordships decided that post-war Divisions should be supplied with Motor Minesweepers (MMS). Early in 1948 MMS 1076 duly arrived alongside Eaglet and was to be renamed HMS Mersey. She was a wooden ship, 126 feet long with a beam of 26 feet, built in Totnes, Devon, in 1943. The design speed was 10 knots being pushed along by a single screw and a 500 b.h.p. gas-diesel engine; the power for lighting, etc., was supplied by a Lister diesel 25 kW generator set. An English Electric 99 kW diesel generator set supplied the power for the magnetic sweeps and in an emergency provided a back-up system.

Tucked away on the portside of the engine room was the domestic boiler. It had to be watched! It was fired by diesel oil dripping onto a piece of cotton waste which was set alight, the amount of oil dripping onto it being regulated at the side by a cock ... foolproof! There was always a fire risk while it was lit if

at any time too much fuel oil was allowed to drip into the pan and overflow into the engine room. A watch keeper always had to be below when the boiler was flashed up.

She was soon transferred across the water to Irwell as it was found that there she could get out of the locks for about eight hours out of twelve.

Lieutenant (E) G. Olver, RNVR, recalls the first trip, a short weekend at Llandudno. All went well ... at first. 'Suddenly there was a frantic hammering on the Wardroom door and a scared looking Stoker Mechanic shouted in "Will the Engineer Officer please come down to the engine room. The place is on fire!" We rushed down the alleyway after the rapidly disappearing rating, and sure enough, large clouds of black smoke were billowing from the engine room hatch. I can't remember who was down first, but on reaching the bottom of the ladder we could see the starting air pipe was red-hot. One of the air start valves had stuck in the open position allowing hot gases of combustion in the engine cylinder to back up along the pipe,

and it was the oil that had been on the outside of the pipe which was causing all the smoke. Someone had eased the engine speed and, after one or two sharp taps on the valve, which was spring loaded, it closed and everything closed down again.'

This does suggest that the rest of us are quite correct in assuming that the only tool required is a hammer and that all that is asked of an engineer is the knowledge of where to use it!

Lieutenant Olver was full of such tales.

'On another famous occasion we ran out of fuel in the middle of the Mersey channel through the fuel gauge on the Ready Use Tank moving right round the clock and on again to three-quarters. With many a rude word the senior engine room rating had to get rid of a nice air lock in the fuel system.'

That proves there are special engineering words to use when the hammer is manipulated. One assumes that no advice is needed. However engineers can blind the rest of us with science and here is an example. Mr. Olver continues. It was 1953, the Easter four-day cruise to Cork. There had been no problems, but!

'About 2030 on Friday the 3rd April, it was reported that the after plummer block was running hot and that the engine room was full of smoke. Speed was reduced to SLOW ahead, and on investigation it was found that the paintwork on the plummer block was glowing, and it was filling the gland space and battery compartment with smoke. A hose was immediately rigged to the fire main and water played on the bearing to cool it and also to reduce the fire hazard. After twenty minutes it was cooled considerably and a solution of soft soap and fresh water was poured into the oil space; by this time the smoke had cleared and it was found that the shaft ring had jammed, and all efforts to get it moving were a failure. The bearing was topped up with lubricating oil, and orders were given that it had to be inspected every fifteen minutes. By 0430 on Saturday, the 4th April, speed could be increased to 275 rpm without the block heating up, and with regular attention, speed was finally increased to 400 rpm at 1700. On arrival, the plummer block was inspected and it was found that a piece of emery-cloth had been left in the oil sump of the bearing. It is thought that the heavy buffeting from the weather had jammed this up against the shaft ring thereby stopping it from rotating and so starving the bearing of oil.'

As most of us have no idea of what a plummer block is, we should not worry about where we dispose of our emery cloth ... whatever that is!

Lieutenant (E) G. Olver had thoughts about the water supply in Mersey.

'One constant source of trouble on the ship was the water supply. To prevent corrosion, fresh water tanks are always coated internally with a bitumen composition to a thickness of one quarter if an inch. This flakes off as the water swishes around when the ship rolls and small pieces of it block the pipes. Perhaps, in future years, the insides of fresh water tanks will be painted with something more adhesive. Nevertheless, the department has nearly always been able to maintain supplies.'

I suspect that his fingers were crossed as he wrote the last paragraph.

On the 5th September 1949, HMS Mersey returned to Liverpool after 14 days' training cruise to Bordeaux, where the seven officers and twenty-six ratings were entertained by the French townspeople. During their stay a detachment of the crew were present at a burial service for the French forest fire disaster. Later they collected 50,000 francs for a relief fund for those made homeless by the fires.

The Commanding Officer, Lieutenant T.K. Alcock, was received by the Mayor of Bordeaux, a former Resistance leader.

Before the Mersey sailed home she was open to inspection by the public.

A few days earlier two MTBs and two submarines of the Royal Navy had visited the port. The RNVR crew received as great a reception as the regular sailors.

Lieutenant-Commander Tom Conway, RD, RNR, has written a cautionary tale which might bear the title, 'Never volunteer to be a cook, if you are not a cook'. Tom joined the Division in December 1951 and started his training in Irwell under the care of CPO Woodall. Incidentally, his first sea experience was in HMS Creole, a World War 2 'C' Class destroyer when they visited the Western Isle, Loch Gilp, The Firth of Clyde and Lamlash. But this tale concerns a training weekend to Llandudno in our own 'Mickey Mouse', MMS 1045.

'I reckon that CPO Woodall must have had a favourable opinion of me and suggested that I might 'volunteer' to sail as the Ship's Cook. At first sight this might appear to be an ideal opportunity to shine and get rapid promotion ... this was not to be.

'We reached Canada Dock when we experienced a main engine break down and an engine room fire. The 'Not Under Command' balls were hoisted and we dropped anchor. In time we resolved the problems, proceeded up the channel to the Bar Light Vessel and eventually anchored in Llandudno Bay for the night..

'During this activity I had taken stock of the galley, the food and the pre-planned menu. I began to hope and wish that the crew had brought sandwiches. I was not happy. The galley was small ... 5 feet by 6 feet ... the size of two GPO Red Telephone Boxes and at the inboard end there was a short ladder to a door which led directly down to the Wardroom. I had the impression that I was under constant observation.

'The galley deck head was very low and the facilities

comprised:-

    A small work surface.

    A Zinc 'Belfast Type' Sink with only a cold water tap.

    A draining-board to the side of the sink.

    An iron coal burning stove with hotplate and oven.

    A large iron kettle and numerous pots and pans..

    Kitchen tools were limited to a ladle, a fork, a spoon and a carving knife.

    A food storage cupboard with a metal mesh screen.

    A small coal bunker and a small shovel.

    A large coal-bunker was located aft of the superstructure on the starboard side.

    There was no accommodation for ashes from the stove.

    The ash generated by the stove had to be dumped over side. That was to a major problem.

    Very fortunately there was a copious supply of chopped wood.

    I cannot recall that the facilities included a refrigerator!

'The menu for teatime was simple ... something like bread and jam. The Sunday breakfast was to be Full English and I will come to the Sunday Dinner later.

'The stove had no draught control so once lit the fire burned very fiercely. That stove consumed volumes of coal. So the harassed Cook spent a lot of time stoking the stove, scurrying down the waist of the ship to the coal bunker, raking the stove and tipping the ashes over the side.

'You can have no idea, unless you have attempted it yourself, of the mess created by 'tipping ashes over the side'. It is very dangerous. The fine ash and hot cinders blow inboard and create an incredible mess and a fire hazard..

'Incidentally, the shovel was too big to fit into the door of the stove and the coal had to be distributed by hand. My hands were black and my body covered by ash. I served breakfast with my hands hidden behind my back! My food was well received.

'Imagine my shock when I discovered the Sunday Lunch Menu for the whole crew of twenty plus was:

Roast Ox Heart. Boiled Potatoes and Vegetables.
Tinned Peaches and Evaporated Milk
(Thank God, nothing to cook!).

Panic! How do you roast a whole herd's worth of Ox Hearts? For one who had recently left University having never cooked anything more than porridge over a Boy Scout camp fire, boiled eggs, custard and mashed potatoes, and had never faced an oven in his life or an Ox Heart, this was a daunting proposition. There were no roasting dishes, no recipe book, all that I had was common sense. Then I remembered as a Boy Scout creating a camp fire-oven by using a large cube-shaped biscuit tin. So I approached the First Lieutenant, Leonard Foinette, requesting two large biscuit tins because there were no roasting dishes. The ship was scoured and I was frankly amazed when a supposedly 'non-magnetic minesweeper' produced two cubical tins. We were a 'Go' for lunch!

'The Ox Hearts were popped into the biscuit tins and put into the oven with a fierce heat around them from the well-stoked stove. There followed a fury of furious stoking, removal of ashes and more stoking. The galley was more like Dante's Inferno than a galley!

'I was frankly amazed when the whole meal turned out to be perfectly cooked. The roast Ox Hearts only needed carving into deliciously appetising slices and served up on trays. The Cook was very dusty and coal soiled at the end of the evolution. My right hand was black, but coal is only carbon and that is inert.

A little bit of coal dust never harmed anybody ... ask any coal miner.

'I had the job of cleaning up the galley on the way up the channel from the Bar Light Vessel to Brunswick Lock to be ready for Rounds before paying off in Salthouse Dock. All was well. I was personally thanked for my efforts by the First Lieutenant and he presented me with a Ten Shilling Note which was the result a whip-round in the Wardroom.

'I never volunteered to be the Ship's Cook again! Incidentally, many years later I mentioned Ox Hearts to Leonard Foinette, but it did not ring a bell! He had forgotten. But I remember every detail of the 'rewarding experience' to this day.'

Thank you Tom Conway.

Wireless Training in Irwell 1951.

No story of Eaglet can possibly be complete without full reference to the NAAFI manager Eric Wolfenden. Let the saga unfold.

To start at the beginning, Eric has deplorable feet and was firmly classified as Grade 3. Happily he chanced to be in Scotland and there he was examined, found to be A1, and joined the 'Andrew' (the RN). They did not ask him to take his shoes off!

He was posted to a ship the day after he joined the Navy. He never saw barracks. He was to remain in HMS Crane until early 1945 as 'a sea-going-grocer'. Next stop was our Irwell where he spent happy days slicing bacon for the sea-going trawlers. Thence he entered the bakery in HMS Wellesley ... better known to us as the old Royal Southern Hospital. On VE Day he was posted to Reaper in Rosyth and sailed via Cherbourg, New York, and Panama Canal into the Pacific in time for VJ Day. The next task was transporting our POWs to a hospital in Sydney. Finally he came home on 7th June 1946. By this time they had discovered his feet via the Fleet Air Arm at Risley and our good friend Eric arrived in Eaglet in September 1949. He is still with us! And now for his memories!

The Olden Days.

'We used a plank to get the ale barrels on board the old Eaglet. One day as one might expect the plank moved. Down went the barrel, down went the plank and down went the drayman. There was a minor problem, the fellow could not swim and we had great difficulty in getting him out. We all assumed that it put him off water for the rest of his life!

'There were tremendous goings-on at our New Years Eve Balls which we started up again on 31st December 1949. Every classroom was decorated ... there were fountains and pools and waterfalls. Wonderful! It was all left for the New Year's Day Ball for the Ratings. Each year we improved and improvised and they carried on for many years.

'Saturday nights were always great fun. We had a pianist and a sing-song and even though our prices were low, we made a bomb on the bar. Once we made a terrible mistake when we were based in Trafalgar ... we advertised in the Echo for a good piano for the messes. The ship was inundated with the things ... over twenty! There was only one solution. We loaded them on every passing vessel in the lock and asked them to dump them overboard in Liverpool Bay. In years ahead divers will be very concerned as they find 'strange artefacts of war' in the deep.

'Anything that moved seemed to find its way back into the ship. One visit by the sweeper ended up with half of the bits and pieces off Llandudno Pier Fairground in my store-room. Once I had a No Parking sign from France. I was tipped off that the police were to 'go over' the ship and I slung all the articles that had 'been won' over the side. Salthouse Dock must be a wonderland of goodies.

'In those early days the lads were great smugglers. After a fourteen-day trip they would come alongside my storeroom porthole and pass the stuff to me. It was all distributed on the next drill night. We were short in this country of all the good things of life and it was an opportunity not to miss. Sadly on one occasion the customs arrived at the lock gates and the ship was fully rummaged. About twelve men had to resign and that was the end of all that! Such is life.'

I trust that Eric will forgive my interpretation of his tales. There were many more!

Eric with bow tie in 1989, celebrating 40 years in Eaglet . . .
and he is still with us!

Bob Barclay (Ordinary Seaman / Able Seaman, MD/4507) gives a graphic account of his entry into the Division as a young man.

'The only certain way of getting into the RN for National Service was to have completed at least Part 1 training in the RNVR. There were two ways of achieving this, the 'Schools and University' entry or general entry. As I hadn't heard of the former entry I went along to HMS Eaglet in Salthouse Dock and enrolled; this was in the Autumn of 1952. I was deferred from National Service as I was training as a quantity surveyor so had up to five years deferment available. In those days Mersey Division was very big having about 1500 men and women. The Division covered a very large area, particularly Manchester and as far as the Yorkshire border, also to the Scottish border and down into the Midlands, and North Wales. It was impossible for the majority of people living further than about twenty miles out from Liverpool to attend regularly on the two drill nights, Tuesdays and Wednesdays. Therefore those living further away from the Division attended at weekends, known as Tuesday and Wednesday weekends. These lasted from 1600 to 1930 on Saturday and from 1000 to 1500 on Sunday. This had one major disadvantage, there were in effect two separate Divisions as those who attended on weeknights rarely saw the weekend attenders. In addition to this there was the RNVR Postal Service, and the Schools and University ratings that did not attend at the Division, but did two weeks training a year in a RN establishment. To make things even more fragmented, in addition to Eaglet in Salthouse Dock, there was another training ship, HMS Irwell, berthed in Morpeth Dock, Birkenhead, and sharing some facilities with the Royal Marine Reserves.

'Having been accepted, I opted to do my training at weekends as my studying involved night school and a lot of homework. As there was no New Entry class due for a few weeks I started on 'Wednesday Weekends' at Irwell in the Seamanship class. The Instructor was Chief Petty Officer Harry Woodall, a little barrel of a man, one of the best instructors I've ever come across. He claimed that he had entered the Navy as a boy seaman in the latter part of the First World War and he certainly seemed old enough for that to have been correct. The use of every knot or hitch was illustrated by 'bits' of life in a coal-burning battleship or some other ship of the era. You had to be able to do every bend and hitch blindfolded and you didn't pass on 'Ropework' until you could splice both fibre and steel wire rope. This was done and done again until you could do a very tiddly splice in any of the common ropes of those days. Anchors and cables were taught on a model of a battleship's fo'cstle complete with three cable holders and a centre line capstan all operated by hand from the back of the model. Anchors could be broken from their cable and catted, using all the correct types of ropes and shackles in miniature and picking up ropes passed and the cable secured to a mooring buoy. You had to have the whole thing completely weighed off before you were examined. So it went on, whaler pulling and procedures for lowering and recovering a sea boat, using only manpower. You had to know all the correct orders for the procedures (because "One day, lad, you might, just might, be a Petty Officer."). Quartermaster's duties in the wheelhouse on the wheel and the engine room telegraphs followed.

'Part way through my seamanship course, I started on my New Entry course at Eaglet. Marching and saluting, how to wear your uniform and maintain it correctly, naval routines, everything in fact to turn you into a matelot. Parade training was carried out by an RNVR Leading Seaman going through for his second hook, but all done under the watchful eye of the Chief GI CPO Gunn (Gunn by name and gun by nature. A fearsome man in the true tradition of the Whale Island gunnery school!). New Entry course completed, I returned to my seamanship course and immediately returned to the tender mercies of CPO Gunn for gunnery. Types of ammunition, types of guns, safety rules, different positions on the mounting, cleaning and then gun drill in Eaglet's Drill Shed on the Ajax 4-inch mounting. Those dummy rounds and cartridges were damn heavy and most of the class lost a finger nail or had a bruised foot to say nothing of aching fists and shoulders when you were loading. Still it was all good fun. The Gunnery course passed, it was over to the TAS School in Bell's Timber Yard, a very genteel place after gunnery where we were taught the ins and outs of ASDIC, depth charges, Hedge Hog and Limbo mortars. The instructor was CPO Charlie

Possenger, another very good instructor who made the lessons come alive with anecdotes of the war in anti-submarine vessels in the Atlantic. We also did minesweeping training with CPO Possenger sometimes done on the sweep deck of HMS Mersey, the old all-wood Motor Minesweeper (MMS), sometimes called Micky Mouse Ships.

'I was lucky enough to be chosen for the crew of Mersey (the MMS) for a trip to Cobh (pronounced Cove - the old Queenstown) in Southern Ireland over the Easter weekend of 1953. I was the most junior seaman on board by a very long way. All the officers and senior rates and a large number of the junior rates had seen war service, so the ship's company was very experienced. It was just as well because as we left the Mersey we ran into reasonably rough conditions.

'I was on watch for the first time for the Middle with two other experienced ABs. Somewhere along the North Wales coast, first one then the other of my mates went out of the wheelhouse to spew up and left me on the wheel. I knew all about the error of chasing 'Lubbers Point', in theory at least, but up till then had never steered a ship. The wheel house compass was seen through a slot with a mirror behind reading the underside of the compass card. All the compasses in the ship (magnetic) were graduated in quarters so that courses were given as say North twenty East (020 Magnetic) or South thirty five West (215 Magnetic). After a few minutes of allowing the ship to wander all round the compass, the OOW started ordering in no uncertain way to watch my course. I did sort things out but not after several more blasts from the OOW. The OOW was a rather rotund, ginger haired Lieutenant-Commander by the name of Harold Duffy. In later years he said that I had replied, "Sorry, Sir, I'm new". I might well have done. You learn quickly under those circumstances. Steering the old Mersey was fairly heavy work as it was a purely mechanical linkage, but she was easier to keep steady on a course than the Ton class CMSs later on.

'We plodded on throughout Good Friday and Saturday forenoon, the weather improving as we progressed at our steady eight knots. I had not been sea sick during the first night at sea, but the following morning when turning to after breakfast I got a waft of fumes from one of the fuel tank vents and the smell of diesel oil put paid to me. The best cure was working on the sweep deck with the Buffer. The Walkers Patent Log had fouled something during the night and we had to recover it, by hand of course, streaming the normal inboard end out again as the log was still turning erratically. When the rotor had been recovered and the gash removed, it was streamed again and the inboard end recovered. Making sure the whole lot didn't run out took some doing. By the time the job was completed I was well over my seasickness. For the benefit of those who never enjoyed the task, every time the log was recovered, the inboard end had to be paid out to allow the turns in the line to run out. It could be a cold and hard job.

'We arrived in Cobh harbour and secured early afternoon on the Saturday. Leave was given to two watches almost immediately. Liberty men were inspected by the Coxs'n before being allowed ashore. The Coxswain was CPO Jumper Collins who gave all the warnings about behaviour and what to do and not to do to keep out of trouble ashore. A train to Cork and an excellent run ashore, I seem to remember that we missed the last train back to Cobh, but were given a lift back in a very large old car by a very large, old and drunken gentleman. Get back we did before leave expired.

'The passage back to Liverpool was relatively uneventful in much calmer conditions. I remember that before we got to the Bar Light Vessel, we were overtaken by a destroyer (can't remember her name) but she was working for ACR (Admiral Commanding Reserves) and had been taking a number of School and University and New Entry ratings from Eaglet for a long weekend training trip. By the time we were getting to the Alfred Locks to enter Birkenhead dock system, the destroyer had unloaded her trainees at the landing stage and had slipped and was leaving the river. The CO for that weekend was Captain Bernard Smith.

'I did my first annual fourteen days training in Mersey. We plodded up round Scotland to Invergordon, which in those days was still a busy fleet base. We worked with other RNVR minesweepers doing both Oropesa and LL sweeping. The Oropesa was a torpedo-shaped steel float used to suspend the cutter on a line sweep. It was single or double and cut the lines on buoyant mines. The LL sweep, an earlier version of the later Loop Magnetic Sweep, was on a powered reel but the sweep wires were on non-powered reels and recovery was by muscle power. Another extremely energetic job in the old MMSs was pumping up fresh water from the storage tanks to a ready use tank on the funnel deck. The semi-rotary hand pump was in the galley alongside the coal-fired range. It was hot and hard work and a job I got frequently as the most junior seaman. The trouble was that by the time I got to the bathroom, all the water in the header tank had gone and I had to go back and refill it.

'Invergordon had very little to offer, just one very crowded pub that closed at nine o'clock and across the road the hotel with a notice 'Officers Only'. It was on this trip that I first learned about HMS Natal. All HM ships entering and leaving the Cromarty Firth piped the Natal BUOY marking the wreck of HMS Natal off Cromarty village. The Natal had anchored off the village at Christmas 1917(?) and given a party for all the children of the village. Whilst the children were on board the ship blew up, there were no survivors, children or ship's company.

'On completion of the working part of the deployment, we headed for Inverness and entered the Caledonian Canal, passing through Loch Ness and berthing at Fort Augustus at the western end of Loch Ness. The following morning we ascended the Fort Augustus staircase of locks then headed west. All was going well until just a mile before the penultimate locks on the canal, the wind got the bow on a bend and we ran aground on the South bank. Every trick in the book was used to try and get off, but eventually we ran a kite wire for'ard and out across the canal and secured it to a very large tree. The Sea Boat was about sixteen feet long and hung on radial davits against a griping spar. It was a whole ship operation to lower and recover the boat so we worked damn hard that afternoon. Using the wire and the foc'stle warping drum we succeeded in freeing our selves, but by the time we got off and proceeded down to Corpach locks, the locks had closed for the weekend. To add to our misery, it started to rain and kept it up until the Monday. It was a long walk from Fort William, but there was a pub nearer in Corpach village. We eventually left the Caledonian Canal on the Monday morning and made our best speed down Loch Linnhe and southwards.

'We berthed in Douglas, Isle of Man, the following afternoon for our 'jolly' but sailed for Liverpool the next morning having lost a day whilst we were trapped in the Caledonian Canal. It was on the passage back to Liverpool that I first encountered explosive fishing. We had some primed AX (an explosive acoustic sweep comprising eleven small grenades a bit like Blue Bell tins in size and shape that fitted in a rack and were ejected by a hand-operated ram. As they exploded under water, they gave a low frequency sound that was supposed to replicate the sound of a slow reciprocating steam driven ship). Whether they actually worked as intended I never discovered either then or later, but if there were any fish around they floated to the surface stunned waiting to be caught in a bucket. On that occasion we only got some very small tiddlers, not worth bothering with.

'Some of the characters on that deployment were Lieutenant-Commander John Anderton, the Commanding Officer, and Lieutenant-Commander George Matthews, the First Lieutenant. Lieutenant-Commander Matthews was a vet and he brought a very large tin of 'Udder Cream,' which he maintained was excellent for cleaning your hands of the waterproof grease that covered the sweep wires. It did, but it did make your hands lovely and soft which wasn't what you wanted working as a seaman on a minesweeper. The Navigator was a young Lieutenant by the name of Trevor Jones; the Engineer Officer was an equally young Lieutenant Ernie Scott. The Coxswain was CPO Jumper Collins and the Chief Stoker was one Tommy Rhodes. It interesting to think that in the fifties, the Division was so large that you had to beg to get onto the sweeper, although admittedly it only normally did one fourteen-day training period each year.

'I continued with my training in the Division, opting to specialise in Radar for my non-substantive rate. In 1954 I did my annual training in HMS Headingham Castle, part of the Second Training Squadron based on HMS Osprey at Portland. The ships of the squadron went out each day with classes embarked to detect submarines that also had classes on board learning how to avoid being detected.

'As one of the number of RNVR Ratings on board, I learned a lot about painting a ship. We had one day alongside when the whole ship's company turned to painting including all the officers. I did a number of wheelhouse watches including going on the wheel. How easy with hydraulics! The Whole Squadron did a weekend visit to Torbay where we had a sailing regatta. I was coxswain of Headingham Castle's whaler by virtue of sailing dinghies at home and had the good fortune to win the ratings' race. Living in a mess in a 'Canteen Messing' ship was a wonderful experience. You were accepted in the mess if the lads saw you were willing to muck in and do your best. They were always willing to show you the ropes if you asked and the Tot was a wonderful currency. I learned a great deal about life on the lower deck and 'Jack'. It stood me in good stead later, both as a rating and later as an officer. It was a very enjoyable training period.

'I was Rated AB in 1954 and in 1955 did my training in the new Ton class Coastal Minesweeper, HMS Mersey (Amerton) M1105. We went round to Harwich and worked with a RN Squadron based on HMS Mull of Galloway, the Minesweeper base, moored in the River Stour off HMS Ganges at Shotley. It was very interesting, operating a brand new ship with all the latest equipment and the high standard of accommodation with showers and plenty of hot water was very much appreciated. We went over to Scheveningen, a wonderful Dutch holiday resort near The Hague for our jolly before returning to Liverpool.

'The Characters on that deployment were:- Lieutenant-Commander David Geldart, Commanding Officer, Lieutenant-Commander Putt, First Lieutenant, Trevor Jones, Navigator, and Sub-Lieutenant John Carter. CPO Jumper Collins was Coxswain, CPO Tommy Rhodes, in the engine-room, the signalman was Cliff Parsons and my oppo, John Wright.

'Back in the Division I continued my Radar training under CPO Jerry Grogan. The class consisted of about ten Wrens and two ABs, me and one other. We concentrated on theory of Radar and types of sets and plotting both surface on simulator driven ARL surface plotting tables and Air displays where you plotted on the back of large vertical perspex screens and wrote in mirror printing. It was interesting and we took part in exercises in the TAS school using their ASDIC and plot simulators. I went to HMS Dryad at Portsmouth in 1956 for my training to do the RP3s course. There were only two RNVR's on the course so we got individual tuition, but we often joined up with our RN counterparts for some lectures and working on the plots. Dryad had mock up ops rooms of a number of different ships, Eagle/Ark Royal for carriers, a cruiser ops room (Gambia) and several destroyer and frigate ops rooms. For training on sets we went to Fort Purbrook, one of the 'Palmerston Napoleonic War' forts built along the crest of Portsdown Hill overlooking Porstmouth Harbour. Here they had working examples of all sets then currently in service and we were taught to switch on, operate, fault-find and use and report. Sets 277 P & Q (Surface and Air search sets), 960 the early warning air guard set and 974, the Decca high definition navigation set.

'The simulator equipment at Dryad was the latest and the best and exercises in the various 'Ops' rooms linked together to form a unit were extremely realistic. The training included a live seaward defence exercise conducted in Southsea Castle ops room with live action out on the Solent. A day-long exercise that really had you on your toes. I was very impressed by the very high calibre of all the instructors and the determination of the men on the courses to succeed. After 'secure' each evening, everyone drew their tot at mismusters. You just could not cope with a tot (2 and 1) at midday and then concentrate on a lecture or work on a plot in the warmth of an ops room. Then after tea we went to our messes to revise the day's work. If you wanted help or clarification on anything, a general enquiry would bring forth all the help you could wish for. It was one of the most satisfying training periods I ever did in all my RNVR/RNR service.

'My deferment ran out at the end of 1956 and in the

November I received my calling up papers to report to RNB Portsmouth on the 7th January 1957. I had served just over four years in Mersey Division and had enjoyed every minute of it. There had been the bad times, luckily very few and the good times, luckily many. These four years gave me a flying start to National Service. I could only say thank you to all the Officers and Senior Rates I had served under and the lads of the lower deck I had lived and worked with. I have tried to remember as many names as possible, but apologise to anyone reading this who was with me and whose name I've missed out.'

Well done, Bob Barclay ... and there will be more to come!

It was a sad day when eventually with deep regret in November 1953 that the old ship HMS Mersey had to leave Merseyside for good as she had to go into dry dock. There was dry rot in her timbers and she was in danger in heavy weather. She had been the Division's first sea-going craft.

The following account covers six pages ... sadly we only have room for snippets. Read on!

Inter Divisional Regatta Sunday
11th September 1949

0820   Met Press Liaison Officer.
0910   Drew alongside Irwell.
0915   Helped stow beer-gear-beer-sails-beer etc. on launch. Engine started, strong smell of petrol. Stowed fire extinguisher.
0918   Engine conked.
0920   Engine started.
0922   Engine conked. 2 ring Chief in natty uniform - shown how to keep engine ticking

0925   Engine now firing on two cylinders. Snarl of whaleboats
untied - re-lashed.
No keys for Admiralty launch. No petrol for other
launch.

0930   HMS Mersey's siren "Where the hell are you." Petrol
cage opened - petrol obtained for launch.

0935   Once round the dock in launch towing whalers.

O937   CPO seen running down quay buttoning-up trousers,
with jacket over arm - hopping mad - wrong boat.
Admiralty launch must be taken. Key found.

0938   Admiralty launch started - came astern - into snarl of
whalers.

0939   Admiralty launch full ahead - into side of HMS Irwell.

0939.30 Admiralty launch propeller fouled loose rope. Engine
stopped.

0940   1 Chief, 1 Stoker, 3 Two Ringers, 1 Steward and 1 CPO
still hopping mad - start cutting rope.

0942   Still cutting rope.

0943   Still cutting rope.

0945   Rope cut.

0946   Engines Admiralty launch started. Slow astern. Stop.
Transhipped beer, gear, beer, etc.

0949   Slow ahead.

0950   Full ahead.

0956   Slow engines.

0958   One bridge negotiated.

1000   Dock-keeper slouches along quay - couldn't walk slower
- or care less.
Much, much later ... second bridge negotiated.

1010   Don't look now, but we are being followed. Hurrah!
Clean looking MTB (motor torpedo boat) with Damsels
in natty uniform.

1011   Into lock. Tie up to Rae's tug. Several rude remarks passed by tug hands.

1030   Enter Mersey.

1031   Engines started - slow ahead - fended off by tug.

1034   Out in river - full ahead - "New Brighton Here we come".

1035   See minesweeper off landing stage.

1045   MTB and beautiful damsels leave us behind. A Wrens farewell?

1046   See HMS Mersey moving down river.

1105   "Where do we tie up at New Brighton?"

1106   "How do we tie up at New Brighton?"

1107   "Can we tie up at New Brighton?"

1108   "Must we tie up at New Brighton?"

1109   Suggest floats at rear.

1109.45 Suggestion accepted.

1112   Tie up to floats at rear of New Brighton Stage.

1113   Manx cat tries to come on board.

1114   Chief boards whalers to tie to stage. "Should he lash line to seat?" Told to drop an anchor overboard and not leave go!

1115   "Shall we rig whalers?"

1116   "No. Insufficient wind."

1117   "But we must rig whalers."

1118   Two 'types' disappear in direction of Wallasey Sailing Club and are last seen swarming up mast with red and yellow flags in their mouths.

1119   "There will be a 'helluva' row if we don't rig whalers."

1120   Decision. "We'll hold conference when we board Mersey."

1121   HMS Mersey now off stage.

1125   Alongside Mersey. "Where's that beer? Bring that on board first."

1126   Beer in wardroom with tomatoes, pears and pies.
1127   Conference on wind.
1128   "What about black balls?"
1128.30 "Black balls not needed on HM ships."
1135   Conference still on wind.
1137   More beer.
1138   No wind yet.
1139   Suggest drifting race.

And so it went on and on and on.
There was to be no race .... just beer and no wind! And at last!

1705   Start tying up at Irwell.
1715   Still tying up to Irwell.
1716   Stop engines.
1720   Tea and sandwiches in Wardroom.
1721   Left Press Liaison Officer somewhere ... we think.

Thought for the Day

Quote.   "Ardship, 'e sez, you dunno wot a n'ardship is"
Unquote

The RNR pulling regattas ruffle many memories of times past and 'glorious deeds'. There were a couple of whalers and each summer battle was joined in West Float. Each department entered a crew and practised in Salthouse. Those whalers had to be boarded from the stern of Eaglet via steel rungs welded to the ship's side. That hull curved out somewhat and upwards; when you were whacked it was always a struggle to climb up the side! Surgeon Captain Kershaw, a great character of some idiosyncrasy, used to take a great interest and when he gave up pulling he used to coach and cox the wardroom crew. He was an exceedingly stern taskmaster as many will remember. The whole

RNR had a national pulling regatta, which most Divisions took in turn to host before it moved to a Royal Naval base where boats were in better supply. It all stopped in about 1970, although the sailing regattas were to continue.

The major conversion and 'clean-up' of Eaglet was completed and the ship reopened for training on 7th January 1950. There was a re-commissioning party held on 20th January.

August 1951 was an important date for the RNVR. Mersey Division took a prominent part at Portsmouth when for the first time a warship was commissioned wholly by officers and men of the Reserves. Her Majesty's destroyer Contest had been selected and the regular naval crew went on leave. Her Commanding Officer, Lieutenant-Commander J.J. Brooks and some other officers remained in the ship in a supervisory capacity. Lieutenant G.A. Matthews, Lieutenant G.H. Burrows, Instructor Lieutenant J. Carey and thirty-eight ratings were from Mersey Division. They were all on board for 14 days.

In Liverpool the date '17th November 1951' is not to be forgotten. Six weeks before, Princess Elizabeth and the Duke of Edinburgh had flown from London Airport for a tour of Canada and the United States. It was the first time that a Royal Tour overseas had started by air and the first time that an heir to the throne had flown the Atlantic.

The Empress of Scotland had berthed at the Landing Stage in the moonlight at 5 a.m. A 21-gun salute greeted the Royal party at 10 a.m. and they were greeted on the Landing Stage by the Earl of Derby, and the Lord Mayor of Liverpool (Alderman Vere E Cotton). On reaching the Prince's Parade the Princess inspected along the RNVR Guard of Honour. The Prince appeared to be delighted by the splendid naval welcome.

There followed a grand tour of the Town Hall and the Cathedral, where they received a fanfare by the RAF. That was the signal for the eight bell ringers to ring the loftiest and heaviest ringing peal in the world ... and they were all youngsters in their teens. After a minute the older team took over the ropes. Thousands of people watched the Royal car drive along Hope Street to Lime Street Station. Platforms 7 and 8 were draped with 'Welcome Home'

And that was that.

Snippets of past history catch the eye in local papers. The heading read: 'Mersey Veteran of Gallipoli dies, aged 87.' The year was 1953. 'The death has occurred at the age of 87 of Mr. George Grant Daglish, who commanded D Company of the Hood Battalion of the Royal Naval Division (RNVR) in the First World War. He will be remembered by many of the old soldier-sailors of the Division that was known as the Mersey Division. He took part in land action at Antwerp and Gallipoli and was wounded while controlling the landing on V Beach at Gallipoli.'

Pat Moran, known and loved by many on Merseyside, tells his story as only he can. 'The seagoing minesweeping trips and the maintenance weekends were in the wrong time of the year. It could be cold, rough, wet and dangerous. On one sweep the wire parted whilst we were underway. No one was allowed on the sweep deck when minesweeping was in progress. We were putting the hammer over the side and needed a shackle and the tool bag was on the sweep deck. I shouted I'd get it and set off aft. I stood between the sweep wires when I heard one begin to go. I dropped on to the deck and felt the coils of the broken sweep wire hitting the back of my life jacket. I got from under and went to the ship's side. Bert Pottinger, the Chief TAS I, came running aft, shouting did it hit anyone and I said it hit me! His face was Quinine Yellow anyway, but it appeared to turn purple as I felt my eyes turn up. He put his hands out flat to hold me up. Recovery was instant, but another shock awaited when I took my life jacket off and found the back shredded with the Kapok spilling out. We recovered the Kite and Otter and carried on. Another Division lost several men in a collision when on exercise so it was not all pleasure and we gave the RNVR plenty in return for all the goodies.

'About this time the WRNVS started up and were regarded with suspicion by the Senior Rates. The suggestion, by the Wrens, that we should have nice curtains for the big square windows (Ports) in Eaglet's side did not help. Us young Petty Officers were in heaven, being regarded with open admiration by all these gorgeous girls, mostly very Posh and much cleverer than we were. They were also very smart in dress and in anything they did. They were not much good on the sweepers, having to be off before dark and not knowing what was what. We were all from the marine industry and did know what was what, which increased our stature in their eyes. Life didn't get much better!

'Also about this time we built a new Chief and Petty Officers Mess, which became very prominent in the social life of the Division. I did help organise some Division dances and remember feeling very sorry for the Wren Officers, who had to wear mess kit / evening dress allegedly designed by Lord Mountbatten! It certainly looked like something designed by a destroyer Captain.

'Gibraltar was wonderful. We had the place to ourselves, there being no other naval ships in port. We were moored right outside the Admiral's Office. Our Quarter Masters watched for him like hawks. The poor man could not come out on to his balcony without being piped and having to salute at attention. It could be louder than that because Commander Smith had brought a bugler along!

'In Quiberon we anchored in the bay in wonderful clear water. Beautiful, young girls swam around in tiny bikinis and the Coxswain fell in. The Coxswain was the traditional rotund shape that coxswains are supposed to be and could not climb the stern ladder! His shorts had fallen off. He could not swim, so getting to the main gangway was out. Eventually, CPO Collins, Chief GI, climbed down with a towel and we hauled him on board with a gantline.

'Outside a chemist's shop there was a six-foot, plywood young lady advertising camera film and not wearing many clothes. This person was 'stowed away' in the steering flat and was not found until we sailed. She was presented to Lieutenant-Commander (E) Currie as he was the handsomest man aboard. He presented her to the RMR in Birkenhead.'

Pat Moran summed up the Reserves of the day beautifully. "You did not have to be good, but you did have to be committed to the RNVR."

King George VI passed away at Sandringham on the 6th February 1952. Lieutenant-Commander R.T.F. Smith with twenty ratings from the Division lined the streets of London as part of the parade for the funeral procession. There was also a Service of Remembrance in Liverpool Cathedral and Captain E.N. Elgood was included in the Civic Procession.

The Division won all the Trophies at Bisley in 1952 ... the Duke of Westminster Challenge Cup (Rifle Team), The Viscount Elvedon Challenge Cup (Revolver Team), the Graham Challenge Cup (Rifle Individual Competition), the Rifle Individual Competition (Junior), the Staff Match, Ratings' Individual Competition, and the Junior Ratings Competition.

A letter was received at the end of 1952 from the Commanding Officer Harry Barnes of the RMFVR. 'We are now in our new headquarters and on behalf of all the RMFVR (Royal Marine Forces Volunteer Reserve) I send my sincere thanks for the extreme courtesy, co-operation and practical help and advice which we have had at all times since the early part of 1949, when it was our good fortune to open a centre under your roof.'

There were smiling faces in May 1953 when about forty members of the Division under the command of Lieutenant Sellers spent most of the week in Portsmouth. They were there training to march thirteen and a half miles! That was to be the distance they would cover on Coronation Day, 2nd June. The whole contingent was away for the fortnight and much enjoyed their Coronation duty as they lined the streets of London.

Incidentally, Mersey was one of the naval vessels at the Coronation Naval Review at Spithead, under the command of Lieutenant-Commander N.P. Brown, RNVR. The Senior Engineer Officer for this occasion was the Division Senior Engineer, Lieutenant-Commander (E) John Smith, DSO, RNVR, an ex-submariner, to whom Mersey's diesels were just childsplay. Naturally Mersey behaved impeccably.

Captain John Knott, Master Mariner, and yet another old friend, has recalled a truly remarkable 'happening' from years back a bit. He was a Brocklebank man and some words of introduction are necessary.

John in July 1948 joined SS Matheran at the age of 16 as an apprentice in Birkenhead. At that time the gun platforms were being removed from her poop deck and the gunners' accommodation stripped out from the half deck casings. In those days the Brocklebank offices in Cunard Building had a pair of guns outside the main doors. Those weapons were typical of the guns that Brocklebank had purchased and fitted to their own ships during the First World War and for which they supplied the gunners. One of those guns can be seen today in our Maritime Museum. After the last war Brocklebank still worked closely with the Admiralty in the design of their ships. But what has this to do with Eaglet? Let John Knott tell his story.

'Based to some degree on their Admiralty links, Brocklebanks, post-war, sent their young deck officers to HMS Eaglet for training in 'ABC' ... Atomic, Biological and Chemical Warfare. And so, in 1953, as a Brocklebank 3rd Mate with a Foreign-going 2nd Mate's ticket, I was duly posted to Eaglet for ten days training.

'In the shore-based facility alongside were the guns of HMS Ajax. Fitted with both cross-wire and gyroscopic gun-sights and all the means of azimuth and elevation, they lacked only one thing for training purposes ... the recoil which would be generated by using live ammunition and the resulting ejection of the brass cartridges. This lack was overcome by fitting the guns with an ingenious system of smooth-acting levers operated by pulling down heavily on ropes fitted to each side of each gun. The resulting problem, however, was how to protect the ejected cartridges (which were needed for loading training) from continuing damage with the concrete decking. Hence, the loading and firing of the guns went something like this.

Gunnery Officer: "No. 1 gun - Load. No. 2 gun - Load".
(Two men on each of the two gun ropes would then pull downwards, the breeches would open, the loader would push in the shell casing, and the gun captains would close the breeches, shouting "No. 1 gun ready, sir. No.2 gun ready, sir.")
Gunnery Officer: "No. 1 gun - Fire. No. 2 gun - Fire."
(The gun captains would then operate the firing mechanisms.)
Gunnery Officer: "No. 1 gun - Recoil. No. 2 gun - Recoil."

'The men on the ropes would then pull down heavily, the breeches would open and those damn long and heavy brass casings would come whistling outwards - not to land on the deck (Oh! No!), but in the arms of the poor guy who had been designated 'catcher'. The trick was to extend your right arm along the line of the casing, taking the full force of the percussion cap against the muscle of your upper arm, and to steady the casing by hugging it with your left arm. Everyone had to take a turn at each duty and I think we all finished up with bruised biceps.

'For years afterwards, Brocklebank officers, who had done this training, would make a party piece out of parodying the gun drill, using a fire extinguisher as the casing, and all hands shouting, "No.1 gun - RECOIL".

'I never did find out what gun drill has to do with Atomic, Biological and chemical Warfare.'

Thank you, John Knott for your brilliant exposition of nothing in particular.

It will be remembered that Captain E. N. Wood, DSC, VRD, was the first RNVR Officer to command a destroyer, HMS Atherstone and the first to command a Fleet destroyer, HMS Tuscan. On his retirement in 1954, the Division welcomed the new Commanding Officer, Captain Alan V. Turner, DSC, RNVR.

Captain Turner joined the Division in May 1939 and had a remarkable wartime career. He was serving in HMS Gurkha when she was sunk during the evacuation from Norway. Later he served in HMS Janus and saw considerable action at Greece, Crete and on Malta convoys. He was the first RNVR to be appointed First Lieutenant in the Eastern Mediterranean. Later he commanded HMS Burwell and HMS Stayner. It was in the Canadian Frigate Stayner just after D Day that he was awarded

Captain Wood and Captain Turner.

his DSC. Deployed with a group of four ships off Ostend, four E-Boats (German Motor Torpedo Boats) were destroyed in one night. Following his discharge, Captain Turner had rejoined the Division in 1946 as Commander and was in command of HMS Irwell at Birkenhead.

In 1954, the Jubilee Year, Eaglet had a permanent instructional staff of more than 20 Chief and Petty Officers and on the strength were 843 Ratings, 167 Commissioned Officers and 42 part-time National Service Officers in addition to 154 members of the WRNVR, which had first been formed 1952 ... there is some problem about this date as there were Wrens in the Division two years earlier. However the Wrens did celebrate their 21st Birthday in October 1973. At that party was Florence Farrell who had signed on in Eaglet on the 10th March 1952. Incidentally, after retirement she kept her Eaglet links by working part-time as assistant treasurer in the wardroom.

Rosie at Morpeth, 1953.

1954 marked the fiftieth year since the birth of the RNVR on Merseyside. This was a time to look back briefly again at the history of the Eaglet sitting in Salthouse Dock. She had been launched in the last months of the First World War and was the first of a class of twenty-four convoy escorts - all named after racehorses - built under the emergency programme. The war ended in November 1918 and although Sir Bevis wore light and dark grey, it is doubtful that she ever saw active service. Laid up in 1920, she was converted in Sheerness into a drill ship for the

RNVR and went to Manchester in 1923. That was when she received her second name ... HMS Irwell. Three years later she took her third and final identity when she became HMS Eaglet. She replaced the old wooden-wall Eagle which name had been changed to Eaglet when the aircraft carrier Eagle was launched in 1918. All that remained of the wooden-wall was the bearded and helmeted figurehead, the ship's wheel and the wooden doors.

Every Reservist was required to carry out fourteen days training each year, either at sea or at a regular Naval establishment, and HMS Mersey went to sea most weekends from Easter to early October.

Since January 1950 when National Service was introduced, Eaglet in four years passed 521 Ratings through to the Royal Navy.

To commemorate the Jubilee Year a reunion was held of all past and present serving members of the RNVR. This was held in HMS Eaglet on March 5th 1954.

The Mersey Division had been set up in 1904 and became the second largest in the country. Birkenhead played a large role in the Division fifty years ago. It was accepted that the 'misuse' of the RNVR during the First World War had had a bad effect upon recruiting. It was not until the RNVR was reconstituted in 1922 and the Admiralty officially declared that the future involved the sea and not the land that numbers slowly began to increase. For Birkenhead, the closure of the Caernarfon Company from lack of support and later the demise of Southport and Manchester meant that by 1931 Liverpool and Birkenhead shared the personnel. The arrival of Irwell (the first drill was on 1st May 1932) much enhanced the vitality of Birkenhead. Irwell had served as a base ship at Manchester from 1926 to 1931, when Manchester had closed. The Division was more than 1,000 strong at the outset of war and within days almost all had been drafted into sea service. About 120 were lost in such sea epics as the Rawalpindi, the Rajputana and the tragic sinkings of Hood and Prince of Wales and the carriers Glorious and Courageous. Eaglet became the flagship for the Western approaches and Irwell in Birkenhead served as a Depot Ship for minesweepers. At the end of the war men returned with strong memories of their service days and rejoined the Division. The WRNVR was formed in 1952 and had a complement of 154 (including nine officers). This could not have been envisaged in 1904. With service in the RNVR from the age of 17 as the sole method whereby National Servicemen could enter the Navy, Eaglet was playing an even more important part then she did before the war. The Jubilee Year saw the Division in good heart.

During the Jubilee Year, the RNVR was reviewed by Queen Elizabeth.

An article in the Liverpool Evening Express, printed Thursday 4th March 1954, is worthy of attention. 'Not enough of the Mersey's merchant ships fly the Blue Ensign, zealously guarded emblem of the Royal Naval Reserve. A much larger number of merchant ships are expected to qualify to carry this coveted insignia as a result of the varying of the Admiralty warrant which permits its use.

'The Admiralty grants this honour expressly to the ship's commander who is a Reservist and who has four other Reservists under his command. This is a big concession as the pre-war regulation had required a far larger figure.

'Captain R.V.E. Case, RNR, Marine Superintendent of Coast Lines stated: 'Requirements to fly the Blue Ensign have been greatly reduced. Our strength is being built up and you can expect to see a great deal of it in future. The Ensign is of great significance and a serious view is taken of abuses of the privilege to fly it. The privilege is allowed to British merchant ships and fishing vessels.'

Captain Case was promoted Captain RNR in December 1953. The opinion of this officer with 34 years' experience - who gained a DSO and two DSCs while commanding escort vessels in the Western Approaches during the war - must be respected. Incidentally, I found myself self-appointed chauffeur to Captain Case after many convivial evenings ... it was an experience and an education for a Padre!

'Exercise 1984' will never be forgotten and was reported by the local press at length. It was the second weekend of March 1954. It actually happened!

Exercise 1984
Marines Invaded Scottish Hills to Capture 'The Professor'
By Anthony Sharrock
(who sailed with the raiding force)

'Exercise 1984 - the largest combined air, sea and land exercise ever staged with the reserve forces in this country - reached a climax in the early hours of Sunday morning when fifty Marines from the Merseyside and Clyde centres waded ashore on the Mull of Galloway and captured a 'mad' nuclear physics 'professor'.

'The orders of the attacking force had been to capture the professor, who was convalescing after nervous breakdown, 'regardless of the cost in men and ships.' Exactly what losses were sustained has not been finally calculated - but there was unanimity after the exercise that it had been a resounding success.

'Commented one of the observers, Captain S. Beattie, who was awarded the VC during the war for his part in the St.

Nazaire raid: "Everything went nearly according to plan. It was very good training."'

The exercise started on the Friday night with Mersey and the Seaward Defence Boat Droxford leaving the river to rendezvous with the other forces from Belfast and Greenock. It was the first sea voyage of the newly acquired Mersey and all apparently went well.

Half an hour before midnight on the Saturday they were anchored near Port Logan beach in preparation for the landing of the marines.

'Camouflaged and with their faces blackened, some of them formed a beach-head while others made their way inland to the professor's hide-out. Seven of them formed the final snatch party to dash through the defending King's Own Scottish Borderers and bring the prisoner back to the beach.

'The four miles' journey inland had taken them two and a half hours. With the defenders harrying them with blanks and thunderflashes, the withdrawal took under half that time. "The enemy were completely demoralised," said Captain Tom Sherman, leader of the snatch party, afterwards. "The journey inland was a bit troublesome through gorse and undergrowth, but we succeeded exactly as according to plan."

'By 3.30 a.m. on Sunday morning, the 'professor' - 49-year-old Commander Jim Tebay from Preston - was on board Mersey. The finale came that afternoon when Mersey and Droxford berthed once more at Liverpool. Complete with whiskers and deerstalker, the professor walked ashore clutching a home-made cobalt bomb; one man around whom a weekend exercise involving over five hundred reservists had revolved.'

A post-script of a memory of Exercise 1984 was given to me in Eastbourne (I was there as Chaplain to the annual 'do' of the Fast Minelayers Association) by Stanley Butterworth, who had enrolled in Eaglet in the spring of 1954 ... a mechanical engineer second class. The memories are almost fifty years on ... but still vivid! And it was late in the evening at Eastbourne and I was totally enthralled. This is the unofficial version of the happening.

'I joined the sweeper at the stage, Pierhead, and it was blowing half a gale. We all felt ill immediately, before we left the stage. I was really suffering from an evening meal of beetroot and brown ale. CPO Proctor had organised that supper. Off we went to Belfast with some of the Reserve Commandos on board. It was cold, so cold that the only place I was warm was when I wrapped myself around the asbestos lagging in the engine room.

'In the morning, I checked the steering engine in the tiller flat and that entailed crawling over the sweep deck to the hatch. When I opened it the tiller flat was full of very grey, sick and as-green-as-their-berets commandos ... it stank of them and of a rather pungent engine oil.

'That night we arrived to drop the raiding party. My task was to man the motor boat engine, so I went with them. We dropped into the water. It was a single-cylinder engine started with ether. There were to be no lights. It was not very amusing as I tried and failed to get the engine started. I was totally surrounded by big marines with guns, big boots and camouflage. There was only one solution. I had to row the damn thing until we hit the sand.

'They jumped into the night and disappeared and we waited a long time. There were flashes and rockets, one hell of a commotion. Then a marine came back with a fellow over his shoulder ... the mad scientist! He chucked him into the boat and we rowed. What happened to the rest of them, I've no idea! I did as I was told. I was totally knackered, but back home and at work the next morning.'

Maybe that was the essence of Exercise 1984.

By this time Stan Butterworth was in full flow and I scribbled his reminiscence as best I could. It really was very late in the evening. 'My medical was in the recruiting office in Manchester and I spent every third week in Eaglet. We slept in the Gordon Smith Institute or if it was full, in Atlantic House or the Sailors' Home. If we were in Irwell at Morpeth Dock we stayed in Red Ensign House, Birkenhead. Most engineering was over the water in Morpeth. There was a steam pinnace called Rosie and it took about four hours to pump up the oil sprayer in the boiler in order to raise a head of steam. Pump too hard and it went out! It was always too cold for that engine in winter.

'In turns we went to a café in Hamilton Square. It was near the main abattoir and we ate watching the slaughter men, covered in blood, coming into that café for coffee. There were about ten gas stoves lined up along the wall with pans of food, cheap food. It was rough and ready, always busy with about thirty people, good grub.'

By this time Stan was totally absorbed in his memories. I scribbled as fast as possible. Midnight had come and gone.

'Once flashed up, the head of pressure up, the engine could be left until the morning. Round Morpeth Dock we would go on the Sunday. That boiler room was so small, only four at a time ... so we learned our trade. We joined at 2 in the afternoon on the Saturday and left for home at 4 on the Sunday.

'Sometime in 1955 the new Ton class sweeper arrived, brand new. Looked great with all the varnish. We had three weekend crews to man her when we went to sea ... the duty ERA, a Petty Officer (three of them), and six Stokers ME2s. Standard kit was a bucket between the knees and, if there was a drop of 'ruffers', the bucket came into use. She could roll on wet grass!

'I remember when we won the Thorneycroft Trophy ... a model of a Ton Class sweeper in a glass case ... sweeping real live mines with limited charges, still dangerous. There was the Oropeza Sweep with mechanical cutters and a paravane, and a Pull Sweep over the stern. My job was to look after the pulse generator (it sent out a pulse of electricity to blow up a magnetic mine). Then there was the Hammer, a big steel box over the side on a crane. There was big clapper inside making a horrendous din for the acoustic mines.

'Once we thought we had lost a man over the side. It was the middle watch on the way to Antwerp. It was my turn to make the Kye about 2 in the morning. Went up to the galley, made the Kye, there were two stokers on watch and me. The guy in the generator room was missing ... couldn't find him. Called the engineer officer and he called the bridge. We turned the ship round, all lights on and started the search. We scoured the ship. I undid the hatch on deck to the gyro-room and there he was fast asleep on a pile of life jackets. I won't tell you about the discussion that followed, Padre, but it was at length and in colour!'

Time was passing but Stan kept going. I had given up on any hope of falling into my cot.

'We had a Seaward Defence Boat, the Dee, she was narrow with three engines. I remember I was sent to collect something, can't recall what. The ordinance artificers were changing the barrel on an oerlikon (a twin barrel 20mm automatic cannon) and had placed it on the foredeck. In my enthusiasm I jumped from the dockside to the deck, young and exuberant. The Dee was light and rolled and the barrel went into the dock. I got a right rollocking, much shouting and swearing. Maybe that was why the division had a diving section! I heard no more about it.

'Then there were the Saturday night socials. Some girls and soldiers used to come on board and crates of beer were under the tables. My mate, Dave, fancied himself and off he went to chat up a Judy. Her soldier friend was not too happy and promptly laid one on Dave. Sadly he fell across the table backwards and all the bottles and glasses arrived on the deck. A slight kafuffle ensued. One of the older Petty Officers sorted us out. My mate thanked him and was firmly told "I'm not worried about you, lad, it's the uniform!" And so we learned. The experience did me good, broadened my outlook and made a man of me.'

Thank you Stanley Butterworth.

HMS Amerton (M 1105) replaced M 1045 and was renamed HMS Mersey. The Division's old vessel was a motor minesweeper, but the replacement was powered by high-speed diesels, had twin screws and a double mahogany hull. Her complement was twenty-six and she sported three small guns. She was renamed Mersey on October 9th 1955 by Miss Ethel Griffin, the daughter of the Lord Mayor of Liverpool. Miss Griffin had served as a Wren in the Headquarters, Western Approaches and after receiving a commission, she was a member of the staff of the Commander-in-Chief, Portsmouth. The old Mersey - speed about eight knots compared to the new minesweeper's fourteen - went into reserve in Chatham.

At the naming ceremony, following prayers led by the Bishop of Liverpool, (Dr. Clifford Martin), Captain Alan Turner, DSC, spoke affectionately of the proud record of the old vessel. 'This fine ship won her first battle honours at the sinking of the Konigsberg, and was again mentioned in the battle of the Belgian coast,' he recalled.

In March 1955 a breath of naval brightness swept up the Mersey. Eaglet acquired a new look. She appeared resplendent in black and white paint. Three reasons were given for the change. 'First, the old drab light-grey made her look more like Noah's Ark than a warship; second, we were reverting to tradition, and third, she will be easier to clean and make smart in Liverpool's murky air.' The old HMS Eagle had been a black and white eye-catcher. Until the Second World War there had always been black hulls and white upper works. It took two weeks to effect the transformation.

In 1955 HMS Droxford, a seaward defence boat, was attached to the Division and was renamed HMS Dee. She was 140 ft long, built at Pimblotts shipyard and was the last vessel built for the Royal Navy launched on the River Weaver at Northwich, Cheshire. She was powered by high-speed diesel

The Worker's.

engines and had a speed of fourteen-and-a-half knots. She carried depth-charging equipment and her complement was twenty-six officers and ratings. Re-named HMS Dee, she was to become the Liverpool University Naval Boat.

The 18th Earl of Derby had a long and happy association with the Mersey Division Royal Naval Reserve, HMS Eaglet, and HMS Mersey. He was appointed as an Honorary Captain in 1955 and exercised this privilege continuously with regular personal contact with the many and varied aspects of the Division until 1990. At sea he would wander around the ship and circulate and chat to the crew. Everyone was entirely at ease in his presence and he was entirely relaxed ... he had excellent sea legs!

Bob Barclay - Ordinary Seaman (1952) to Lieutenant-Commander (1989) - continues his experiences. 'In September 1954, Mersey Division had a brand new Coastal Minesweeper, HMS Amerton, renamed Mersey, to replace the old war time Motor Mine Sweeper. First impressions of her were that we had suddenly joined the modern navy. Fifteen knots, all mod cons, it was wonderful.

'Only a month later we were to receive another vessel, a Seaward Defence Boat (SDB). I had been unable to go in the ferry crew that brought Amerton up from HMS Diligence at Southampton but made sure my name was down for Droxford. The volunteer crew had to meet at Lime Street Station to catch the 5.30 London Train. We arrived at Euston at about 9.30 and were taken across London in service transport to Waterloo to catch the Portsmouth train. It must have been nearly midnight when we arrived at Harbour Station where we were told to go down to the Gosport ferry stage where a pusser's launch was waiting to take us across to HMS Hornet in Haslar Creek. Hornet was higher up Haslar Creek above Dolphin and was the base for Coastal Forces, the MTBs and MGBs (Motor Gun Boat). Tucked in there was Droxford. The advance party had a supper ready for us when we arrived.

'A very early call on the Saturday morning and a hectic round of familiarisation before we sailed at 0900. It was little enough time to get to know the equipment and throughout the passage there were a number of things that should have worked or performed better if there had been more time for learning about the vessel. One of the most serious was that the rudder indicator was not working and there was doubt as to how many turns of the wheel were needed from midships to full rudder. The steering was mechanical shafting all the way to the rudder head and needed a good bit of effort to use particularly when going full chat. Despite this problem we left Haslar Creek without incident and proceeded westwards through the Solent and out through the Needles Channel. The sea was not too high and the ship had a very clean entry into the water and pitched easily. This was just as well as it gave the ship's company the chance to get their sea legs.

'Throughout the day we made fairly good progress down the Channel, but into a rising Southwesterly wind and increasing sea. I had been on watch in the wheelhouse since 2000 with two other ABs. By about 2300 we were coming up to Lands End and the wind had increased to gale force out of the Northwest with a big sea running. My watch-keeping mates had succumbed and I was on my own in the wheelhouse. As we rounded the land, speed had to be reduced very considerably until at times we were apparently only just making headway. Calling the middle-watch men was out of the question. The mess deck hatch was on the fo'cstle and had a canopy to protect it, but the fo'cstle was by now almost continuously awash. Water was finding its way in through every joint in the wheelhouse windows. So there was water sloshing around on the deck. I was one of those lucky people who rarely suffered from seasickness, but I must admit that during the Middle that night I was apprehensive to say the least, in fact bloody scared at times.

'One factor making matters worse was the lack of knowledge over the rudders. We were using the wheel with a maximum of two complete turns from midships to hard over. I learned later that in fact it was four turns in each direction, so we were using no more than half the rudder movement available. Even so it was very hard work. I was eventually relieved by one of the officers, I can't remember who it was but I went and got my head down in the ASDIC caboosh for a few hours, then relieved the officer. Between us we saw the night out and it was only with the approaching daylight that the weather moderated and we were able to open up the mess deck hatch. The ship was still very lively but I turned in, in my own bunk, and only surfaced for a scratch midday meal.

'In mid afternoon on the Sunday we sighted the South Wales coast at the time we should have been berthing on Eaglet in Salthouse Dock. We entered Milford Sound, but were too late for the tide to enter Milford Haven so we proceeded up the Sound to Pembroke Dock to the Admiralty depot. Milford Sound looked beautiful on a sunny winter afternoon after the turmoil of the night before. (There were no oil refineries then, it was a beautiful unspoilt natural harbour).

'We berthed on one of the Admiralty jetties, but were quickly advised to shift by the crew of an Admiralty tug and in fact we berthed on the tug. Half an hour later, jagged rocks were showing clear of the water where we had been. After securing and a very quick clean up, the rush was on to get to Pembroke Dock Station to get the train, the last of the day. We all caught it and started the long trail home leaving Droxford in the hands of the Commanding Officer and the small permanent staff who had been the advance guard when we joined at Hornet. We changed trains at Carmarthen and Cardiff; we were lucky at Cardiff, our train from Carmarthen just got in before the station refreshment room closed. We managed to buy the last few remaining pies, sandwiches and biscuits before they shut shop. The Liverpool train left sometime after midnight and got into Lime Street Station around seven on the Monday morning.

'A quick dash home, a bath and breakfast then another dash back into town to get to work. An apology to the Boss for being late and an explanation that I don't think he really believed was true. He didn't think any one would be daft enough to do what we had done! And then it was a struggle through the day to work without dropping off to sleep. I'm afraid I can't remember any names from this ferry crew, but I think the Commanding Officer was Lieutenant-Commander John Anderton.

'As far as I can remember, Droxford was collected the following weekend by another crew, but I wasn't in it, I only had one Saturday per month off. In fact, I never sailed in Droxford again, not because I was put off by my experience on this trip, but I was lucky and selected for Mersey, the new CMS for its deployment the following summer. That was to be a start of a very close association with the 'Ton' class up to the end of their time with the RNR in 1985.

'In keeping with the practice of the day, Droxford was renamed Dee during her time with Mersey Division.

'The Seaward Defence Boats were 120 ton steel vessels designed for coastal patrol work against submarines or other smaller vessels. They were 117 feet long by 20 feet beam and drew 5 feet and powered by a pair of 550 bhp Paxman flank diesel engines giving a speed of 18 knots plus an auxiliary centreline Foden engine of 105 bhp. They were armed with 40mm Bofors and depth charge rails, 974 Radar and ASDIC (that's what it was called then, now Sonar). There was accommodation for 26 on board but the normal complement was 19.

'They had very fine lines and from my above experiences, seemed to be good sea boats. As Droxford had been built by Isaac Pimbolt Ltd of Northwich on the River Weaver, the Mersey Division was an apt home for her.'

Thank you Bob Barclay.

Lieutenant-Commander Bob Barclay at Brodick Arran, 1987.

THE THORNEYCROFT TROPHY 1955

The Portsmouth Navy News told the story in its October edition. Authorship is not indicated. The Captain of Mersey was John France and the First Lieutenant was Roy Humphreys Jones. This is the way it was.

'The Engineer Officer was superstitious about sailing on a Friday. It was one minute past midnight on the Saturday morning before we slipped from the landing stage to begin an interesting and instructive two and a half weeks in one of Her Majesty's minesweepers. Six hours previously the entire ship's company had been finishing up in their offices and factories before setting off on what civilian colleagues termed holidays. In this short space of time a ship had been commissioned, stores had been checked, and confidential books been mustered. HMS Mersey, one of Mersey Division RNVR's sea-going tenders, was in all respects ready for sea.

Competitive Exercise

'We were bound for Invergordon to take part in a competitive minesweeping exercise with the eleven other RNVR Divisions in the British Isles. There was a trophy to be won and we were, I was told, going to be very unpopular with our RN Staff Officer ashore if we did not return with it. The trophy was given not only for skill in sweeping, but also for smartness both in appearance and a particular form of naval torture known as general drill. The First Lieutenant, who was by no means happy that the ship was as clean as she might be or that everyone including himself knew all the answers about minesweeping, had ordained with the Captain's approval that the forenoon should be spent cleaning what appeared to be an already spotless ship and the afternoon and dogs should be devoted to streaming the very complicated and dangerous looking bunch of knitting known as minesweeping gear.

Divisions

'At 0800 on the Saturday morning when most of the ship's company's civilian colleagues were enjoying one of their bi-weekly lies-in afforded by the five-day week, the seamen including those who had been on watch from midnight to 4 a.m., fell in dressed in No. 8s, the naval rating's working clothes. The Engineer Officer detailed his off-watch ratings to do some job not connected with very much of apparent importance, to the disgust of the First Lieutenant, who was endeavouring to match his decks with the Royal Yacht we were to escort later. At 0900 the Captain opened the first of the little buff envelopes, each of which contained some evolution or item of general drill thought out by the RN Staff Officer to keep us on our toes before we reached Invergordon. The contents stated briefly 'hands to go to Divisions at 0920, dress of the day No.2s and medals. Report by signal the number of officers and ratings adrift at 0920.' This meant changing into best uniform and cleaning boots and medals in less than twenty minutes. One rating was adrift, one forgot his medals and the First Lieutenant had a few streaks of metal polish on his sword. These envelopes were opened at hourly intervals throughout the day. Sometimes it was 'rig sheerlegs' to lift some extortionate weight, sometimes it was 'fire the Bofors gun' - it took three minutes to find the key of the ammunition locker on the first occasion, another time 'prepare to be taken in tow forward,' which meant breaking some very reluctant cable. Even the stewards were not exempt and they prepared and served scrambled egg to the Captain in three minutes two seconds. In between these evolutions the sweeping gear was streamed and the ship was cleaned to such an extent that it ill behove any member of the engine room to tread on the upper deck in oily boots. Good weather favoured us and the officers who had volunteered to paint the funnel were afforded a good view of the Queen Mother's Castle of Mey as we steamed through the Pentland Firth. The Doctor, who undertook the job of cleaning and painting the motor-boat, showed considerable annoyance when a (clumsy) rating allowed a hose to spray on his wet varnish in the course of washing down. We were proud of our paint-work when the ship arrived at Invergordon on Sunday night. Within seconds of securing alongside another minesweeper, the First Lieutenant and his right-hand man, the Buffer, went ashore to assess the merits and demerits of our rivals. The former, an incurable pessimist, and the latter, who was a confirmed optimist, returned to the ship with very different opinions, and the ensuing altercation made interesting hearing to the most casual observer.

General Drill

'The following day was spent doing competitive general drill in harbour and it was most enlightening to see the high standard set by our rivals. Needless to say, few of the evolutions we had already practised were ordered, and although the watchful eyes of the shore staff from the signal tower missed nothing we managed to attain third place amongst the reservist minesweepers. Tuesday, Wednesday and Thursday were spent at sea, sweeping mines laid by the RN a few days previously, and staff officers acting as umpires, transferred from ship to ship by helicopter, watching and, no doubt, awarding points. Sailing at 6 a.m. and returning just before midnight can be hard going when concentration and hard work are the order of the day. The Captain and Navigator spent all their time on the bridge where meals consisted of a hurried sandwich, and the minesweeping experts nearly took root on the quarter-deck whence most of their equipment is streamed. It was, however, encouraging to see the mines surface after being swept and to know that the gear did work efficiently. On Friday the Admiral took the squadron to sea for manoeuvres and even more general drill. Our RNVR Yeoman of Signals and his assistant who also had their meals on the flag-deck throughout the exercise, culminated several days of first class-work by receiving a well-deserved recommendation. It was quite fantastic the way two pairs of hands coped with the complicated signals by flashing, flag and voice. They were allowed a well-earned rest, when we sailed alone for Antwerp that night. On the last day the ship returned to harbour at 1 p.m. in time for a comic relay race to a public house half a mile inland.

The relay, involving several 'legs', called upon an amusing variety of fancy dress loved of all sailors. The highlights were the Commanding Officers being carried on stretchers at great speed by none-too-careful members of their ship's company, and stewards running half a mile with a tray bearing a cocktail for the Admiral. The Admiral, who was supposed to sample each concoction, must have been dismayed to note that spillages were few.

Antwerp

'We arrived at Antwerp on Sunday evening after the uninteresting passage up the Schelde and threaded our way through the smart Rhine barges whose length and speed can make ship-handling something of a nightmare to those in more conventional craft. Official calls were made and received and the fact that many of these calls were repeated informally during our five-day visit to the port indicates the mutual friendship and understanding we had with our Belgian friends. Those members of the ship's company, who remembered their francs were rationed, made haste to buy presents for their wives and girl friends and everyone relaxed after the rigours of Invergordon. The ship's soccer XI playing together for the first and probably the last time was beaten 9 - 1 by the local RASC Unit ... the previous HM ship had suffered an even greater defeat. Those who were so-minded took in the superb architectural sights of Antwerp and Brussels, to say nothing of the beer, which was quite reasonable in price. A visit to General Motor Corporation's assembly plant - one of the largest in Europe - with its palatial showroom containing a unique spiral staircase which is supported by balance alone and had gold-plated banisters - and to a carpet factory in St. Nicolas, were amongst the interesting excursions arranged for the ship. We left Belgium with regret and fully appreciated the hospitality we had been given. It was perhaps fitting that shortly before we slipped from our berth a middle-aged woman who kept a bar within stone's throw of the ship arrived with a bunch of flowers for the coxswain, who was thereafter alluded to by his short title of 'swain'. The Officer of the Watch was not far wrong when he described the English Channel at night as Piccadilly Circus, and I was surprised to see the amount of extraneous lighting shown by merchant ships to the detriment of their navigation lights. We arrived at Plymouth on Saturday afternoon, and the flashing from the shore signal station sent the Commander-in-Chief's congratulations on winning the minesweeping trophy - our efforts had not been in vain. Half our ship's company had to leave us at Plymouth in order to resume their civilian jobs on the Monday and a relief draft was waiting to take their place.

Royal Yacht Britannia

'Most of the passage from Plymouth to Holyhead, where we were to embark our Honorary Captain, Lord Derby, was spent once again cleaning ship. There was some light relief as one officer mistook a large tube of toothpaste for hair-cream and a junior steward served cold tea in lieu of clear soup. At Holyhead we met the Division's HMS Dee and sailed to rendezvous with Britannia and her destroyer escort HMS Orwell and took up our stations. We noticed that we were watched with interest from the bridges of the two RN ships. At Douglas the Queen and the Duke circled us in their barge before going ashore and we cheered ship. In spite of several rehearsals in the course of which one or two caps had been lost overboard, the volume of cheers was spontaneous and the Queen later congratulated us on our seamanlike appearance and ordered us to splice the mainbrace.

Liverpool

'We sailed with Britannia that night and then were detached to our home port, Liverpool. The training and experience absorbed during those two and a half weeks was considerable and it is not surprising that the Admiralty places such reliance in their Navy of civilian sailors.'

Captain John France and the First Lieutenant Roy Humphreys-Jones were well pleased with the commitment and dedication which had brought the Thorneycroft Trophy to the Division.

Operation Venus

If you were there, you would ever remember the exercise 'Operation Venus' on the second weekend of March 1956. It was based on the novel and film 'Appointment with Venus' by Jerrard Tickell. He actually sailed with the troops and remarked "It made my book come to life." Abersoch on the Lleyn Peninsula became a place of fantasy and deserves further explanation. About five hundred Naval, Army and Air Force reservists turned that quiet resort into a pantomime stage.

The thirty-eight pages (restricted, of course) were issued well in advance. This was to ensure that everyone (I repeat 'everyone') would know precisely where, what, when and how this exercise would function, down to the last positive jot and tittle. The missive bore on page one the grand title 'The Bull for Exercise Appointment with Venus 1956'. It was neatly divided into Conduct of Naval Operations, Air Orders, Raiding Forces Orders, Army Orders and finally, Intelligence. Nothing was to be left to chance.

This is the story of what actually happened.

The objective of the Commandos, who splashed discreetly ashore and up through beach huts, was the seizure of a pantomime cow from a farmyard two miles inland. The animal was played with realism and relish. Some local inhabitants who saw the unfortunate animal careering up the main street before zero hour were heard to remark "It's almost human." They were, of course, correct. Two gentlemen from Mersey Division, Lieutenant Ronald Sutherland at the sharp end and Lieutenant Dick Cattle (sic) at the blunt end, successfully indulged in bovine-eye-rolling and rather erratic tail twitching. Mr. Cattle, at the stern, apparently attempted the impossible with four milk bottles and had to be restrained.

The good inhabitants of Abersoch were neutral, but confused. One Commando states that arriving on the shore with the second wave, he found the locals were convinced that they were organising a barbecue with the roasting of something which might have been a 'sucking pig'.

It was apparently a good-natured raid out of consideration of the lambing season and the sensibilities of the local natives. One senior officer said "It may look a bit of slap-stick, but it took four months to plan and it is first class training. They were all rather keen!"

However, it was not all plain sailing. Two boats broke down and sea-air contact was somewhat frail. The whole operation was plotted by the Wrens in Liverpool and it was acknowledged that the Air Divisions of the RNVR might have caused a little trouble to the ships with their puffs of smoke! Although the ships claimed that their puffs of smoke were equally damaging to the aircraft. Ashore the defending forces comprised about a hundred men drawn from the King's, the South Lancashires and the Liverpool Scottish Regiments. Liverpool's Rosie made waspish E-boat-type attacks on Mersey simulating torpedo attacks by firing Verey lights. A ketch was also spotted from the Outward Bound School at Aberdovey, under the command of a Merchant Navy officer. No-one was quite sure of the purpose of the ketch.

But, what of the cow?

By eleven that Saturday night the commandos were prowling inland and under the protection of a moonless night had no difficulty in evading the defences. So they approached the barn where both halves of the cow were being stifled in their brown and white costume, surrounded by twenty other really smelly, but rather puzzled live beasts. The arrest was achieved with strong purpose and the cow went quietly. It was reported that from the inside of the shapely Venus as she waded through the surging water to embark for the homeward voyage, two voices spoke as one in most un-cow-like language. It was probably the language picked up from those Welsh cows!

The last word came from one of the Abersoch villagers: "I don't know what they thought they were doing, but it wasn't a bit like the film."

Third Officer Cassandra Cornelius was to lead the poor beast ashore in Liverpool and had apparently volunteered to be the back-end only to be told that 'it was no job for a woman'. She did not accept the rebuff too kindly! (She was to marry the front half of the cow!!)

Back home a few lines of doggerel were composed.
'When you sailed with the Mersey,
The cow came not from Jersey,
The plot bore small relation
To your excellent narration.
But the Wavy-Navy's version
Included your immersion,
Which caused more than a giggle
In our wardroom, Mr. Tickle,
We are delighted you have seen us
... Come again, true sire of Venus.'
Perhaps, that had better be the last word on the subject.

There was much excitement in June 1956. The ACR, Rear-Admiral Thistleton-Smith was to embark in HMS Rosie, the Division's 52ft. steam-harbour launch, and she was to be 'manned' by nine Wrens under the command of Third Officer Cassandra Cornelius. The plan was to convey the VIP up-river to HMS Eaglet where he was to inspect the 1,000 strong Division.

The Wrens had worked extremely hard for ten days, cleaning, polishing and creating 'nice blue and white cushions' for the Admiral's launch.

This is really a sad story!

A local paper put it rather simply. "It was called off, yesterday, because the Admiral didn't want to get wet." An officer said, "We'd picked the prettiest crew ever." But storm signals stopped the cruise. "We didn't want to go round like drowned rats," said the Admiral. So the girls in navy blue were just ... blue. And the last word came from an unnamed male rating. "It would have been like a flippin' harem, anyway!" '

There had long been a connection between Eaglet and the RNVR Northern Air Division at their parent station, HMS Blackcap on the Royal Naval Air Station, Stretton near Warrington. They took part in many a sea exercise with ships from the RNR Divisions, including Operation Venus. The Division comprised two RNVR Air Squadrons - No. 1831 (fighters) and No. 1841 (anti-submarine patrol). Both were first-line operational units that were ready to go into action if required.

The RNVR Air Squadrons were disbanded in 1957 with due ceremonial and dignity!

Admiral Sir Caspar John, Flag Officer (Air) Home stepped out of his aircraft at Stretton. Three Fleet Air Arm officers sprang to attention. Then they smartly snapped bugles to their lips and played ... the Boy Scout March. Each officer was wearing a bowler hat (the pilots' symbol of being grounded). The

Admiral passed on to the Guard of Honour. This consisted of pilots and observers wearing toppers and bowlers. Two Wren officers were among the men in the front rank. Captain Ted Armour doffed his trilby as the Admiral reached the centre rank. The rear rank consisted of officers' wives and four small children clasping hands. Admiral John solemnly carried out the inspection while the buglers switched to the tune of a rather rude ditty.

Rear-Admiral G. Thistleton-Smith was asked to take the salute at the march past parade. He walked out glittering in medals and sword. The band broke into the Dead March in Saul. A car went past carrying a coffin draped with a Union Jack. Inside was the effigy of the 'last RNVR pilot' dressed in the second best uniform of Commander Gilchrist. Behind the car, in slow march, came forty officers in toppers and bowlers, and wearing false moustaches and false noses.

A grave had been dug. Lieutenant-Commander Peter Rougier read the oration:

> Ashes to ashes, dust to dust
> If the grog don't get you,
> The Admiralty must.

The Last Post was played. Wreaths from the Cheshire Constabulary and Warrington Licensed Victuallers' Association were laid. A 'volley' was fired from a 6-inch shell case stuffed with thunder-flashes and mud. Five Senior Officers, including a Rear-Admiral, saluted with umbrellas. And then a tombstone was put up to the memory of the Northern Air Division, RNVR.

> RNVR
> FORCES DESTROYED
> BY BRUTE FORCE AND
> IGNORANCE
> 10 MARCH 1957

Hear lies the Northern Air Division
Disbanded by their Lord's decision
Is it for us to deem unwise
Their efforts to economise?

As the bearer party filed past, beside them marched a sailor carrying a wreath from "All at the Kremlin". And that was their last word.

On November 9th 1957 Captain A.V. Turner, DSC, VRD, DL, RNVR, was relieved as Commanding Officer of the Division by Commander Bernard Smith, RNVR. The new Executive Officer (an old boy of HMS Conway) was to be Commander A. Letty, DSO, DSC, RD, RNVR.

It was a great day on Thursday May 8th 1958 when Her Majesty the Queen Mother sailed down the Mersey in the Royal Yacht Britannia. The proud escort was HMS Mersey and ten river tugs, all newly painted and gaily dressed overall, chosen from the five principal towing firms in the port. Thousands of people packed the outside of the high iron fences of the Princes Landing Stage and clung to every vantage point on both sides of the river. Thousands more on the ferry steamers and down river at New Brighton cheered the Queen Mother after one of the most splendid visits ever paid to the city.

HMS Mersey escorted the Royal Yacht to the Liverpool Bar Lightship. As Britannia moved away she sent this signal on behalf of the Queen Mother. "It has given me great pleasure to have had a ship of the Mersey Division providing part of my escort. I wish you and your ship's companies all good fortune in the future. Elizabeth R."

The Mersey replied, "Please convey our sincere thanks to Her Majesty Queen Elizabeth. It has been a great honour to have formed part of your escort." The Mersey went alongside before HMS Blackwood relieved her. The Mersey Docks and Harbour Board No. 3 pilot boat, The Arnet Robinson, sent a launch to pick up the Admiralty pilot, Mr. Terence Collins, and then hoisted the signal "Pleasant Voyage". In acknowledgement the Queen Mother came on deck and waved.

Many of us have fond memories of Commander (E) Ernie Scott. At the end of the 1950's the Division was well blessed with Technical Officers. Ernie insisted that all Engineers went to sea for 14 days and that they had a bunk and not a camp bed! He also insisted (he was good at interpreting the word!) that contrary to MCM Standing Orders the stokers when in harbour did not do gangway watches as well as engine room rounds.

And here are some of Ernie's tales! They must be true because he told me they were true.

'In 1958, HMS Mersey (Commanding Officer Tony Suthurst, First Lieutenant Trevor Jones) was on passage from La Rochelle to Portsmouth. We were in the lead. St. David signalled that Mersey's stern glands must be leaking lubricant because there was an oil slick in the water behind us. The Engineering Officer was sent for and told this and after a full communication, consultation and third degree with the Chief it was concluded that nothing was amiss. The EO requested that St. David be told that "My engineer is washing his overalls!" That concluded that matter.

'Keeping a weather eye on the other lot was important. On one trip Jolly Jack (Mersey lot) decided that since the Welsh Division had a Red Lion from its masthead and the Belfast Division sported a Red Hand, action was needed. We acquired a

bed sheet and painted on both sides a Liver Bird. It was quite artistic. It was thereafter flown every morning as a recognition symbol and also on the approaches to the River Mersey. It is difficult to get one over a Liverpool Jack!

'Back in '67 or '69 we were on an Exercise and anchored in Gibraltar. A large American cruiser was secured to the outer mole. One morning it was merrily observed that on the cruiser's Black Boot-topping (just above the water line) was prominently painted in RED the words 'HMS Kilmoney, Mersey

Divn. RNR'. Our Commanding Officer Olaf Collis was promptly hauled out of his bunk and Roy Humphreys-Jones, who was in charge of the RNR Squadron. Both were badly shaken as the American's deck watch carried loaded firearms on duty. After inspecting Mersey's crew for paint on their hands and clothing, also life belts and other life saving equipment, nothing was uncovered. Later that day the American cruiser put to sea for a repaint. There were smiles all round. So much for the Deck Watch Keeping security of our Very Good Friends!'

Here endeth the Plumber's Tale.

Changes were around the corner for HMS Eaglet.

Changes? Note headgear in 1910.

SHERRY

Chapter Seven

1958 - 1972
THE RNR

On November 1st 1958 the RNVR and the old RNR amalgamated into a new unified RNR. The name Royal Naval Reserves was retained because it was the older title. The various lists under which the officers served could still divide into professional seamen and civilian volunteers. Happily the merger went smoothly and was purely a matter of administration. Uniforms, aims and much of the training were identical. At the same time the WRNVR became the WRNR, though by legislation it had to remain as a separate Reserve, and remained as an integral part of RNR

In Mersey Division several of the officers considered as civilian volunteers were ex-professional seamen who had 'swallowed the anchor' to take up shore jobs as marine superintendents and such like. Captain Smith - an accountant by trade - borrowed a phrase from the Duke of Edinburgh at a medical dinner by saying that he felt like a 'poacher at a gamekeepers' re-union.'

The chief 'gamekeeper', Commodore J. Whayman, RNR, of the Booth Line, who had taken the chair at a similar function in the Painted Hall at Greenwich a few days previously, actually flew his pennant in Eaglet. This honour had only just been granted to RNR Commodores. The blue cross on a white background would be remembered as the wartime pennant flown by commodores of convoys.

The old RNR under the new arrangement became RNR List One. These were the 'Professional Seamen'. The old RNVR became RNR List Three. These were the willing 'Amateurs', giving time to the Royal Navy and being trained to fill in a number of RN slots, both ashore and afloat.

The role of the List One originally was to serve in Royal Navy ships, but this had to change over the passing years as warships became more sophisticated, and the training requirement higher. Captain Robin Woodall, after forty years at sea, was appointed in July 1990 to be the Master of Queen Elizabeth 2, surely the world's foremost passenger liner. Finally in October 1994 he retired from Queen Elizabeth 2 and from the sea. His RNR career had started in June 1961 and he was to retire from the Reserve in December 1993. During his time he served in many RN shore establishments and in HM Ships Londonderry, Undaunted, Lincoln, and Tiger, seeing service in Home Waters, the Baltic, Mediterranean, Indian Ocean and the Far East.

Happily he has shared with us some of his tales. Is this the inside story of a List One? Read on.

'There was a phase when the idea was that List One would remain in his own Merchant Ship to provide on-board liaison with the RN, or to become Naval Control of Shipping Staff, again to liaise with the Merchant Navy. Senior Officers, i.e. the oldies like me, would become convoy commodores. Now the role seems to have changed again, and amphibious warships seem to be the 'in-thing'. The main theme being to provide the considerable expertise of their profession to advise the RN. I must stress that this is my personal observations and may not be the party line. One thing I must say is that I always considered the terms Amateur and Professional as slight misnomers as my experience was that the RNR List Three were very professional in all they did within the RNR.

'With regard to my own career in the Reserve, I always said the only similarity between a warship and a merchant ship was that they both have a sharp and blunt end, and float (hopefully). As a result I found my naval experience fascinating. I joined as Lieutenant because I held a Masters Certificate, lesser mortals would join as a Sub-Lieutenant. Promotion up to the rank of Lieutenant-Commander was automatic, after that it was by selection only. The P (for probationary) course was carried out in shore establishments. Victory, teaching us to be Naval Officers; Heron, for flying (I am glad to say I was too big to fit into a fighter plane); Mercury, teaching communications, England expects etc.; Drake, the nasties of war; Dryad, how to fight a ship; Vernon, submarines and all things under water; and Excellent, square bashing, gunnery and bulls**t.

'In HMS Londonderry, where I served for ten months, we started with a 'work up' at Portland, and then went to the Far East. RNR Officers were not supposed to serve abroad at that time, but the Captain asked me if I wanted to go, and I said 'yes', so off I went. As an 'officer under training' I had no specific role, but the ship lost its navigator, so the Captain said to me, "I could make you Navigator, but that would be too easy. I will make you Communications Officer, and Sub-Lieutenant Bloggs Navigator. All I ask, Robin, is for God's sake make sure that we get to Singapore." (We made it!!!) As a result I became SROAFE (Senior Reserve Officer Afloat Far East). When we were escorting Eagle on Sundays, the Chaplain would arrive by helicopter, land on the quarter, doff his bone-dome, put on his surplice, hold the church service, and then fly off to his next appointment. Good runs ashore in the Far East.

'HMS Undaunted was Captain 'D' of the Portland Squadron, so a bit strict, but I managed to hitch a ride in a submarine for a few days, but kept banging my head. HMS Lincoln saw me in the Baltic, where we were shadowed by the Russians all the time, and in Germany. Good runs ashore, and discovered what a real sauna was! HMS Tiger was a helicopter carrier, where I flew in Sea Kings. Because I was attached to QE2 at the time I was known as the 'Queen's Airy Fairy'. What worried me at one stage was after one 'interesting' flight in horrible weather, I went into the wardroom that evening, the gin pennant was out, and when I asked who for, I was told it was my

pilot celebrating his 21st birthday! Ouch.'

The last word about Captain Robin Woodall can only be written by the Commander-in-Chief, Naval Home Command, Admiral Sir John Kerr, GCB, ADC. "The Royal Naval Reserve has benefited from having such a senior and distinguished Merchant Navy Officer in the Service. I am particularly grateful for the expertise which you brought to bear on all aspects of RNR activities and for your active involvement with the Royal Naval Reserve life of HMS Eaglet."

That might have been the last word, but I felt that there were more stories to tell and I asked Robin to give the 'lamp another swing'. Here we go again.

'Whilst in HMS Londonderry the ship was based in Portsmouth prior to going to the Far East. In those days there were lots of not only RN ships, but foreign naval ships in harbour. On one occasion I was 'volunteered' as the Officer of the Guard to attend the visiting Italian Naval Sail Training ship, Amerigo Vesspuci, a great 'wooden wall' sailing ship, rather like Victory.

'As Officer of the Guard I was representing the Commander-in-Chief Home Fleet, (Admiral ... who's name escapes me), and as such I had to go out in the Admiral's Barge to meet the ship off Spithead, board her, and technically show her the way in, (thankfully the ship did in fact have a harbour pilot on board). Then I was expected to advise her captain on anything he wanted advice on.

'I joined the Admiral's Barge at the King's Steps in Portsmouth, in my best bib and tucker, complete with sword, and as I boarded the Admiral's pennant was hoisted at the masthead. His coxswain advised me to 'sit there and do what I tell you', and I, being a lowly Lieutenant RNR, thought that was the best advice

I had had that day. As we went down Portsmouth harbour all the ships we passed 'piped the side', and I had to return the salute. I felt very grand sitting in the Admiral's seat like Lord Muck, thinking this is a doddle of a job, little knowing of what was to come.

'As we cleared the harbour the sea became somewhat choppy, and when we approached the ship I could see that she had the accommodation ladder down, but with no platform or guard-rails, and a nasty lop alongside. Slowly we got nearer with the Barge bucking and rearing like a rodeo horse, the coxswain said, "We will only get the one shot at this. I will put the bow in, you stand ready, and when I say 'jump', you jump SIR, and I'm off."

'As I stood at the bow hanging on for dear life, we approached the gangway, then I heard this roar 'jump', and I jumped. Landing on the bottom step of the gangway in an untidy heap, one hand holding on to my hat, (it was windy), the other grabbing the next step of the gangway to stop me falling in, my sword hanging and banging between my legs, (not a pretty sight), and me scrabbling to climb up before the next wave came to soak me. This I managed, and I went up the ladder on all fours, sword banging against the steps, and cap jammed on my head.

'At the top was an entry port fit for Lord Nelson, but not somebody my size. So having squared myself off, I stooped down to go through to be greeted by serried ranks of side boys in shiny knee high boots, white breeches, blue tail coats, and shiny top-hats, piping me on board with a ruffle of drums in the background. (Straight out of C.S. Forester.) As I saluted I was greeted by the second in command, and escorted to the bridge to be greeted by the Captain, again with much fanfare and saluting.

'After all that it was rather an anti-climax going into Portsmouth, and alongside the South Railway Jetty. The Captain then asked me to his cabin, saying he imagined I would like a drink, and that I did, a bloody big one. His cabin was magnificent, the Grand Cabin, as it is called, extending right across the stern gallery of the ship, all polished brass and beautiful wood. I then went ashore in a much easier fashion than boarding, but still with the full ceremony of the pipes and drums. Such was a day in the life of a RNR List One Officer.

'Going back to my previous memories, there are just a couple of things to enlarge. When in HMS Undaunted at Portland we were at sea in a hurry one day, the weather was bad, the bridge on that ship is very low, and I was used to the high bridge on passenger ships. Spray was blowing continuously over the bridge, and you could not see a damned thing. By some peculiar whim of the Naval designers the bridge radar on all RN ships is situated at the back of the bridge, facing aft, so when gazing into it ones backside is facing for'd, a great way to keep a lookout. Anyway on this day because the bridge was covered in spray I had my backside facing forward. When the Captain came on the bridge I remarked on this, and said he should get a periscope fitted so we could see where we were going. He was not amused, and I got all the s***y jobs after that. Not a good day in the life of a RNR List One Officer

'HMS Lincoln was more fun in the Baltic when we were there in October. As I mentioned I found out what a real sauna was, and more importantly I discovered an alternative to having to swim when in water. We were in Helsinki on a flag showing visit, and to entertain Prince Philip at a 'Baron Strangling' cocktail party. Whilst there the Finnish Navy kindly invited several of us to go for a sauna. I, never having been to a sauna before, read up all about it, and discovered that you go into this thing, get very hot, and when you get too hot, you go out, have a cold shower, then repeat the process. Fine ... I now knew all about it. Our Finnish hosts collected us, and off we went in a mini bus up into the mountains outside Helsinki, up above the snow line, to a lovely log cabin.

'There we ate reindeer sausage, and drank beer, then into the sauna. We are all sitting there, beating each other with birch twigs, and I got very hot, so said to one of our hosts, "I would like to have a cold shower." "No shower," says he. "Follow me." Whereupon he opens the door, and we all run out into stygian blackness, then down a path lit by glow-worms in jam jars. If you can imagine the sight of sixteen naked, hairy, naval officers running down this path with steam billowing out behind them, that was us. At the end of the path was a lake. I would remind you, it is October, we are four hundred miles from the Arctic Circle, we are above the snow line and it is freezing cold. I can assure you that when I hit that lake I walked on it instead of swimming. Just another day in the life of a RNR List One Officer.

'To end on a nice little note. When I was in HMS Tiger the captain was Captain M.L. Stacey, a very nice gentleman, and I got on well with him. He was later promoted to Rear Admiral, and became Admiral in Gibraltar. Some years later when I was Staff Captain in Queen Elizabeth 2 it was my pleasure to welcome him on board when he joined us outside Gibraltar for an official visit. We had a most enjoyable meeting. That afternoon he invited Eileen and I up to Admiralty House for tea and tabnabs on the lawn, a most pleasant occasion. It shows just how the RN and the RNR can mix, even when the RNR officer is in his civilian role. And that was just another day in the life of a RNR List One Officer.'

So ends just a glimpse at a List One Officer ... the rest of Robin Wooddall's story deserves a book on its own merits.

Another List One Officer is Captain Peter Woods and here are some of his recollections. 'My days at Eaglet go back to my time as a Sea Cadet at T S Mersey, which was very close to Eaglet and Irwell as they sat in Salthouse Dock. This means that my association with the Division goes back to 1956 with a career path from Ordinary Seaman to Captain RNR. In 1961 I became a Midshipman List One. When I arrived on board, chaos and consternation reigned. What was this strange beast called a Midshipman doing when it appeared to me that everyone was a Commander? But they made me feel welcomed. When I got my Second Mates 'Ticket' in 1963, I was immediately sent off to do my six months Initial Training.

'Memories!

'An Air Course at RNAS Yeovilton was an attempt to lure me into the Fleet Air Arm. 'OK, Lad, this is the throttle, this makes you go up and down, and these make you go left and right, off you go!' Nobody had told that man that we were Merchant Navy Officers and game for anything. So the look on his face as we became airborne was a picture followed by an immediate 'I have the aircraft, get your hand and feet off everything ... now!'

'Then there was a Whale Island Gunnery Course. As our brand new commando rubber soled boots came down on the gravel with hardly a sound, the Drill Instructor's face went a variety of shades of colour, finally ending up with a deep purple and I first understood the phrase 'steam coming out of his ears'. One look at our brand new boots and we were doubled off to the cobbler to have studs hammered into the rubber soles so that the DI could hear a satisfying crash of feet on gravel. The whole effect was somewhat marred by a passing Iranian Navy Junior Officers' Course doubling past without a sound. As they were in carpet slippers complete with gaiters, apparently their feet hurt in boots, the lack of noise was understandable until the DI opened his mouth. I had never expected a Gunnery Course to improve the breadth of my vocabulary so quickly, but not quite the sort of vocabulary one would impart on family and friends.

'At Whale Island they had what was called a 'Battle Teacher' which consisted of a hand loaded 4.7-inch gun on a moveable platform. The course was expected to load a separate shell and cartridge whilst being doused with some 200 litres of water a minute and having thunder flashes thrown at you to simulate the other side's gunfire. In the middle of the battle, my course was amazed to see what appeared to be one of our members doing a violent dance routine. Completely baffling until he plucked a thunder flash out of his sea boot with the fuse still burning! Some high ranking Air Force Officers were watching all this and one Air Vice Marshal gave his opinion that the shells were dummies and suggested that I threw one to him. The Course Officer nodded. Off went the shell in a graceful arc into the arms of the VIP who promptly went straight backwards out of the door! Fortunately he had a sense of humour and my RNR career did not suffer.

'The first time I arrived at a naval establishment as a commander for a training course in HMS Dryad, I was totally ignored by the porter until he asked for my name. He immediately dropped everything and took care of my joining procedures. At that time I was already a Captain in the Merchant Navy and that small incident really brought home to me that I had now 'joined the club'. Senior officers who had only recently called me Woods now referred to me as Peter.

'I had good times serving in the RNR. I recall a seagoing appointment in HMS Badminton and I expected to be a normal watch keeper as the ink was barely dry on my Second Mates Certificate. I was informed that I was not only the Navigator, but also the Squadron Navigator for the Vernon Squadron of which

Badminton was the senior ship. It was a very steep learning curve, but one made very pleasant as two other RNR Navigators in the Squadron were both from P & O and had Extra Masters Certificates! It was marvellous training for a Junior Officer, which my colleagues in the Merchant Navy sadly missed out on.'

Thank you, Peter.

There was a strange 'happening' that started in February 1958 ... it could have been peculiar to Merseyside! The tug Applegarth, which had been high and dry at a Birkenhead graving dock for the past ten weeks because of a demarcation dispute between the AEU and the Boiler-makers' Society, had been sitting there trapping HMS Mersey. The dispute arose over a cast iron rope guard that both unions claimed was their duty to fix. The guard-rail was eventually fitted by members of the Engineering Union and it took them less than two hours! Mersey missed her annual Easter voyage. The response from the boiler-makers was prompt. "The work has been carried out by AEU workers in direct contravention of a promise from the employers." Their spokesman added, "We will now have to decide whether to 'black' all the tugs in the fleet". And that is what they did!

Perhaps the final comment must be given by Roy Humphreys-Jones who presented his thoughts to a local paper. "It may be childish to suggest that such a matter of union 'principle' could be decided by spinning a coin, but nevertheless, it would appear to have been a most appropriate solution." The naval rank of the author of this so obvious pearl of wisdom was not disclosed, lest the whole Fleet be 'blacked'.

After all that there was much cleaning up to be done in Mersey before the engine and generator trials. It was a race against the clock. Lieutenant-Commander Roy Humphreys-

Jones again went on record: "Our chaps are helping out, but it will be touch and go about our training voyage next weekend to Portsmouth and the Brittany ports."

1959 was the Centenary of the old RNR and in that year HMS Amerton was replaced by HMS Pollington and was naturally renamed HMS Mersey. The arrival of Pollington was not unnoticed by the Liverpool pilots. As it was known that seven of the junior officers on board would be taking their equivalent of a driving test when they next ventured out into the river, the pilots took action. The ship was to leave Wapping for the first 'test' at about 11.30 that morning and was to spend the day meandering about the Mersey. It is not recorded what the naval reply was when a pilot boat pulled alongside and enquired as to whether any advice was needed.

Pollington was the last naval craft to be refitted by the Sheerness dockyard before its closure. She had a closed-in bridge and Deltic engines which gave a maximum speed of 17 knots. She was a big advance on previous ships allocated to the Division. It was planned that she would carry out five long cruises in 1960, including two NATO exercises and was to be manned by RNR officers and ratings only.

The Centenary of the old Royal Naval Reserve was celebrated in November 1959 by a centenary dinner in Eaglet. The guest of honour's life spanned three quarters of the centenary! Vice-Admiral Sir Gilbert Stephenson was known to thousands of Reserve officers and men as the wartime Commodore-in-Charge at Tobermory. He was dubbed the 'Terror of Tobermory'. His speech at the dinner expressed his admiration for the Reservists who had 'hoisted in' in the short space of two or three weeks much of the knowledge he had acquired in the whole of his career as a professional naval officer.

When asked about the innumerable stories about his time in Tobermory, he thought that they might have been distorted and then began to add more tales from his own memory! The fact is that all who had served under him had good reason to be thankful for the training they received when they subsequently carried out such evolutions as rescuing survivors and abandoning ship in grim reality.

Sir Gilbert Stephenson must be regarded as much a character as Field Marshal Lord Montgomery and other generals, many of whom had to exalt their own careers with authorship as a sideline. Stephenson was a great man.

Apart from the dinner on board Eaglet, the Centenary was also marked by a Service in Liverpool Parish Church at Pier Head and by a Roman Catholic Service in the pro-cathedral (the new one was not in existence at that time) with Archbishop Heenan in attendance. 200 members of the RNR were guests of the Liverpool Steamship Owners Association at a cocktail party on board the Cunard liner Britannic.

One cold and dark night in February 1959 a reporter from the Liverpool Echo agreed to go diving. Inexplicably, his name was not revealed.

In front of him was thirty feet of stone-cold, dock-murky water. He was well prepared by Lieutenant-Commander Tony Sutherst, the Diving Officer in charge and by Chief Petty Officer Robert Leonard as they eased him into a rubber suit over a pair of long, nylon 'combs' and a full length woollen pair of stockings. A tight fitting rubber head mask was clamped to the neck of the one-piece suit. It was to be a surface swim so no breathing apparatus was worn.

'Feeling like an underwater monster, I struggled down from Eaglet on to a barge and fitted on the massive fins. Getting in looked easy. The members of the team just put their hands round their facemasks to keep the air in the suit when they hit the water and jumped gracefully backwards from a nearby whaler.

'I tried it from the barge, putting my hands over my face and shutting my eyes tightly, I launched myself backwards and went into the dock with an almighty splash. My first pleasant surprise was to find myself still alive and floating. My second was that I was quite warm inside the suit, although the water was bitterly cold on my hands.

'Following Commander Sutherst's instructions, we lay on our backs, flipped the fins and moved silently across the dock towards the Mersey Docks and Harbour Board salvage ship Dispenser. After the shock of getting in, it was quite exhilarating and abandoning the navigation to others, just visible in the darkness, I had just settled down to enjoy the swim when a quiet voice warned "Mind your head". I looked up to see the side of Dispenser looming up into the sky about 12 inches away.

'The journey had been surprisingly quick. Turning around proved something of a problem. "Try moving the port fin and keep the other still" advised an unidentified voice in the darkness. It worked and we were on the way back.

'I had thoroughly enjoyed myself and once back on board we climbed one after the other into a bath of hot water to clean the suits and get out of them.'

The unit had only been formed two weeks. The first volunteers were Telegraphist Paul Kenyon, Steward Albert Arkwell, Leading Electrician's Mate Brian Lloyd, EMI James Sweeney and another not recalled.

Commander Sutherst: "There is nothing slap-happy about our unit. Everyone takes the training seriously and we work as a team with first class discipline. We don't do this diving for fun. It's hard work working in four feet of mud at the bottom of the dock trying to break a chain with a hammer and chisel."

A story appeared in the Yorkshire Evening Post on Monday June 20th 1960. Five boys from Dewsbury Sea Cadet Corps completed a 700-mile voyage in HMS Mersey and an Evening Post Reporter sailed with them and produced this cautionary tale.

'HMS Mersey, a 440-ton minesweeper, left Port Edgar and sailed under the Forth Bridge with the cadets forming the traditional line of smartly-dressed seamen for a warship's farewell salute to a port.

'No man is a sailor until he's been to sea. These boys, aged 13 to 15, were bound for a baptism by salt water. Ahead of them was a 700-mile voyage around the North of Scotland and down the West Coast to Liverpool. The seas are quick to anger. They sort out the landlubbers from sea dogs. And in HMS Mersey they have an ally who will jump to their slightest bidding.

'She is a light ship, built of aluminium, wood and alloys - so as not to trigger off magnetic mines. And because she is light, she bounces. She also sways, plunges, soars and corkscrews.

'HMS Mersey put her nose out of the Firth of Forth and into the North Sea. A message reached the bridge. "One of the cadets," it said, "has already been sick." And so the boys fell, all but one of them. Each sick boy 'died' his private little death in that seamen's mess down below, where a man's whole world can be the inside of a bucket. Or perhaps he lurched upwards, through the bucking ship to get to the deck and fresh air. And there he stayed, alone and palely loitering between spells of hanging over the rail.

'The boys were not alone in their agony. In the wheelhouse and on the mess decks seasoned seamen wore the telltale look of pinched pallor, with just a tinge of pink at the tip of the nose.

'The first night ended with HMS Mersey fighting through a four and a half knot tide race between Stroma and Swona, twin islands lying between the Orkneys and the Scottish mainland. And she heaved her way around Cape Wrath, on the Northwest tip of Scotland, and started the long haul to the South.

'The wind freshened and whipped white horses into life on the wave-tops. Down below, on the mess deck, 'Housewives' Choice' blared through loud speakers. Able seamen slept on, unheeding. For they have learned in the long, long ago of watch-keeping how to hug-to-themselves the precious gift of sleep at sea.

'The cadets were in various states of awareness. He of the strongest stomach, 15-year-old Jim Foley, from Woodsome Estate, Batley, sat on his bunk with the chirpiness of the strong-stomached. The brothers, Stanley (aged 14) and Jim Ellis (aged 12), from Savile Town, suffered and sailored on. Trevor Oddy (aged 13), Staincliffe Road, Dewsbury, could still force a grin because his worst moments were to come.

'And that fifth cadet? He was the smallest, but his sufferings were the greatest. Kevin O'Donnell (14) was only 4 ft 7 inches tall, a true 'three pennyworth of copper'. His mates called him 'Lofty'. And 'Lofty' was stricken, terribly stricken. He had that withdrawn from life feeling that only the very seasick know.

'Down by the Hebrides, past the Mull of Oa and the Duok on the Island of Islay, ran H.M.S. Mersey, slapping her bows on the long rollers coming in from the Atlantic. Night came again, and with it comparative peace. One by one, on the morning of the third day, the cadets emerged from below. They were smiling now ... wanly it is true, but smiling. The ordeal was over.

'The Skipper of HMS Mersey for this voyage, Commander John France, RNR, of Mirfield, said: "In spite of having been sick, these lads will be able to stick their chests out in Dewsbury and say 'I've sailed all the way from Edinburgh to Liverpool, right around Scotland.' "

'The five boys who lined the forecastle deck as HMS Mersey saluted her home port of Liverpool were better boys than those who had lined the deck in the Firth of Forth ... though you would have had a hard job proving it to them in that early stage of their convalescence.

'For no man is a sailor until he's been to sea. And they had received their salt-water baptism'.

The Inaugural Service in the Anglican Cathedral to commemorate the Battle of Atlantic was held on Sunday, 3rd May 1959. Whilst the records refer to this as an 'inaugural' service, other records state that the service organised on Sunday, 27th October 1957 is 'an opportunity to inaugurate an Annual Naval Service in Liverpool Cathedral comparable to the Services held yearly by the Army and the Royal Air Force.' The size of the contingents invited is of interest. RNAS Stretton 30: HMS Scarborough, Whitby, and Hardy 30 seats each; HMS Eaglet six contingents of 60 and Sea Cadets two contingents of 30. The total was 510. One must assume this was really the pre-inaugural service that led to the establishment of the first Battle of Atlantic Sunday in 1959 and this led to the decision that the Service was to be held thereafter on every first Sunday in May.

Commander-in-Chief, Plymouth, Vice-Admiral Sir Richard Onslow, KCB, DSO, during the 1959 service presented the bell of HMS Liverpool to the Cathedral in memory of those who lost their lives in the Second World War. The Dean used these words as he accepted the Ship's Bell of HMS Liverpool: "I receive this Bell on behalf of the Dean and Chapter for safe custody within this Cathedral. Here it will find a place of honour within a worthy shrine of remembrance. May all who look upon it and hear it sound in days to come find in it a sign and symbol of watchfulness, of discipline and of faithful service."

The address was given by the Archdeacon of Warrington, Eric Evans, whose wartime record of sea-going excelled all other Naval Chaplains. He was Chaplain, RNVR on active service 1940 - 46. Also at the service was Canon C.B. Naylor, Chancellor of the Cathedral, Chaplain RNVR on active service 1943 - 46. The Chaplain of Eaglet, Padre G.C. Cutcher had served as a Lieutenant (S) RNVR in HMS Liverpool, 1945 - 46. HMS Liverpool was laid down in 1936 and completed in November 1938. During the Second World War she served in the Far East, the Mediterranean and in the Home Fleet. In the Mediterranean she was twice torpedoed by enemy aircraft and seriously damaged, but was repaired and returned to service in October 1945. Until 1952 she formed part of the Mediterranean fleet and was for a time flagship of the Commander-in-Chief.

An article in the Liverpool Daily Post in 1959, whilst pointing out that the Service was 'a joint effort of the RNR and the Sea Cadets', added this important statement: 'It is hoped to make it an annual service on the lines of the RAF Battle of Britain.' This firmly suggests that the Commemoration of the Battle of Atlantic Services actually started in 1959.

Organisation for such a service was immense and the burden was upon Eaglet. As it was a 'first' much had to be learnt at speed. HMS Chaplet came to the Liverpool Landing Stage, the Liverpool Police Band 'did' the fanfares and Last Post in the Cathedral, the Royal Marine Band dealt with the March Past, everybody who was somebody had to be invited, the clergy had to pray for fine weather, and a wall bracket for the bell had to be designed, approved and installed. Item 5, Ref. 46/5/A, has an air of desperation: 'Lord Derby has been alerted as to the service and to Captain Smith's earnest hope that he can attend, watch the march past and have a slug in Eaglet with Commander-in-Chief.' In the end all was well. But there is no information available about the weather on that day!

The Battle of Atlantic Service in 1960 brought two Navy ships to Liverpool ... HMS Dainty and HMS Battleaxe. In the Cathedral were contingents from the Royal Navy, the Royal Naval Reserve, the WRNR, HMS Conway, Indefatigable, the Sea Cadets and RAF Coastal Command. The address was given by the Right Rev. G.A. Ellison, Bishop of Chester. He was a former Naval Chaplain who had served in the Atlantic Battle.

It was announced in 1961 that Captain Angus Letty had been appointed Commanding Officer of the Mersey Division on the retirement of Captain Bernard Smith. By tradition the retiring captain was pulled across Salthouse Dock on the 14th January 1961. The whaler was manned by commanders and above. It was one of the foggiest nights in memory and the Captain truly 'disappeared into the mists'. Captain Letty had trained in HMS Conway and was the first professional seaman to take command of Eaglet. He had been awarded the DSC for special service in France in 1940 and the DSO while serving with light coastal forces in 1943. After a short staff course, he was appointed Senior Officer (Operations) in the Freetown Escort Force, where he remained until being demobilised at the end of 1945. He also held the Reserve Decoration with clasp. Captain Letty after the war returned to the Cunard Company as the First Officer of the Samaria and later served in the Aquitania, Queen Mary, Queen

Elizabeth and Mauritania. He was appointed to his first command in July 1953 and came ashore the following January as Assistant Marine Superintendent.

It was a happy chance that last December 2002 I encountered a recently-retired General Practitioner, Doctor Michael A.J. Holland. We stood at the bar of the Skelwith Bridge Hotel in the Lakes and chatted. And you can guess what happened.'National Service was still with us and whilst medical students were deferred, we still did a year as officer cadets before our time at university. At the end of medical training we would have been expected to serve for two years as Medical Officers, but sadly National Service was over. That truly did sadden me.

'Whilst at school I did 14 days in a carrier at Portland and then during my training for six years I put in 14 days each year at sea mostly in frigates. Even when I was qualified I did my fourteen days yearly in Mersey ... not as a doctor, but as an Ordinary Seaman. I cannot recall what List I was on, but was always available to be 'called up' for ten years.

'Part of my task was to mop up the officers' gangway and accommodation, they were always throwing up ... I just got on with it. I was on board during the Suez crisis. We set out into the Atlantic to meet two submarines in order to transfer charts of the Med. We were at full speed into really bad weather, the screws were often out of the water and the ship would shudder violently. My station was outside on the wing of the bridge with spray right over the top. Apparently my task was to keep a look out. All that happened was that I was soaked to the skin and did my best to hold on. They were warm inside the bridge! Our main diet was hard-boiled eggs. I also continued to mop up ... they were all at it! I suppose that I was there to do nothing very much because I had no knowledge.

'The return journey was wonderful with clear skies and calm waters. We dropped a depth-charge and the cook was sent out in a cutter to collect the fish. It was a magical trip back to Weymouth.

'Our annual bounty when I was a student was, I think, a grand total of seven pounds. Another memory is the daily tot at sea. If it chanced to be your birthday, you were 'asked' to partake of 'sippers' from everyone else's tot. The victim ever fell over at the end of that.

'Whilst I was a student, I spent three months as a sailing instructor at Dartmouth. I much enjoyed the College. Britannia came in with herself on board. As there was to be a Ball, they dressed me up as a Surgeon Lieutenant complete with two rings and a dash of crimson and, like Cinderella, I attended the Ball on board. The next night I was told to look after the Royal chauffeurs and we decided on a pub crawl ... I was young at the time! I told them where I would be standing during the Queen's · Parade the next morning. The next day along trundled the limousine driven by a chauffeur with an immovable catatonic stare. As the machine drew alongside me, my friend of the night before managed to close his right eye and waggle his lower jaw. That really was a Royal moment to remember!'

The Magazine of the RNVR Officers' Association entitled 'The Wave' contained as usual a report on the affairs of the Mersey Division. That of Autumn 1959 is of some interest.

'At the time of writing this report, HMS Mersey has completed two of her fourteen day cruises and has visited Norway and the Channel Islands. The Admiral Commanding Reserves was dined in the Mess on the eve of his Annual Inspection during July. During his inspection of our Wrens' Division the band played "Thank Heaven for Little Girls," but this was not an adverse comment on the male members of the Division. The BBC Northern Dance Orchestra's broadcast mentioned in the last edition of Wave was subsequently made from HMS Eaglet, and Miss Sheila Buxton sang the pick of the 'pops' suitably attired as a Wren rating.'

One must assume that this made sense to those who had been involved.

The Lawson trophy, which is presented annually to the most efficient Wren Reserve Unit in the United Kingdom, was awarded on March 19th 1962 to the Mersey Division of the Women's Royal Naval Reserve. The Director of the WRNS, Commandant Jean Davies, presented the trophy to Chief Wren Joyce Melsom.

There were eleven Wren Reserve Units in the United Kingdom and Commandant Davies, a native of Liverpool, also presented a long-service medal to Chief Regulating Wren Florence Farrel. She served in the Wrens from 1942 to 1948 and joined the Mersey Division in 1952. In fact she was the first young lady to sign on.

Dining Out Nights play a vital part of the life of any Division. It is a time to look back with gratitude for loyal service and friendships. On the night of January 28th 1963 farewell was offered to two good servants of the Division. Surgeon Captain W.R. Kershaw held the Chair of Parasitology and Entomology at the famous Liverpool School of Tropical Medicine. He joined Eaglet in 1938 and was Medical Officer on board the destroyer HMS Harvester while she was employed in the Western Approaches and at Dunkirk. Lieutenant-Commander Harrison, who was an electrical engineer, commanded several trawlers and the corvette HMS Snapdragon, and took part in the evacuation of Norway and the invasion of Sicily.

HMS Irwell ended her career in April 1963. The Drill Ship had spent 31 years of her port-bound life in Merseyside. She was a ship that really never went to sea! Little was known about the possibility of selling her to an Italian firm for scrap and there was no fuss as she was taken across the Mersey to Herculaneum Dock in Liverpool and placed into the hands of the ship-breakers.

Irwell was built in 1918 as a Fleet minesweeper, but was not completed. Her engine space was concreted in and she was converted as a training ship in 1926. Then she was stationed in Manchester until 1931, when she was transferred to Birkenhead. That arrival had been marked by a ceremonial march past in Hamilton Square, Birkenhead.

The vessel had provided facilities for training in engineering, seamanship, radar plotting and store-keeping. In 1953 there was a complete overhaul with additional lecture rooms, cabins, showers, a canteen and a radar plotting room. In this general uplift she was given the dignity of her first funnel!

Irwell was the centre of attention in 1953 when nearly 1,000 officers and ratings of Mersey Division were on parade in Birkenhead for the annual inspection. The inspecting officer, Vice-Admiral A.K. Scott-Moncreiff (Admiral Commanding Reserves) arrived at Morpeth old entrance lock in the 'barge'. He was received by Captain E.N. Wood, who was on the point of retirement and by Commander A.V. Turner, his successor.

In the February of 1956 she was rudely disturbed when she was taken from her moorings in Morpeth Dock, Birkenhead, and towed by tugs on her first voyage for 25 years across the Mersey to Liverpool's Salthouse Dock to join the drill ship HMS

Eaglet. This simplified the RNVR training schedules and saved the men having to cross the Mersey.

Irwell had served her purpose and was fondly remembered.

In June 1963 HMS Mersey joined the Royal Navy, the Royal Danish Navy and the Federal German Navy in a 14 day minesweeping task to clear a path across the bed of the North Sea so that telephone cables could be laid to Esbjerg, Denmark and Borkum, Germany. This was felt necessary because during the war it was estimated that 14,000 mines were laid and any of the magnetic variety on the seabed could still be dangerous.

As a protection against possible blast, the men on board lived in the upper part of the ship and wore crash helmets. However, the task was completed without casualties. The Commanding Officer of Mersey was Lieutenant-Commander John Woodhouse and the Navigating Officer was Lieutenant Robert Barclay.

The exercise was no picnic. Each section of the area to be swept had to be gone over nine times. The reason for this was because some British mines contained an arming device that would not detonate the mine until several ships had passed over it. To sweep for magnetic mines the minesweeper had to tow a giant electric cable loop astern through which heavy shots of current were passed from a generator on board the ship. There is probably nothing to equal the monotonous and almost deafening fading and swelling moan from a minesweeper's generator going on for hour after hour.

There was a strong effort in 1964 to replace the obviously ageing Eaglet with HMS Starling. On Merseyside Starling was regarded as the flagship of Captain F.J.Walker, famous for master minding the destruction of the U-Boats during the war. The campaign was led by Alderman Simon Mahon, the Labour MP for Bootle, but a letter from John Hay the Parliamentary Under-Secretary, responsible for Royal Naval Affairs at the Ministry of Defence, stated that it would cost £150,000 to refit her for this work! The intention was to establish a shore base.

There was obvious disappointment. The original request to the Ministry of Defence had put the basic case. 'When Starling and the Second Support Group returned from patrol during which six U-Boats were sunk, the First Lord of the Admiralty at that time Mr. A.V. Alexander compared that exploit to the Battle of Trafalgar. Captain Walker and his Group were actually responsible for the destruction of 21 U-Boats during the war, of which Starling helped to account for no less than 15.

'If HMS Victory can be maintained from public funds to commemorate Trafalgar, would it not be reasonable to expect some similar support to ensure that the victory of the Atlantic, upon which the survival of our country depended, is not forgotten?'

Commodore R.H. Walker, RD**, RNR, DL has penned some random notes which give a vivid insight into the life of an RNR officer. It was the Sixties. 'Joined 1959 after National Service. Many ex-N.S. Mids and Subs who have remained good friends ever since. Training Tuesday and Wednesday nights and Weekends each month. Division many hundred strong with 400 WRNR. ACR's Inspection Ship's Company fell in threes by Ships Book Number and stretched along the road.

'Tenders Mersey (Amerton) open bridge!, Dee seaward defence boat, and the picket boat Rosie, beloved by all for boat handling practice, engines controlled by whistle! Sea-going billets hard to come by had to enter name at training office and hope! ... even though I had navigated a CMS in the Med for nine months. Drivers Norrie Sellars, Ronald Smith, Tony Sutherst, Tom Fox.

'Classroom instruction in Navigation by Schooly Hill, who sadly rather a large nose, but was most committed. This took place in the TAS School where we looked at the equipment and tried to imagine how it had been used in the war! No sea-going-fortnights for the first two years of the sub-lieutenants' courses, navigation then minesweeping and gunnery.

'Monday lunches well attended but not by R.H.W. who needed to be at his desk! Evening supper cooked by George Williams, Captain Walker's steward, and Bert Myers, food welcome but origin uncertain at times! George was a strong character and better not to cross him. The polished tables were his love and he ran the Wardroom as though his own. They were well supported by their wives when more help was required.

'The Mess life was friendly and lively, many RN visiting ships to entertain before and after drills. Mess Dinners were very formal to a youngster and not a little daunting as one might be called to account for oneself at any time. The hard wing collar and day uniform did not help! There were bunks in the Casbah to sleep in if it was to be a very late session.

'Eric Woolfenden ran the NAAFI Canteen and was always helpful, the Rebate was a major contributor to the Welfare Fund. The Chiefs' Mess was their own!

'Mess games after dinners were enjoyed by all. Deck hockey on the old wooden drill slopping deck, round the wardroom without touching the deck was particularly hazardous for Mike Tomkinson who managed to "break a leg" climbing out of the window to cross the deck above, and table races with the tables upside down and the passengers jumping them along the carpet! The usual tests of strength with bottles and chairs.

'Whaler pulling was the main out of class activity, they were reached by a vertical descent down the steel hand-rails fixed to the side of the bow. Of course we never knew whether it was the bow or the stern as Sir Bevis was sharp at both ends to confuse.'

And at that point Rod Walker stopped, but there could have been so much more! He had first joined the RNR in 1957 as an ordinary seaman for National Service and was commissioned the same year, serving as Navigating Officer for HMS Wilkieston in the Mediterranean and Red Sea. National

Service over, he returned to the Division and after a time he was Navigator and First Lieutenant of the Coniston Class Mine Countermeasure Vessels; he passed for command in 1969. Then he was to become First Lieutenant, Training Commander and Executive Officer. Promoted Commander in 1981, he assumed command of the Division in 1985 and was promoted to Captain in 1986. In April 1988 he became Captain Sea Training and in April 1991 he was appointed Commodore of the Royal Naval Reserve. He retired in 1993

Lieutenant-Commander John V. Duckett, RD*, RNR, recalls being interviewed in 1963. As National Service had ended it had been decreed that it was necessary to re-introduce Direct Entry Commissions for Technical Officers. Amongst these was Tom Cunningham (a future Captain of Eaglet) and the joining rank was Probationary Acting Lieutenant. John Duckett remembers being interviewed by Commander (E) the Honourable Edward Broke-Evans, son of 'Evans of the Broke'. They all felt that having the son of an Earl and a distinguished Admiral added a touch of distinction to the Engine Room department. Commander (E) Ernie Scott was in charge of the Junior Engineer Officer training. He placed great emphasis on knowing the ship in every detail, taking the watch-keeping certificates required of the Ratings and developing a pride and 'esprit-de corps' in the Engine room department ... in a word, to become a genuine 'plumber'! John talks of many a cold drill night spent in a boiler suit crawling round the sweeper to be able to sketch the Engine room system into his journal, getting to know every pipe and valve so that they could be found in the dark. John Duckett served in Eaglet for twenty-six years and became Head of Department as a Marine Engineer and was the Senior Technical Officer.

On Saturday, January 11th 1964, Captain Angus Letty was dined out by his fellow officers. He was a Marine Superintendent with Cunard Line and the first professional seaman to command the Mersey Division. He held the Reserve Decoration with clasp and was appointed an ADC to the Queen a year before retirement.

His successor was Captain G.N. Sellers who had joined the RNR as a midshipman in June 1938. He served in HMS Ramilies for the first four years of the war. He also served in the destroyers Quality and Penn and commanded Versatile. Captain Sellers was an adjuster of claims with a group of insurance companies based in Liverpool.

An article in the Liverpool Daily Post, January 30th 1964, spelt out the purpose of the RNR. Whilst the Territorial Army's principal function was to reinforce the regular units, the Naval Reservists played a more individual role. They were trained to man minesweepers and in an emergency they would supply the crews for a number of operational sweepers, which were lying cocooned in reserve. Commander France, Eaglet's executive officer, pointed out; "Our job would be to keep the approaches and the harbours of this country clear of mines and to free members of the Royal Navy for other functions." To help in this, the Division had full time use of HMS Mersey, a modern £650,000 coastal minesweeper carrying the latest equipment. Commander Harold Duffy, who was in charge of communications, stated that his branch was the biggest in Britain and could maintain a link with the Mediterranean. There were 90 members of the branch and many did their 14 days training at Malta or Singapore or Gibraltar.

HMS Mersey on the last weekend of June 1964 carried Lord Derby to the Isle of Man. Minesweeping exercises were carried out around the Island before docking at Douglas. Lord Derby received Sir Ronald Garvey (Lieutenant-Governor) and other senior Manx officials at a reception in Mersey and on the Monday he addressed the IOM Chamber of Commerce.

At the end of 1964 HMS Beckford, a 125-ton seaward defence ship, arrived in Liverpool and berthed astern of Eaglet. Although built in 1956, the new arrival was 'brand-new', for soon after being handed over to the Navy she was 'cocooned' and her trip from Barrow to Liverpool was her first sea-going journey. She was to be used for training junior officers in ship handling and training new entry ratings. Beckford had twin diesel engines, a third centre line engine for slow running and accommodated a crew of 26.

On the 6th February 1965 fourteen men from Mersey Division took part in an operational visit to the West Indies. Four coastal minesweepers, manned by men from the eleven RNR Divisions and from the Wireless Reserve, UK, set out from Plymouth. HMS Mersey was commanded by Lieutenant-Commander L.T.A. Foinette. The vessels arrived in the West Indies on the 23rd February, having refuelled en route. Visits were made to Grenada, St. Vincent, Antigua, Barbados and British Guiana, before sailing home via Bermuda to arrive on 23rd March.

During 1965 the Communicators of the Division won the Mountbatten Trophy, which was competed for annually by all the various Communications/Wireless Districts in the RNR. Earl Mountbatten said that he would present it in Eaglet, when he came up to Blackpool to the Burma Star Association Reunion, but unfortunately was taken ill whilst staying at Lord Derby's home in Knowsley. Not wishing to cancel all the arrangements that had been made, he said that he could not get to Eaglet, then at Princes Dock, and asked that the Division went to him. A fleet of buses was hurriedly assembled, got to Knowsley Hall and the Division fell in.

To everyone's surprise Mountbatten appeared in front of the Hall in pyjamas with a pusser's raincoat over them and proceeded with the presentation. He thanked us all for coming out there and promptly disappeared back inside.

The unique photograph includes Captain G.N. Sellers, VRD, RNR, Commanding Officer of HMS Eaglet, Captain H.T. Duffy, MBE, VRD, RNR, Senior Communications Branch RNR and Commander John Felice, VRD, RNR.

John Felice recalls the conversation. "We spoke about the Old and Bold weekend trips in HMS Mersey. Those took place almost every year during Roy Jones' time as Commanding Officer, usually at the end of the Training season, and when the weather was bad. I can recall a couple of such trips to the Isle of Man in dreadful weather. We usually finished up in the Casino, once ashore, as accommodation was not available for all on board."

Life is rarely running on straight lines and Mr. Murphy's laws are ever with us. In the middle of July 1965 HMS Mersey was on her way to Morlaix in Northern France for a minesweeping exercise. She called in at Portsmouth Harbour when there was a collision with the yacht Sunitu that sank in six minutes. There were no casualties and the survivors were rescued by a British Railways launch. It was a task for the Navy divers to start the salvage operations.

A brief article in the Daily Post on November 1966 looks back on a particular voyage of HMS Mersey. 'The calibre of HMS Mersey, her officers and crew, was tested severely one day in 1966, when she was caught up in the tail-end of Hurricane Betsy in the English Channel. Both came through extremely well. Mersey was battered about the superstructure and badly flooded, and many of the men ... some of whom had never been to sea before ... were ill.

'Mersey was returning from a NATO exercise at Emden, Germany, and had started the homeward trip in flat, calm seas. The she ran into dense fog, and 24 hours later she was battling through 25-30 foot high waves in a hurricane.'

I joined the Division as Chaplain in 1966, having been an Officiating Royal Navy Chaplain since 1961 and retired from the RNR in 1981. I started my ministry with the Mersey Mission to

Seamen in 1961 and eventually retired in 1989. Before all this nautical activity, I had served in wartime as a Royal Air Force pilot and then about ten years as a Padre with the Air Training Corps. The sea and the air have much in common ... both demand respect and bind men into a remarkable fellowship.

My memories of the 'floating hulk' are fond, but distant. The first duty of the Chaplain on Drill Night in Eaglet was to conduct prayers at Divisions. The drill deck was large and decidedly ill-lit. With the full ship's company assembled after much shuffling and restrained shouting, the order came ... 'Off caps'. Forward I went and for two minutes or so the stage was mine. It was a challenge. Quickly I realised that a piece from the Liverpool Echo was more likely to grab their attention than Cranmer's best prose. I knew that I had communicated when during my tour of the ship, my leg was pulled and the topic dissected. There was one bit of Cranmerian prose that never failed. Too often the lights invariably dimmed from fatigue and old-age. That was the cue for me to make use of the Evensong Collect, 'Lighten our darkness we beseech Thee, O Lord' ... and there was always a fervent 'Amen'.

May 5th 1968 was an important day for Liverpool. Admiral of the Fleet Earl Mountbatten of Burma was present at a service in the Anglican Cathedral to commemorate the twenty-fifth anniversary of the turning point in the Battle of the Atlantic. Eaglet has always been at the centre of the organisation of the service and Liverpool was the central control of the Battle.

It is generally considered that the start of the victory over the U-boat fleets was marked by the passage of Convoy ONS 5 in May 1943. But it was not the end of the Battle. Churchill stated that the Battle of the Atlantic was "the one campaign of the Second World War that lasted from the first day to the last."

Many lives were to be lost in the Atlantic as the result of enemy action after May 1943 and it is unfair to their memory to suggest that the Battle of the Atlantic was over by that date. In fact two vessels were sunk by U-boats off the coasts of Britain on the eve of the Armistice.

Earl Mountbatten, who had sailed to Liverpool in his flagship for the ceremony, later took the salute in the march-past by contingents of the Royal Navy and Royal Marines from the naval frigates Zulu and Danae, which visited Merseyside for the event.

The address was given by the Bishop of Liverpool, the Right Reverend Stuart Blanch. (He was to become the Archbishop of York). He took as his theme the achievement of all-round victory against the enemies that beset the modern world. 'We can be successful in business or public life, but lack success in private life. We can build Concord, but cannot solve a strike. We can send men into space, yet our prisons are as full as ever before.'

The University Connection

In most universities you will find the Army Officers' Training Corps and a University Air Squadron, but in Liverpool no attempt had been made to create a Naval Division, although during the last war one had been established to give initial training and had then been disbanded. In 1968 there was a discussion between the Commanding Officer of Eaglet and Colonel D.R. Morgan of the University Army Training Corps and the University authorities with the purpose of establishing a Naval Unit. There was very heavy weather ahead and much tribute must be paid to Captain Duffy for the eventual success of the venture. In October 1971 it was decided that there should be a regular naval officer as Officer in Charge and a regular naval petty officer as Coxswain. A member of the University staff Lieutenant-Commander Philip Kemp, who had served in the Merchant Navy as Second Officer and who was responsible for the afloat activities of the Liverpool Unit of the RNXS, became the First Lieutenant of the University Unit. The first Commanding Officer was Lieutenant-Commander Peter King, RN. Everything at first was based in Eaglet. Eventually the centre of the work was at 18, Oxford Street, adjacent to the Army Officers Corps.

It was proposed that the Naval Unit would have the use of Dee, which had been used by Mersey Division, as a training ship for navigation and seamanship. The first trip was memorable. With the Staff Officer of Eaglet, Lieutenant-Commander David Allen, RN, and the new Unit Commander, Peter King, Dee duly slipped from Princes Dock. Lieutenant-Commander David Allen gave the appropriate orders to the engine room, but the engine room quickly informed him that they could not comply because a control lever had "come 'orf in me 'and, Sir!" Dee nudged the jetty and was secured later and ignominiously to her berth. Thus began a series of mishaps and defects, which, with one brief interval, kept Dee from playing her proper part in the development of the Royal Naval Unit for some eighteen months.

To aid recruiting, the students were invited to HMS Eaglet to learn something of what was on offer. Incidentally, it is worth recalling that at this time Dee was being loaned to Clyde Division, RNR, and was damaged in a grounding! The Autumn Term of 1971 saw classes being held in seamanship in Room 202 in Eaglet. The Executive Officer of Eaglet, Commander (later Captain) W.T. Jones, afforded every possible co-operation.

By 1972 there was a total strength of fourteen and the

Unit began to take shape. Naturally it was necessary to create a social life. Phil Kemp, the First Lieutenant was ex-officio President of the Mess and recalls the briefing by Peter King, the Commanding Officer. "You will have to make a speech, don't go on all night!" Sound advice!

I recall the commissioning service that I shared with the late Father John White, my fellow chaplain and good friend in Eaglet, when in a biting wind we sent the Unit's new vessel HMS Waterwitch on her way. 'For those in peril on the sea' seemed appropriate words as we battled with the elements on dry land. The year was 1981. Philip Kemp was Sub-Dean in the Faculty of Engineering Science and had just retired from the unit after ten years as First Lieutenant.

The story of Liverpool University's Naval Unit has been well documented by Philip Kemp. The work continues and is happily a peripheral part of the Eaglet saga.

The Annual Inspection Parade by the Admiral Commanding Reserves was always formal and exacting. Every department would be inspected and the whole Division would be on parade. One of the most famous Admirals to be appointed ACR was Rear Admiral B.C. Godfrey Place, VC, RN. His appointment covered the period about 1968 - 69.

The Admiral won his Victoria Cross as Lieutenant in command of the Midget Submarine X7, an X-Craft, in a successful attack on the German Battleship Tirpitz in Kaa Fiord, Norway, on 22nd September 1943. X5 was commanded by Lieutenant H. Henry-Creer, RNVR, and was probably sunk by gunfire and there were no survivors. X6, commanded by Lieutenant D. Cameron, RNR, and X7 succeeded in laying the high-explosive charge on the seabed underneath Tirpitz. The charges seriously damaged the German ship, but did not sink it.

The survivors were to spend the rest of the war as Prisoners of War.

The photograph shows the Rear Admiral in an earnest conversation with Lieutenant-Commander Thomas Conway who received the Reserve Decoration in 1968.

The Black Hand Gang

Minesweepers run on diesel oil and love it or hate it its odour is all pervasive. It clings to all the members of the Engine Room branch and just about anything they touch. Here are a few "Dieso" stories written by Commander Tom Cunningham.

Gibraltar

'In about 1968 I was the Engineer officer and we were outboard ship on a trot of three fuelling by hoses from the jetty. The hose snaked over the ships sides dripping dieso at each joint until it reached our fuelling point. There was a hose joint just inside the ships side adjacent to the "Garden Gate" and the area of deck underneath it was soaked in fuel. I was not concerned about this; the upper deck was the province of the First Lieutenant. I was however much more concerned about the impending visit of the Squadron Engineer Officer who was none other than our own Commander Ernest Scott, a Yorkshireman of great veracity.

'A few minutes later he emerged from the wardroom of the inboard ship and fixed me with a baleful glare whilst striding over ships side. He immediately turned right towards me and at that moment both his feet went from under him on the fuel soaked deck and he was instantly lying full length on his back. The deck was caulked with pitch, which the heat and the fuel had softened. Ernest climbed to his feet, not a happy man, with not only a fuel-soaked set of whites but black tramlines running from the heels of his white buckskin shoes up to the collar of his shirt!

'I could not contain my mirth and decided to make myself scarce rapidly. Ernie could not carry on with his inspection and returned ashore with as much dignity as he could muster!

Fuelling

'To achieve this evolution required that as the tanks were being filled they were dipped via sounding tubes in the Officers' cabins, and the person dipping the tank shouting to his oppo on the valves to switch over, stop etc. One such dip pipe was accessed via the First Lieutenant's cabin and if there was a foul up such as misreading the tape or opening the wrong valve fuel, oil spurted out of the dip pipe and very rapidly covered the cabin carpet. Without doubt such happenings were accidental, but it was never easy convincing the First Lieutenant of this, particularly if he was not known for his love of the Engine Room Branch.

Transferring fuel at sea

'Fuel was transferred from the main tanks to the engine tanks by the manipulation of a complex series of valves in the generator room. It was very easy to overfill an engine ready-use tank, particularly if the duty stoker had nipped off to his mess whilst leaving the pump running. When this happened, as it regularly did, dieso swilled all around the waist of the ship in the vicinity of the fresh vegetable lockers. With every passing wave the vegetables were further impregnated.

'One weekend when I was the Engineer Officer we had serious problems in this area and the potatoes received a really good soaking. When they were served they were a pale yellow colour. "Butter Potatoes," said I as the steward served them. "Marvellous," said the Captain. They tasted awful, but I manfully consumed my share and did not let on, suggesting that it might be something to do with the butter or margarine used in the galley. The First Lieutenant was instructed by the Captain to have a word with the Chef who was in future to serve only plain boiled!'

Engineers have their problems as illustrated in part of a report written by Lieutenant-Commander (E) Dick Cattle after one 'cruise' in Mersey. It all seems to be a matter of 'timing and urgency'.

'Port main engine ready-use fuel tank gauge has been missing for some time. HMS Vernon has ordered one urgently and advise Mersey Division to write in approximately one month to Sub-Lieutenant Martin, Base Engineers Office, HMS Vernon.

'It is understood that Mersey has no priority for this item when ordered direct so this method might prove useful. The absence of this gauge means that the only way of knowing that the tanks are full is to overflow the fuel on to the deck, much to the disapproval of the First Lieutenant. If gauges cannot be obtained at all, then consideration should be given to modifying the fuel lines so that the sump tank gauge can be used as a gauge glass.'

We can assume that the person who received this report understood it perfectly and that the matter was dealt with ... eventually!

Many old friends have said initially, "There's nothing to remember," and then we start to talk! Commander Gordon Milles, VRD*, RNR, put pen to paper. 'I was demobbed as a Hostilities Only Rating in July 1947 and enrolled in Eaglet in September 1947 as a PO Radio Mechanic Air ... not much use to the Division as we had no aeroplanes! Thanks to the deviousness of Commanders Horsfall and Stewart, I reverted to being Supply Assistant and then became to my surprise a Probationary Acting Lieutenant (S), RNVR, on 26th June 1951.

'There were sailing picnics on Sundays and we cooked and ate sausages on Burbo Bank until the tide came in. There was one occasion when Rosie proved by experiment that it was not possible to navigate the Rock Channel at low water, to the chagrin of the Commanding Officer. There we sat on our bilges until the tide refloated us.

'The change to commissioned life took some getting used to as there were very few lower deck promotions and most of the officers had war experience. One of the high lights was the lunch (3 shillings) put on by the Chief Stewards Davis and Williams with Mr. Myers in the galley. Dinner was the same price on parade nights.

'At one of the New Year Dances Cassandra Cornelius dressed as an old salt for the Old Year and she wheeled in a builder's barrow a rather chubby Harold Duffy in baby clothes for the New Year. There were lots of fun and games in those days, deck hockey on the drill deck, games of skill and chance and brute force ... happily there was always a doctor on hand!

'My first RNVR sea-going experience was in the old Mickey Mouse to St. Malo. As our navigator, no longer with us, occasionally made mistakes, my joining instructions to the remaining officers was to bring Dutch guilders, Belgian and French francs in addition to sterling. He was ill pleased. Some time later we were lost near the Channel Islands and by chance spotted the St. Malo Ferry ... so we followed her in! On this occasion the Staff Officer was a captain and much to my surprise I was ordered to put on a sword and medals and then visit all the British boats in the harbour. The point of this escaped me at the time, but further thought made me think that he was looking for the inevitable free drinks. It worked.

'Some years later we were the first RNVR ship to visit Gibraltar ... Bernard Smith was the Commanding Officer. On the way we had 'hands to bathe' in the Bay of Biscay, a risky operation in the swell that was running and lowering the sea boat was even riskier. We managed without casualties. On arrival at Gibraltar and berthing opposite the Tower, the Captain's motor scooter was parked by the gangway, giving Mersey an air of distinction! That was our opinion.

'At one Battle of Atlantic Service Prince Charles and Princess Diana were present. To add lustre to that occasion our Rear Admiral of Southport (the inimitable, lofty and irrepressible Lieutenant-Commander Mike Barnes) organised a guard of Sea Urchin Officers with swords and medals and ever tightening uniforms to protect the Royals.

'Eaglet had become a way of life. This was when we were paid only subsistence, but we would have attended for nothing!'

Captain Harold Duffy was dined out in October 1969.

Everyone was relieved that he was not baptised in Canning Dock. It was the traditional jack-stay transfer. In case any reader is puzzled just let him accept it is a means of transferring a body from ship to ship ... they sling a line and the victim is hauled across. Eaglet's new Commanding Officer was Captain Roy Humphreys-Jones.

October 1968, Mersey, Eaglet, Dee.

No account of naval activities can omit reference to the 31st July 1970. That was the last day of the Royal Navy grog issue. We must pause and look back into history.

The term 'grog' arose in 1740 when Admiral Vernon, Commander-in-Chief, West Indies, who was appalled at the drunkenness of seamen, ordered that the daily rum ration should be diluted with water. The Admiral's nickname was 'Old Grogram' on account of his habit of wearing a grogram cloak. His orders were, 'Whereas the pernicious custom of the seamen drinking their allowance of rum in drams, and often at once, is attended by many fatal effects to their morals as well as to their health; the daily issue of half a pint is to be diluted with a quart of water to be mixed in one scuttle-butt, kept for that purpose, and to be done upon deck in the presence of the Lieutenant of the Watch.'

In 1884 the ration was reduced to a gill once a day. Grog (2 parts water and 1 part rum) was issued daily to every victualled Member of the Ship's Company who were over the age of 20 years and who were not into temperance.

Chief Petty Officers and Petty Officers had their gill of rum neat and added their own water.

There are still amongst us those who would wish dialogue concerning the Draconian edict of the 31st July 1970 and who will undoubtedly question the details of my account.

Another 'end' was at hand.

An old friend, long gone, Don McKinley of the Liverpool Daily Post, wrote a fitting obituary for the old Eaglet. 'For 44 years the old Eaglet had been berthed in Salthouse Dock and on April 13th 1971 she was on her way to Birkenhead for sale to the ship-breakers. With a skeleton crew of ten ... and a Mersey pilot ... she was eased from her berth and through the locks to the river by two Alexandra Towing Company's tugs.

'As she moved slowly along the waterways, dockers and riverside men waved farewell to the ship that had for so long been part of the Merseyside scene.

'The move from Liverpool to Morpeth Dock, Birkenhead, took about three hours. It was a tricky manoeuvre, carried through by close liaison between Mersey pilot Mr. William Owen and the tug crews. In the river there were some anxious moments with the fast running flood tide.

'In command aboard Eaglet was Lieutenant-Commander Eric Verge, RN, who has been with the ship for the past three years as Staff Officer of the Mersey Division RNR and has charge of the arrangements of the new shore base at Princes Dock, Liverpool, opening next month.

'Saddest man aboard was 59-year-old Fred Dalton, Head Ship-keeper for the past seventeen years. "I've been with her for so long, I'm really going to miss her," he said. Missing her, too, will be Tramp, a big brown and white stray dog that Head Ship

Tramp & Fred.

keeper Dalton found shivering and homeless in the dockside snow a couple of years ago. Since then Tramp, the ship's mascot, has had no real home and no food problems.'

The skeleton crew numbered ten and they needed feeding during the three-hour trip. The volunteer cook was Wren Second

Officer Jacqueline Bennett, but it was no easy task. The fire had to be made in a stove with pieces of furniture and timber. Apparently 5lbs of bacon was devoured in sandwiches. It is not known whether Tramp was on board.

Chief Petty Officer George Williams, a veteran of the Battle of the Atlantic, joined Eaglet in 1939 and became the Chief Steward in 1952. His last farewell thoughts were: "I think it will be sad to leave her. This ship has all the character in the world. As long as you can look out of a porthole, you can feel that you have the right atmosphere. But maybe if we can take some bits and pieces with us from the ship, we can brighten up the new headquarters. Every 'brass-hat' who has come to Eaglet has been enthralled with her."

A cable giving information was sent to the ACR - Ref: Disposal of Eaglet.
'Eaglet has been transferred to the custody of the buyers Messrs Pemberton and Carlyon Shipbreakers Garston Liverpool at 1000 25 May 71.
'Ship will be towed to the breakers yard on 26 May 71.'

Liverpool humour always is topical and smacking of the truth. It was said at the time that a certain Naval Officer overheard a conversation as Eaglet left her berth. It went like this:

"How long's she been here mate?" asked one dockyard worker.

"Since 1926," replied a sailor. "We couldn't move her before because of the strikes."

Another wag pointed out that she was very difficult to move off her berth.

"Why's that then?"

"She's locked in by all the empty bottles!"

A visit to the Dance Hall at Poulton Victoria Club, Wirral, will reveal a secret. There on the wall is a plaque that tells you about the porthole, which is fitted to the cellar room door behind the lounge in the bar. It belongs to the old Eaglet! The Club Secretary had watched Eaglet on the way to the breaker's yard and had decided to rescue that porthole as a memento!

There must surely be a better last word than all that porthole hearsay!

Eaglet received the following flimsy from HMS Eagle on 23rd March 1971.

1   Here's to the maiden of bashful nineteen
    Here's to the widow of fifty
    Let the toast pass
    Drink to the lass
    I'll warrant she'll prove an excuse for the glass

2   The knackers are waiting for the bodies of both of us,
    But they are unlikely to get at the spirit.
    Good luck from one old bird to another.

        Staff Officer Eaglet replied to Eagle.

Thank you kindly maiden fair
My maiden name's the one you bear
Don't forget it was your Mum's
When your final moment comes.

        And that was that.

Captain Roy Humphreys-Jones waves farewell as Eaglet leaves Salthouse
for the final voyage.

HORSE'S NECK

Chapter Eight

1972 - 1998
THE SHORE BASE AT TRAFALGAR DOCK

When in 1971 the old ship was declared redundant and we moved to the new shore Headquarters in Princes Dock, the official opening on Sunday the 2nd May was conducted by Vice Admiral Sir Gilbert Stephenson, KBE, CB, CMG. The Admiral was in remarkable form ... at the grand age of 93! The Service took place in the Anglican Cathedral and from that distance I read the Dedication Prayer for the new Eaglet. The ship's company marched proudly through the City to our new home.

The New Eaglet

That Sunday was also the annual Commemoration of the Battle of the Atlantic and as ever the Cathedral was full. The destroyer HMS Cavalier was in Canada Dock. The headline in the Daily Post said it all: 'It's All Shipshape in Liverpool ... As the Royal Navy make a Big Day of it.' It was a day of memories.

I had first met Vice Admiral Stephenson (nicknamed, with affection, 'Monkey') when I attended the Annual Battle of the Atlantic Service in our Cathedral for the first time in 1966 as Ship's Chaplain. At the outbreak of the Second World War the Admiral had been recalled from retirement, even though he was sixty years of age.

The Admiral was sent to Tobermory on the Isle of Mull off the West Coast of Scotland. Here the various groups did their final warm-ups before tackling the North Atlantic, the convoys and the hunting packs of U-boats. As the majority of each ship's company were 'hostilities only', they had to be given a quick, sharp shock if they were to survive. Trades had to be mastered in weeks and months, not in years as in the peacetime Navy. 'Monkey' Stephenson was the man chosen to put the fear of God into the final training at Tobermory.

A story, which probably has gone the rounds as long as there have been Navies, has also been attributed to him. He would board a ship unannounced, at an impossible hour, and create havoc. The legendary story is that on one such occasion, 'Monkey' placed his cap on the deck and indicated to a passing matelot, "That's a bomb!" Naturally, the quick thinking lad promptly booted it over the side. The Admiral did not flinch, announced "Man overboard!" and started his stopwatch.

Another such tale tells of the Admiral climbing over the side in the small hours and, having made his way to the bridge without being accosted, pressed the alarm button. Nothing happened. Not a soul appeared. Nothing! Eventually a dishevelled engineer stuck his head around the door and announced, "If you keep pressing that so-and-so button, you'll flatten the so-and-so battery!" The Admiral's response has not been recorded.

So it was that I met the Admiral for the first time at the back-end of the Cathedral at the start of the Battle of the Atlantic Service. There he stood, five feet nothing tall with his ceremonial sword tucked in like a crutch, as it almost dragged the ground. He strode towards me.
"Who are you?"

"Evans, sir, Chaplain Superintendent of the Mersey Mission to Seamen."

That did not seem to impress him one little bit. He gave a sort of a grunt.

"Are you any good?"

I knew that this was the moment that had faced many a young officer in Tobermory. If I showed humility, he would have kicked me over the side. I was amazed to hear my instinctive reply to his challenge.

"Yes, sir, I'm the right man for the job!"

"Quite right, my boy, shouldn't do it, if you weren't!"

No wonder decades before, the men were relieved to escape from Tobermory to face the dangers of the North Atlantic storms and the U-boats. He smiled. Gave a nod of approval and

stumped off to his place in the procession. This was the 'Terror of Tobermory', then in his nineties!

The ship's company, following the Service in the Cathedral, marched through the City to the new Eaglet. The building was system-built and largely prefabricated. Back at our new Headquarters, on the edge of the Mersey, we all lined up on the quayside. 'Monkey' mounted the dais, so that we might see him, and switched off the bank of microphones. He ordered us to 'break ranks' and come about him. In simple language, he told us who we were and what we should do and how to achieve it. His voice cleared the Mersey and I was certain that the dockers on double-plus overtime in Birkenhead thought he was getting at them!

After inspecting the Guard, the Admiral cut an RNR hat ribbon and unveiled a plaque in the drill hall to declare the new Headquarters open. We had, in fact, 'moved in' a month before. Rather wistfully the Admiral remarked: "I only wish I was as young as you and with you ... and could do my part again."

After the formal opening and 'all was done and dusted,' we all sat on the sea wall by Princes Dock lock gates, eating lunch out of boxes, dangling our feet over the edge of the wall in glorious sunshine. Those lock gates were to prove a source of great mirth. You could guarantee that during the most important part of a Principal Dinner Guest's speech in the Wardroom or on the Drill Deck there would be a horrendous blast of a siren from a departing Irish Ferry. The timing was invariably superb.

Vice-Admiral Sir Gilbert Stephenson, KBE, CB, CMG, died at the age of 94 in May 1972. He was a legend in his own day and remains in our memories.

The new Eaglet was built at Princes Half Tide Dock. It cost £200,000 and overlooked the Mersey. There were some 400 members including the Wrens in the Division. The ships were HMS Mersey, the sweeper, and HMS Dee, the seaward defence boat. Some of the woodwork and panelling from the old Eaglet had been used in the construction. The figurehead was placed outside the main entrance. The Admiral Commanding Reserves, Admiral Iain D. McLoughlan said: "I know that the old ship's spirit will live on in the new Eaglet, and I wish the Commanding Officer and his ship's company continued good fortune and success for the future."

No Division would survive without the expertise and commitment of the permanent staff. We all shared pride when on 8th September 1972 Commodore W.R.D. Gerard-Pearse, Chief

Staff Flag Officer Plymouth presented the British Empire Medal to Chief Petty Officer Francis Rose. The citation praised the Chief for his work in leading diving teams in operations involving unexploded bombs in 1968 on the seabed in St. Helier Harbour, off the coast of Jersey. He was stationed in Eaglet as a permanent diving advisor to all the Reserve's Divisions. Such were the men that kept a 'weather-eye' on the RNR.

May 1973, Lord Derby relaxes on the bridge with the
Commanding Officer, Lieutenant-Commander Tom Conway.

A very good example of the RNR's use of their tenders is the cruise of Puttenham with Lieutenant-Commander John Billington in command. The first problem was that the intention had been to sail in Dee, but she was held up in her refit and the smaller RNXS Puttenham was called upon. The crew had to be reduced from 27 to 17 and in order to carry out the objective of the exercise ... to train new entry Cadets and the Combined Cadet Corps ... the permanent crew was severely cut to 1 coxswain, 2 engineers, 1 radio operator and 1 electrical rating. This left two officers under training and five cadets. We let the log tell the story.

Saturday 7th July 1973.

The crew joined early, stowed stores and left the river at 1300 and arrived at Douglas at 2230 after a very wet passage.

An immediate problem was an almost complete lack of pillows on board! This was solved by a smart visit to the Captain's mother-in-law in Douglas ... presumably leaving her without!

Also note that Puttenham's bridge was at the very front of the vessel and most waves ensured a shower for all.

Sunday 8th July.

The weather much calmer; reached Port Askaig in 12 hours steaming. Training with navigation and emergency steering.

Monday 9th July.

Called at Oban to drop RNXS engineer ashore and received help from HMS Reclaim with minor problems. Low visibility and bad weather forecast, scrapped plans and went alongside at Kyle of Lochalsh.

A Wild and Lonely Loch.

Tuesday 10th July.
Moved to Loch Ainort, a wild and lonely loch and anchored.
Cadets ashore with stornophone radio and communicated with
ship hourly during trip up local mountain. Next anchored at
Portree in heavy rain.

Cadets Ashore.

Wednesday 11th July.
Day very calm and man overboard drill carried out with oil drum.
After manoeuvring practice, each cadet fired 10 rounds with SLR
(single loading rifle). Ship secured at Stornaway.
Here the chiefs threw a bit of a party for visitors. Sadly one of
the ship's name-plates went adrift. A signal was sent to shore
base indicating displeasure. It was fourteen days later that a chief
was sent from the Base to Liverpool at his own expense to return
the missing name-plate.
Thursday 12th July.
Refuelled in morning and make and mend in afternoon.

Friday 13th July.

Wet passage to Oban and went alongside Reclaim at 1800. Navigation training on passage and final examination for the first week cadets.

Saturday 14th July.

First week cadets left ship and second week arrived. Slipped at midday and moved into Caledonian Canal at 1600 and secured at Banavie.

Sunday 15th July.

Make and mend as canal way closed on this day.

Monday 16th July.

Long and difficult day going through canal. Considerable care required as gale force headwind caused problems with only one engine in use because of the excessive power of two.

The gearbox was difficult and it was hard to tell whether it was in gear or not. Ship moved by her own volition! Once she backed into a lock rail and bent it. Bottle of whisky given to lock keeper. Damage not put in report ... big mistake! That lock keeper put in a claim for £9 to RN. Happily the RN Officer concerned had been an old boy friend of the Captain's wife but this did not stop John Billington receiving a major rocket for not reporting the incident! There is a lesson tucked away somewhere in that story.

Techniques were gradually improved as crew gained confidence with rope work. Secured at Inverness late in the evening.
Tuesday 17th July.
Ship warped round in canal with ten feet to spare. Once back in Loch Ness opportunity was taken to conduct man overboard exercises. Secured alongside Fort Augustus and Lieutenant Cyril Barnes sent ashore to buy ice cream for the crew.
Wednesday 18th July.
Passage to open sea down Neptune's Staircase with no further problems and finally anchored at Tobermory at 2000.

The Pub at Port Askaig.

Thursday 19th July.
Bad forecast so stayed at anchor and carried out second week expeditionary and communication training at Tobermory instead of Port Askaig. At 1900 alongside in company with Clyde Royal Naval Auxiliary Service (RNXS) and a Landing Craft Tank (LCT).
Friday 20th July.
An early start in view of bad forecast to go as far south as possible. Anchored in Stranraer loch.

Saturday 21st July.
Weather cleared and passage of Calf Sound possible.   In afternoon SLR shooting was carried out and ship berthed alongside at Douglas at 1700 to return pillows.
Sunday 22nd July.
A start was made just after mid-night in order to dock at Birkenhead at 0730. Ship was then cleaned down and paid off at 1200.

The inshore vessel Puttenham was not the ideal ship for such a venture, mainly because she carried no central engine and the power of the engines at slow speed with a weak old dock gate only a few feet clear of the stern made the canal venture difficult. But, the exercise had proved to be an invaluable training run.

Commander John Billington, CBE, RD*, DL, RNR, joined the Division in 1952. He was High Sheriff of Liverpool in 1990 and is now Deputy Lord Lieutenant of Merseyside.

Lieutenant-Commander Tom Conway, RD*, RNR, tells a tale and has kindly afforded us the copyright to publish it for the first time. The copyright probably belongs to the Colgate Palmolive Company Ltd! The date was September 1973. Read on.

Night Encounter Exercise

To set the scene, it must be noted that HMS Mersey had been sent to Halifax, Nova Scotia to exercise with the Canadian Royal Naval Reserve for four weeks. We borrowed from Solent Division a rather tired, German World War II Inshore Operations Vessel, HMS Isis. She was fitted with two very powerful Mann Marine Diesel engines driving two shafts with the very specialised Voight Schneider Propulsion Gear. This made her a very manoeuvrable platform.

Tom Conway was in command, Tony Branthwaite was the First Lieutenant, John Archer the Navigating Officer, CPO Knight was the Coxswain and the Engineer was Chief ERA Richard Warburton.

HMS Isis sailed for Portland to join the 10th Mine Counter Measures Squadron and 'Exercise Rolex'. The Mersey Division crew began to hit problems. Here are one or two examples.

'The controls for the main engines were located side by side on the starboard side of the bridge. They were a simple combination of throttle and clutch. The problem was that the clutch was very worn and the 'teeth' would not stay engaged. When the clutch became disengaged, which was frequent and always at times of high risk, the main engines were at full power and it was necessary to employ the 'trip'. This meant total power loss!

'There were water problems. On one particular day at sea off Portland Bill, the inevitable happened and the ship's Townswater System, which cooled the engines, was totally emptied. There was no cooling water for either the crew or the engines. The ship was not under control and we were towed back to harbour. This and other difficulties led to the phrase 'The Crisis in Isis'. This leads us neatly into the story of the 'Night Encounter Exercise'.

'To summarise: the Blue Forces were to search for and destroy the Orange Forces and the Orange Forces, including Isis, were to get close inshore at Lulworth Cove, Dorset and land an Orange Force Agent. Simple!

'The operation commenced after dark and late at night. All ships operated a 'darken ship' policy, which required no upper deck lighting and red night vision lighting on the bridge. It was a very dark night with no moon and fair weather, but a choppy sea state and a light westerly wind. In Weymouth Bay off Lulworth Cove the wind and tide were together with the flood tide running eastwards along the coast. HMS Isis crept slowly inshore and found the passage to Lulworth Cove blocked by a continuous procession of 10th MCMS sweepers passing along the coast continuing their search and presenting no chance of a break through. With all lights extinguished the ship was just a dark shadow on the sea and remained undetected.

'During the early stages of the exercise, it was observed on Radar that one of the charted buoys in the set of four buoys which marked Lulworth Cove 'Naval Gunfire Support Firing Range' was missing. It was concluded that it had either been sunk by shellfire or it had been removed for maintenance by the Portland Bar Boat. It was decided to take advantage of the missing buoy by moving into its position until such time as there was a substantial gap in the patrolling forces.

'This deceptive position was maintained for several hours with the variations of wind and tide being accommodated by minor adjustments to the heading. It was planned to land the 'Orange Agent' at dawn.

'During the later stages of this carefully controlled operation, the Cox'n informed the Captain that Leading Seaman Armstrong had reported to him that, after going off watch at midnight, he had cleaned his teeth as usual before turning in, but has actually cleaned his teeth using his 'Pile Ointment' instead of his toothpaste.

'Leading Seaman Armstrong further reported that he had checked the label on the tube and noted that it carried a warning that the contents were marked 'Poison'. That was why he had spoken to the Cox'n at the double because he thought that he had poisoned himself!

'Leading Seaman Armstrong was a very tall, well-built young man. He had to stoop low to pass through the screen doors. He was a strapping fellow of a man with a powerful presence as a Leading Hand. But in the red light of the 'Darken Ship Routine' it was possible to see that he was concerned and his pallor was ashen.

'On hearing the Cox'n's report the whole of the bridge staff dissolved into laughter and with the loss of concentration the ship lost its position and we had great difficulty in resuming the correct station to avoid detection.

'The Captain checked the label on the tube of 'Pile Ointment' and confirmed that the 'Haemorrhoidal Prophylactic Ointment' was marked 'Poison'.

'Since HMS Isis did not carry a Medical Officer the Captain decided to report the incident to the Senior Officer of the 10th MCMS in the surrounding patrolling ships and request the assistance of the Squadron Medical Officer in order to resolve Leading Seaman Armstrong's problem.

'The following signal was drafted:

To: 10th MCMS.

From: Isis.

1. Rating reports cleaning his teeth with Haemorrhoidal Prophylactic Ointment (Pile Ointment) instead of toothpaste.
2. Tube containing Pile Ointment marked Poison.
3. Request assistance of Squadron Medical Officer to recommend antidote.
4. Rating now complains of receding gums at one end and 'Ring of Confidence' at the other

'On hearing the contents of the signal as the Signalman read out the message in clear voice on the bridge on the tactical operating channel the whole of the Bridge Staff again dissolved into fits of laughter. This time the whole position was lost. It was late. It had been a long night. The Captain gave the order to switch on the navigation lights. The game was up.' The Blue Forces had won!

Tom Conway states that there were two incidental outcomes to the sea training period in HMS Isis.

'Firstly, I submitted a comprehensive Defect Report on completion of the training. I never heard officially of any outcome of this report. I did hear hearsay information that HMS Isis was withdrawn from service and given a lengthy and very expensive refit and overhaul before she returned to service.

'The second outcome was that I wrote this story and sent a copy of it to the Chairman of the Colgate Palmolive Company with an apology for using their Company 'Punch Line' and asking if the Company wanted to use the story!

'The reply from the Chairman of Colgate Palmolive Company Ltd was very kind and unexpected. He sent me a cheque for £50, which I donated to the Royal National Lifeboat Institution.'

Thank you, Tom, we cannot take any more! Or can we?

In August 1973 the Canadian Royal Naval Reserve

celebrated the 25th year of its founding in 1948. To support the celebrations the Navy sent four Coniston Class Minesweepers from the Reserve to Halifax, Nova Scotia for four weeks. HMS Mersey was selected, but she was not to be manned by a Mersey Division crew.

At the end of the exercise Mersey returned to Cardiff and Tom took his 1973 Sea Training Crew to bring her back home. Lieutenant-Commander Tom Conway takes up the story.

'The 10th Mine Countermeasures Squadron was accompanied by RFA Brown Rover on both the outward and return trip across the Atlantic. The weather was proverbially bad and everyone, including Brown Rover, was tossed about quite a bit. For stability reasons each coastal had to refuel every day in a standard RAS evolution which was good practice.

'During both outward and return voyages to Canada, I learned later, a significant number of the minesweepers experienced frequent engine breakdowns of both engines and, gearboxes. This information had not been circulated.

'Once aboard Mersey in Cardiff the crew in their various departments started ship commissioning procedure and start up preparations and essential operational checks. We had not been on board very long, maybe an hour, when MEAP 2 John Downs - Chief Downs - came to the Captain with an oil sample from Mersey's fuel oil tanks. CPO Downs had sampled all the tanks and they were all heavily and seriously contaminated with seawater. The Engineer Officer advised me that we should not sail with this degree of fuel oil contamination, as there would be a serious risk of breakdown.'

The Admiralty Fuel Oil Supply Contractor from BP in Llandarcy made arrangements for the tanks to be pumped out and for the vessel to be refuelled. The crew came back to Merseyside and returned a week later. Nothing was ever revealed about the cost and operational consequences of the Canada trip. No comments or compliments were ever made about the Cardiff episode.

'The origin of the contaminated fuel oil problem was eventually attributed to RFA Brown Rover and the state of her tanks. In the shake up she received in the North Atlantic weather her fuel oil became thoroughly contaminated with water and this was pumped over to the sweepers.

'The "And they all lived Happily Ever After" bit came a little bit later. Months afterwards the Admiralty decided to scrap Brown Rover. The poor ship, which had done long and faithful service for the fleet was clearly beyond redemption and repair. It was a relief to hear that. I would have turned tail and ran if I had met Brown Rover at sea after that.'

One suspects that those four minesweepers experienced good fortune to arrive safely home.

Lieutenant-Commander David Allen, RN, was Staff Officer from 1971 to 73. His only previous knowledge of Eaglet had been gained as First Lieutenant of the 'Ferry Crew' that delivered Pollington from Southampton in 1959. She replaced the ageing Amerton. Little did David dream that he would return as the Staff Officer.

He recalls particularly the enthusiasm of the Reservists who regularly travelled from as far afield as Nottingham and Caernarfon to attend their drill nights. The Staff Officer had a number of duties, but perhaps the most important was his command of the minesweeper and the need, therefore, to ensure that the ship was properly equipped and manned when she was taken away by Reserve COs at weekends. Within the Reserve Training Centre he was essentially the RN adviser to the Reservist Captain.

David left Eaglet to return to sea in HMS Hermes, but then retired from the Royal Navy in 1975. He next spent two years working for Land and Marine Engineering, a Merseyside Company, burying pipelines in the North Sea. During this time he was in command of a dumb barge, i.e. it was not self-propelled. He then returned to deep sea sailing for Mobil, the oil company. He had already been granted a Master's Certificate of Service on leaving the Royal Navy but also successfully completed his Masters's Certificate of Competence, studying in Liverpool, in 1980.

In 1981 David was again attached to Eaglet as a List One Officer. Six years later, however, he had to relinquish that commission when he became Deputy Naval Regional Officer, West Midlands and North West; this was to be redesignated DNRO, Northern England in 1994. He retired finally in 2003. He also served as the Chairman of both the Liverpool and Manchester KGFS committees.

He is an example of a Naval Officer who became a Merchant Navy Master and a RNR List One Officer and in the process a Scouser!

The first inspection of the new Headquarters was on Wednesday 22nd July 1971 and was carried out by the ACR, Rear Admiral Iain D. McLoughlan. He congratulated our Commanding Officer, Captain Roy Humphreys-Jones and Commander Trevor Jones and applauded the increase of recruitment since the move to the new headquarters and above all the speed with which the Division had settled in our new home.

One personal memory I cannot forget. We were all lined up with our wives alongside in Knowsley Hall for an evening with His Lordship. At the far end standing in full Captain's rig was our Honorary Captain, Lord Derby, together with our good Captain Roy Humphreys-Jones (a truly charismatic character) at his elbow, ready to introduce his crew. They both looked quite elegant. As we shuffled forward, my beloved D'rene in a loud whisper asked, "Which one is Lord Derby?" It became a matter for debate as we all thought that Roy had the edge with his rather aristocratic bearing. It was a good evening.

All Aboard Puttenham.

HMS Dee was commissioned for service with the Liverpool University Royal Naval Unit on Thursday 23rd May 1974. The Captain called on the Ship's Company to ask for God's Blessing on the ship, using this ancient call.

From the Gaelic Blessing, 1589

The Captain: I call upon you to pray for God's blessing on this ship.

May God the Father bless her.

Ship's Company: Bless our ship.

The Captain:	May Jesus Christ bless her.
Ship's Company:	Bless our ship.
The Captain:	May the Holy Spirit bless her.
Ship's Company:	Bless our ship.

The Chaplain: O Lord God Almighty, let Thy Blessing be upon this ship, and upon all those who serve and sail in her. May good success and Thy Protection and the Guardianship of the Holy Angels always be with them, In the name of the Father, Son, and Holy Ghost.   Amen.

Incidentally, the Mersey Division always provided two bridge watch-keepers to HMS Dee for deployments and weekends.

Captain R.M. Eddleston, OBE, RD, RNR, assumed command in March 1976 at a time of considerable change for the Reserve. "We were already coping with hull-sharing with other Divisions, but on 1st January 1977 the last Admiral Commanding Reserves, Rear Admiral Hugo Hollins, handed over responsibility for the Reserve to Commander-in-Chief Naval Home Command, Admiral Sir David Williams.

"This initiated a hectic and in some ways exciting period for the Reserve in which the Royal Navy as a whole discovered it still had a Reserve.

"In a short period of time the Division managed to survive visits from Admiral Sir Gordon Tait, Flag Officer Plymouth, responsible for CinC Naval Home Command for all aspects of the Division except training, Mr. Patrick Duffy the Secretary for Defence for the Navy, the Minister responsible for Naval Affairs, and CinCNH himself Admiral Sir David Williams ... probably the heaviest load of brass any RNR Division had fall upon it in such a short period!

"During this time we also brought to fruition a competitive crew system for manning the Ton Class Tender which greatly improved crew performance at sea and ashore. This had much to do with the Division winning the Thorneycroft Trophy for 1978/79."

The Thorneycroft Trophy is the top RNR award. It was won for excellence in operational sea training in HMS Crofton, for the efficiency of the Training Organisation, the voluntary attendance record of the Division and the general maintenance of equipment. The Division was also awarded the Collingwood Trophy for the best Weapons and Electrical Department in any RNR Division, as well as being runners-up for the Supply Department for the third year. The Manchester Communications Training Centre (CTC), which is attached to Mersey Division, was awarded the Mountbatten Trophy for the best CTC Unit in the country.

The complement of the Division was over 300 Officers and Ratings, including a large section in the WRNR. This was all achieved under the command of Captain Bob Eddleston.

Commander Harry Harley, RN, who joined Eaglet on 14th June 1976 as Staff Supply Officer has memories to share. "When I arrived, the Annual Inspection by the Admiral Commanding Reserves was a mere six weeks away (that was only six drill nights!) ... one glance told me that we were not ready! I also noted that, like all other sailors, Reservists were dedicated-collectors-of-things-whose-only-claim-to-fame-was-that-it-or-they-might-come-in-handy. Within the 100 spaces that made up Eaglet there were mounds of such 'stuff'. There was no time to sort it out, but having been a member of the fo'ward messdeck for ten years before becoming an h'officer I was well practiced in the art of allowing VIPs seeing only what I wanted them to see. A phone call to our buddies at the Royal Marine Reservist Centre in Birkenhead secured the use of a large truck which we loaded to the 'Plimsoll' line with Eaglet's Come-in-Handy-Stuff.

"That truck was parked in the RMR Centre until ACR was safely back in Whitehall and when I called for its return I quickly elected (very democratically of course!) a Committee of Taste and instant decisions were made to Retain or Ditch each item unloaded. That '48 hour lorry' innovation was repeated in '77 and '78. Several years after departing Eaglet I was informed that the HARLEY LORRY EXERCISE was still in operation. Probably my most influential act during my Eaglet appointment!"

Harry's recollections continued.

"The Queen's relative, belted Earl, etc., etc., was an Honorary Captain in the Reserve and would attend the Annual Bounty Night Parade ... but did not own a Naval Officer's Sword! I learned that each year there was always a debate among Junior Reservists of whom would 'volunteer' a sword for the Lord's use. I solved the problem in '76 and '77 by offering him mine. I felt that it was the least that I could do because as a youngster I had raided his apple orchards countless times! In addition my sense of history told me that I was the only pupil of Longview Secondary Modern School, Huyton, that had earned the right to wear a Naval Sword. That school was built on land given by Lord Derby's father to the local council. What goes around ... comes around!"

I rather liked Harry Harley's final words in that particular tale and decided that no editing was needed. Harry was now in full flow.

"I had arrived at Eaglet knowing very little of the RNR and was filled with some trepidation, facing a new challenge, fresh from the highly organised world of the Ministry of Defence. I was 'in zone' and hopefully ambitious. I entered the building on Day One as RN Staff Supply Officer. I departed the building that night as RN Staff Supply Officer, First Lieutenant of the Building, Captain's Secretary, Transport Officer, Public Relations Officer, Press Relations Officer, Sports Officer, Civilian Staff Divisional Officer, RN Staff Divisional Officer, Deputy Custody Officer of the Tender, Liaison Officer for the Shipkeepers of the Tender, and Morale and Laundry Officer. I likened my first Drill Night to a farmyard full of the inevitable headless chickens. I learned to do nothing on such nights other than make myself available to the Reservists ... and keep my office door jammed open. The mornings following Drill Nights I would ask Martin, the Civilian Clerical Officer, to 'go around and collect it all please'. 'All' were the packs and Files that 'they' had had in use during the Drill evening. My task was then to complete the letters, requests, statements and minutes that 'they' just hadn't got around to completing before heading off to points of the Northwest compass. The Reservists tested me, taught me, and, some sorely tried my patience. However, I quickly grew to appreciate what they were trying to achieve and saw my job as being a friendly witness to their juggling of too many balls in too short a time, which the Regular Navy, particularly too many Whitehall Desks, failed to fully appreciate, nor, to their shame, take seriously. I was there to catch the balls that they dropped. I became very protective of Reservists and rocked a few 'boats' in later years by sounding off in strong support of the Reservist World. When I joined CincNavHome in '82 I was the only Staff Officer who had served at an RNR Centre! The CNH Reserve Dept. Staff used to dread my occasional visit.

"Human nature is strange and has to be understood. In 1977 I was entering my second year as Staff Supply Officer, when I was approached by the Reservist Stores Chief, complaining that his department was understaffed because there was a Trainee Stores Wren who was still in Part 1 Training after six months (a very long time). The following Wednesday Drill night I investigated the matter and discovered that the Wren in question was an incredibly attractive young lady, who was a very efficient member of the John Lewis' Public Relations Department (very bright indeed). But the officer in charge of her Trainee Class informed me that it was not possible for her to move on to her professional training because she was unable to pass her Anchors and Cables Examination! She retook the exam that evening. I marked her paper. She passed. Maybe human nature is not so strange!"

The Loss of HMS Fittleton

The loss of HMS Fittleton was a deep sadness for the RNR. It was the third week in September 1976. These thoughts are guided by David Miller's chapter on Fittleton in his excellent book entitled 'Commanding Officers'. Two of the survivors were from Eaglet.

As the eleven RNR Divisions in 1974 were reduced to manning eight minesweepers, the process known as 'hull-sharing' had been introduced. The two ships involved in the affair were HMS Mermaid (displacement 2,520 tons, 339 feet long) and HMS Fittleton (displacement 440 tons, 153 feet long). For technical reasons with the Napier Deltic diesel engines, the Admiralty in the late 1950's advised all 'drivers' of the Ton-class minesweepers to avoid, if at all possible, travelling at 11 knots as a build-up of partly-burnt oil could result in a fire. The normal complement of Fittleton would have been 29, but on this occasion there were 44 on board.

Fittleton was commanded by Lieutenant-Commander Peter Paget, RNR, aged 44, an experienced Master Mariner who had served for years with P&O shipping company. He had served in London Division for sixteen years and was respected for his well-proven seamanship and leadership qualities.

The Nato Exercise Teamwork involved some 300 warships, of which the 10th MCMS contributed seven Ton-class sweepers. The Senior Officer was Commander Ian Berry, RNR of Mersey Division, who was on board Fittleton, but not in command. At the rendezvous the minesweepers would be joined by ACR, a regular Rear-Admiral, flying his flag in the frigate HMS Mermaid. The Admiral would then assume command and they were to proceed to Hamburg for a courtesy visit.

At 0945 on 20th September Commander Berry received a signal stating that Mermaid was behind schedule and that they were to proceed to the mouth of the Elbe at 10 knots. By 1428 the minesweepers were in two columns when the signal came that Mermaid was approaching astern at a speed of about 15 to 20 knots. Commander Berry ordered his force to change course to that of the larger vessel. At this point two messages were received from the Admiral. The first was a communications check. The second, far longer, ordered a line ahead of 100 degrees and at half distances (760 feet) and that the speed should be 11 knots (the prohibited speed).

It took some minutes for the second message to be decoded and to inform the Captains. Commander Berry, currently in command, ordered a reverse of course to lead his small group towards Mermaid, planning to order line ahead and then hand over to the Admiral. Before this could be achieved, the Admiral sent a further signal ordering immediate execution of the previous signal. The result was a melee as ships moved across and around each other and then reversed course to comply with the Admiral's directive.

Happily it was achieved with no major incident and soon they were all at 100 degrees in line ahead at a parallel course with Mermaid.

At this point the Admiral issued a further signal and a warning order ... it was lengthy and in code. The signal ordered all seven ships to close on Mermaid one after the other for a heaving-line transfer with Fittleton leading. It was assumed that written orders would at that time be passed to each vessel. Again they were told to maintain 11 knots.

It took some time to decipher the new orders and to 'close-up special sea duty men'. This involved most off-duty men coming on watch and moving to their places above and below deck. All this was necessary for the line-transfer. The first lieutenant, the chief boatswain's mate and a group of seamen fell in on the forecastle, where they would be responsible for the actual transfer. Engine control was transferred to the bridge and watertight doors had to be closed.

To achieve this state of readiness, clearly each ship needed time and it had not been completed in Fittleton when the Admiral sent a further signal, demanding "What are you waiting for?" At this point it was obvious to Commander Berry that the Admiral had assumed command which he signified to Paget by moving off the bridge on to the flag deck with his yeoman. Unfortunately the 'hurry-up' signal had been incorrectly coded in Mermaid and it was not entirely clear for whom it was intended. Paget assumed it was meant for him and, even though engine control transfer had not been completed, he began his turn to starboard, only to discover that both Crofton and Hodgeston were also wheeling. To avoid a collision Paget took immediate action and order was maintained.

Fittleton edged near Mermaid to a distance of three hundred feet and increased speed to 12 knots. The standard naval heaving line is 17 fathoms (102 feet) long and the Manual of Seamanship suggested that 12 fathoms (70 feet) was a good cast. Paget edged closer knowing that his part-time sailors were out of practice and also that Mermaid's forecastle was much higher and well forward. The first cast at 40 feet failed and they prepared for a second attempt.

Suddenly without any adjustment to helm or engine controls, Fittleton, was sucked in sideways towards Mermaid. She hit broadside on and then bounced off.

David Miller takes up the story.

'As she did so she also veered to port, with the bow moving outwards and the stern inwards towards Mermaid. Berry, who was standing on the flag deck, quietly told Paget to 'watch your stern'. Paget ordered 'helm amidships', followed by 'starboard 20 degrees', with the object of pulling the stern off. This succeeded in straightening the ship, but then, without any alteration to her engine speed, Fittleton began to move forward relative to Mermaid, giving Paget the distinct impression that she was surfing. His order for a reduction of speed to 10 knots had no effect as Fittleton continued to surge ahead.

'At this point Berry suggested to Paget that he might try to break free by increasing speed and steering to port, that is, away from Mermaid, but by then Fittleton had drawn abreast of Mermaid's bow. At that point she suddenly and apparently of her own volition, swung around 90 degrees to starboard, directly into Mermaid's path. The frigate's captain immediately ordered 'full astern', but it was too late. The larger ship rammed Fittleton amidships, her bow pushing the smaller ship over on her port side.

'These events were so sudden and unexpected that no-one on Fittleton's bridge had time to warn those below of what was about to happen. Within seconds the ship had reached an angle of about 70 degrees, at which point those on the upper deck were thrown into the water. The ship continued to roll, pushed ever further by Mermaid's momentum and almost hitting those already in the water, until she came to rest upside down but still afloat.

'Those below at the time were placed in a terrible predicament. They had been given no warning of impending disaster and found themselves, suddenly and without explanation, with the deck where the deck-head should have been, equipment and debris falling around them, and their compartments flooding very rapidly until only small air pockets were left. Some managed to work out an escape route, which involved swimming underwater along passageways, occasionally finding an air pocket for a quick gasp of air, before continuing until they reached what would, under normal circumstances, have been the upper deck, when they headed for the surface.

'At the moment of impact Mermaid's captain brought his ship to a very rapid standstill and then stopped the propellers in order to avoid injuring any survivors in the water. Fortunately, Crofton, which had been in the 'waiting position', now found herself very close to the upturned hull which had passed down Mermaid's starboard side. Crofton's captain stopped engines to allow his ship to drift down among the survivors. Some were pulled aboard on ropes, while others were rescued by two small boats that had been lowered into the water. The West German frigate Bayern, having seen that something was amiss, came up very quickly and sent her medical officer to Crofton, where he helped to treat the shocked survivors. Altogether thirty-two survivors were recovered and by about 1600 all had been transferred to Mermaid which, being much larger, was better able to handle such numbers.

'Most of the men who had been on the upper deck, including Paget and Berry, were rescued, and a number of those trapped below decks managed to escape. Two bodies were also recovered. That left ten men unaccounted for.'

Every possible means to check the inside of the hull were taken, but at 1830 Fittleton suddenly sank stern first and came to rest on the bottom. At 2100 another British frigate, HMS Achilles, arrived, to which the Admiral transferred to continue his responsibility for the recovery operation.

Recovery vessels raised the hulk some days later and took it to a Dutch port where it was dried out and three bodies removed. The hulk was then returned to England where a few months later it was scrapped. Seven bodies were never recovered.

A Board of Inquiry was held 'in camera' and its findings have never been published, but it must have found a prima facie case against Paget. A court martial was convened at Portsmouth on 20th February 1977.

There were four charges. The first was 'negligence in altering course towards Mermaid when it was not justified'. The other three charges concerned failure to 'take early and positive action to correct a dangerous alteration of course', 'to ensure that his wheel orders were obeyed', and third 'to reduce speed and alter course to extricate his ship from a dangerous position'.

The main prosecution witness was the Admiral. He stated that there had been no apparent reaction from Fittleton to his signal to start the heaving-line transfer. He had then sent the signal: "What are you waiting for?" He accepted, however, that it had been incorrectly 'coded-up', which had resulted in three leading minesweepers all pulling out of the line almost simultaneously. When the Defending Officer asked the Admiral if he would agree that there had been a muddle over the signal, the Admiral replied, "If the captain of Fittleton was unhappy about the situation, he could have hauled down his signal indicating that he was not ready to start the evolution", adding that Fittleton's Captain need not have made the approach until she was ready. The Defending Officer claimed that the prosecution case was so weak that no reasonable court would convict and it was quite clear that Fittleton had been 'sucked towards the bigger ship by underwater currents'. However, the Court decided that there was a case to answer.

Paget then recounted the scene of the first collision and that he then realised that she was continuing to go forward, that he was conscious of the lack of directional stability and that he had the sensation that the ship was surfing.

After several hours the Court found Paget not guilty on three charges and guilty on the fourth of failing 'to reduce speed and alter course to extricate his ship from a dangerous position while she was close alongside the frigate Mermaid during the mail-transfer operation'. The sentence was a reprimand, which was the lightest punishment available to the Court.

On 11th May 1977 the Admiralty Board 'decided that the conviction was unsafe and unsatisfactory and accordingly quashed the conviction and annulled the sentence'.

There have been a number of instances where ships have been 'sucked in'. This 'interaction' is aggravated when there is a significant difference in the size of the vessels involved. During the Second World War the cruiser HMS Euryalus and the destroyer HMS Worcester were just 300 yards apart at a speed of 30 knots when they were suddenly drawn together to a matter of a few feet and narrowly avoided disaster. In another incident, the cruiser HMS Curacao was 'sucked' under the bow of the passenger liner RMS Queen Mary, sliced in two and sank with considerable loss of life. In the 1960s and 1970s there were several recorded instances of tugboats being hit and capsized by the Very Large Container Carriers.

Paget was a highly skilled Master Mariner and at no point had the Board explained the phrase 'error of judgement'. In fact it was clear that Paget had done all that was within his power to do. A commanding officer 'is fully responsible for the unit's efficiency, for the proper and timely performance of any task and for the safety of both the unit and its members. When there is potential hazard everything depends upon the professional skill, judgement and technical expertise of the commanding officer.' However, an equally rigorous responsibility rests upon higher command to ensure that the demands placed upon commanding officers - whether regular or reservists - are both practically and technically feasible! This surely is the fundamental nature of command.

Mal North, a Marine Engineer Mechanic, was the other Mersey Division man on board Fittleton. He had joined the Division in 1961. We chatted as old friends do. The memories were still vivid.

"We had closed up in the wardroom flat ... the wardroom damage control party ... next thing there was a loud bang. I went out on deck and all that I could see was the bow of Mermaid embedded midships behind the motor boat. I looked up and I could see anchors like a pair of eyes.

"Then we were pushed over. I was leaning against the Samson post and had a smack on the head. I suppose I must have passed out. Really cold water brought me round. Next thing I knew I was back in the wardroom flat, upside down, and there were five of us. We talked about where we could go. I took a deep breath of air and went aft. The water was crystal clear. I got to the 'garden gate' and tried to unclip it. Then realised there was no need. By this time I was in trouble, but the ship rolled and there was more air. I swam down about three feet and suddenly came up alongside the hull.

"I saw a mate scrabbling along the keel of Fittleton. I was afraid that when the ship went down she might pull me down with her. I swam away and drifted. Next thing that happened was Crofton appeared and the crew threw fenders over the side to help us ... that was dangerous! Then they dropped a life-raft. I was dead beat. Couldn't get into it. A crew member came and helped me. He grabbed me by the underpants. I had no strength to climb the Jacobs Ladder into Crofton so they lowered straps and got me out. I was very sick. I was put on a German (it must have been the frigate Bayern) motor launch and they took me to Mermaid.

"They gave me pencil and paper and asked me to list what I had lost. The answer was everything! The crew had piled up some clothes in the conference room and we helped ourselves. There was plenty of food, but I could not eat. Whenever another survivor appeared we clapped and cheered. Wherever I went, someone stayed with me. We all got our tots off everyone. I had stitches on my head.

"Back at Harwich we telephoned home off the ship and were sent to a military hospital for a check. Then we were given warrants and a bus ride to Euston. I remember standing on Euston Station and looking at myself. A shirt, no underpants, trousers, no socks, plimsolls and a warrant!

"We arrived in Lime Street. My mum, my wife and kids were there. My six-year old lad looked at me and said, 'Where's my pressy, Dad?' I looked at him and replied, 'It's me, son!' "

That about says it all.

Apart from the Falklands War, the loss of HMS Fittleton on 20th September 1976 was the Royal Navy's most serious surface disaster during the Cold War. In 1951, seventy-five men died when the submarine Affray failed to surface during exercises off the Channel Islands. A year before, the submarine, Truculent, went down in the Thames estuary after a collision off Sheerness with a Swedish tanker. Sixty-four men lost their lives.

On 1st January 1977 Rear Admiral Hollins struck his flag as Admiral Commanding Reserves, being the last to hold that honoured appointment, which had been in existence for 102 years to the day. The Command was transferred to the Commander-in-Chief Naval Home Command, Admiral Sir Terence Lewin, GCB, MVO, DSC, ADC. It was felt that the Royal Navy's vital contribution to the deterrent power of NATO would be much strengthened by this closer link with the Reserves. "We are in an era of change and challenge and I am sure we shall best rise to meet it as one closely-knit team."

1977 certainly was the year of major changes for the RNR and it was felt in Eaglet. The primary objective of the eleven Divisions was for each to supply three minesweeper crews, but the complement of each Division was reduced and the hulls reduced from eleven to six. Two vessels were allocated to the Northwest group, Belfast, Clyde and Mersey ... one Mine Counter Measures Vessel and one Bird Class Patrol Craft. The intention of bringing the activity level of the hulls to the RN standard was actually achieved. In Eaglet the crews were named Horton, Noble and Walker.

Under the new order the Division rated a Commander as Commanding Officer. Department Heads were to be Lieutenant-Commanders and could be retained to the age of fifty. No officers were carried purely for administration.

One must never forget that the main objective of the RNR since its inception in the nineteenth century as the Royal

Naval Artillery Service was to support the Royal Navy. That aim was certainly retained. The main tasks were to be minesweeping, patrolling, naval control of shipping, medical needs and communication. This was to be achieved through the eleven Sea Training Centres and two dozen or so Communication Centres.

Eaglet was to have a complement of some two hundred reservists and twenty permanent staff. The Headquarter building was ear-marked as the port Headquarters in time of conflict. The minesweeper, HMS Hodgeston, was to be the tender for the three Northwest Divisions and was based at Eaglet.

The work continued and hull sharing was here to stay.

The 'Last Command' of Lieutenant-Commander Brian Parr, RD, RNR. deserves to be regurgitated (that might be the correct word!). The report was written in HMS Hodgeston at Gibraltar on 3rd March 1978 and will mainly tell the tale. The objective was to take the vessel to the Rock for a refit. Hang on to that statement!

'Leaving on the 17th February, the passage from Liverpool to Gibraltar, calling at Portsmouth en route to leave the loop at Vernon and to refuel and de-ammunition, was dogged throughout by severe weather conditions. Due to a storm in Cardigan Bay shortly after leaving Liverpool, I was obliged to seek shelter in Fishguard Bay and to remain there for 36 hours. Snow and ice made conditions on deck hazardous. Later the weather moderated but thick fog was encountered off Lands End and again off Portland. Having only a three mile range available on the 974 Radar due to a defective component caused progress to be even slower.'

One can sense some restraint in the telling of this saga, but to continue ...

'The initial stage of the passage from Portsmouth to Gibraltar with HMS Hardy as escort was uneventful but once again the weather deteriorated and on rounding Ushant we decided to turn due East to seek shelter in the lee of Belle Isle. Unfortunately, when only thirty miles off shelter, the sea-state (from the SW) was such that I was unable to maintain the required course and the ship broached to. As a result I hove to on a SW heading at 1802Z on Saturday the 25th February, going slow ahead on both engines. I remained hove to for more than 24 hours and the wind speed remained at Force Ten and above with high seas and swells. HMS Hardy was obliged to return to L'Orient to refuel at 1100Z on the Sunday and escort duty was taken over by the RFA Gold Rover. Later the weather moderated slightly as we approached the North Spanish Coast. After consultation with Captain Cooper of Gold Rover, we decided to seek shelter in the Bay Rea Del Barquero for 24 hours to permit the crew to rest up and eat, as it had been impossible to prepare a hot meal for more than 36 hours. Diplomatic clearance was first obtained for the anchorage. We sailed from the Bay at 0800Z on Tuesday the 28th February and continued to meet bad weather. RFA Tidereach took over escort duty from Gold Rover at 1040Z on Wednesday the 1st March 1978, and we berthed alongside the Supply Wharf in Gibraltar at 1745Z on the 2nd March 1978.'

That is not all the story.

A young padre, Brian Hackshall, had just joined the Division and declared that he would welcome 'a bit of experience at sea'. It is no surprise that the crew, those that were still 'alive', were getting a bit depressed as they crossed the Bay and they presented him with a bag of bones to see 'if you can do better with these!' The Captain stated that he felt rather sorry for that padre at that time and even more so when the Captain of Gold Rover on learning that we had a padre on board suggested that it was bad luck and that we should have thrown him overboard!

And there is more.

This cable was received by the Naval Liaison Officer in Liverpool.
RESTRICTED
REF FO PORTSMOUTH KMO/KLA 131616Z FEB
1. IN VIEW PREVAILING AND FORECAST WEATHER IN BAY OF BISCAY HODGESTON PASSAGE TO GIBRALTAR IS POSTPONED

2. FO PORTSMOUTH IS REQUESTED TO CANCEL REF A NEW NAVMOVE WILL BE ISSUED TO COINCIDE WITH MORE FAVOURABLE WEATHER CONDITIONS AND AVAILABILITY OF DISTANT ESCORT

No-one had thought that there was need to pass this minor detail of information to Hodgeston! It is not recorded how the cable was eventually discussed, but the Divisional Report written by the Commanding Officer of Eaglet, Captain R.M. Eddleston, contained a restrained paragraph:
'When the ship arrived at Gibraltar, the Ship's Company showed little sign of tiredness and merely a sense of relief and satisfaction in carrying out the passage. On arrival the internal state of cleanliness was good.'

One of the problems facing many Reservists is simply getting 'time off' from their employment for RNR activities. The Commanding Officer of Eaglet received this communication in March 1980.

Statement by the Prime Minister
The Territorial Army and the Volunteer Reserves of the Royal Navy and the Royal Air Force are essential to the nation's defence. They must be well manned, well trained and well equipped. The Government is taking all steps within its power to this end by improving the pay and conditions of service of reservists and enhancing their equipment. But Government can only do so much. The co-operation of employers is also essential in allowing men and women to carry out their training commitment with the Reserve. Volunteer reservists make a major contribution to the nation's security and I believe their training also enables them to play a more positive role in their civilian lives. I hope that all employers will recognise the importance and value of service in the Volunteer Reserves, and give these Forces their full support and encourage their employees to enlist.
Note. This statement was sent to Employers' Association on 20th March 1980.

In 1981 the Mersey Division was converted to mine-hunting and a number of vessels were attached to the Division. HMS Eaglet also became over the years the administrative centre for the RNR in the Northwest and served a number of major towns and cities including Preston, Manchester, Coventry and Sheffield.

It was a sad headline. 'The Navy Mourns Old Salt Tramp.' February 1981.
'Members of the RNVR (sic) in Liverpool have been saddened by the death of an old friend ...Able Seaman Tramp. The old sea dog died quietly after twelve years proud and active service since she was found huddled, starving and exhausted, in the stern sheets of a boat. Chief Petty Officer George Williams,

now retired, but active as steward in the wardroom at HMS Eaglet, Liverpool, remembers the day that Tramp came on board the old Eaglet in Salthouse Dock. She had the finest life any dog could have.'

And talking about 'dog collars'. One of the privileges of wearing a 'dog collar' as an RNR Chaplain is that, even in retirement, I am able to maintain my contact, not only with Eaglet, but with the various retired officers' and ratings' associations and in particular with the Walker's Old Boys Association, the Submariners' Association, the Sea Urchins (Eaglet's retired officers), the Fleet Air Arm Association and the Wren's Association and many other Service groups on Merseyside and elsewhere in the country. We are all great at 'swinging the lamp'!

Father John White and Father John Williams.

When I retired as the RNR chaplain in 1981, my successor was the Reverend John Strettle Williams, BA, MBE, RNR. He is much loved on Merseyside. John was made a Member of the British Empire for his services as Chaplain to the

Navy and the Army on Merseyside. Most Merseyside families have Service connections and for this reason the Padre is always accepted by them. The 'man-to-man' work of the 'dog collar' is rarely seen, but we establish friendships that last a lifetime.

There was a full alert in Liverpool in September 1981. One rather unusual able seaman had gone AWOL ...'absent without leave' He was last seen near Pier Head skipping his guard duty and obviously intent on doubtful business. It was a seven-months-old cross-Labrador answering sometimes to the name of 'Kenny'. An official spokesman said "Kenny came here at six weeks old after being saved from drowning. He was given to us as a replacement for Tramp who had stood guard over the ship for ten years." It was a sad day.

It took time, but eventually it had to happen. 'Bruce', a Rhodesian ridgeback, in 1983 was chosen as a mascot and guard dog. He was a stray, confined to barracks at the RSPCA kennels in Halewood and seemed a natural for a dog watch. His future life-style was assured.

All our memories were stirred when we heard that Chief Petty Officer George Williams was to retire in December 1981. He had been Wardroom Chief Steward since 1953 and was retiring after 43 years service. A presentation was made to George by Lord Derby.

George joined the Royal Navy in 1938. He served in HMS Stork commanded by Commander Frederick John Walker from 1940 until torpedoed at the occupation of Algiers in 1942. He spent two further years in the North Atlantic with Captain Walker in HMS Starling. He joined the British Pacific Fleet based in Sydney and was in King George V at the bombardment of Okinawa. George was also present with Admiral Sir Bernard

Rawlinson in the USS Missouri at the signing of the Japanese surrender in 1945. Returning to Drake he next joined HMS Superb in the Second Cruiser Squadron with Vice-Admiral Russell for three years. His final three years were almost local at HMS Blackcap at Stretton, near Warrington. Finally discharged in 1953 he joined the Division as Chief Steward to Captain Wood.

There are many stories. Here is one of them. George was fully aware that his Wardroom Stewards' Contract allowed him first choice of control over any function and he had no hesitation in doing them all himself. His cooking was well known for its portion control ... just enough and no more! There was one memorable dinner when in the absence of a chaplain Surgeon Commander Capps was asked to say grace. He was well up to it and was quite succinct, "For this salt, thank God!" It was

Just another jolly in the old Eaglet!
George is in the middle on his knees!!

a mistake. The Good Steward was fully alert. On this occasion, there was no problem about the size of the portions. It was the content. When the first course, the soup, arrived, it had been laden with blessed salt.

No wonder that we all felt that we should keep on the right side of George Williams, BEM, RN!

There are always the characters. Commodore D.H. Stewart, RNR, (List One), flew his pennant in Eaglet as he was Liverpool-based with Blue Funnel. His home, however, was in Northern Ireland, and before leaving for home after a voyage in his container ship, Liverpool Bay, he would invariably dine in Eaglet before joining the Belfast Ferry in Princes Dock. The Wardroom arranged for CPO George Williams to stand on the edge of the Princes Dock lock gate into the Mersey. As the Belfast Ferry levelled up, Williams handed over a Pink Gin on a silver salver to Desmond Stewart, who was standing precariously on the Ferry to receive his drink. A seaman handling the Ferry's ropes, seeing this, said to Williams, "Whoose dat den?" Williams replied, "He is the Captain of the Liverpool Bay." The seaman retorted, "He wants to be bloody careful he doesn't fall into it!"

The Daily Telegraph (January 3rd 1984) expressed the feeling of many in the RNR Divisions. 'There is a growing frustration and disillusionment among the 4,000 volunteers of the Royal Naval Reserve, who man 90 per cent of the Navy's minesweepers, over the Government's failure to sanction any increase in their numbers.

'Over the past six years the number of male volunteer Reservists has declined from 4,500 to 4,300. In the same period the strength of the Territorial Army has risen from 57,400 to 66,800 male soldiers.

'Although the Reserve's nine coastal minesweepers, some nearly thirty years old, are to be replaced over the next three years by new trawler-type minesweepers and each of the 11 RNR sea training centres around Britain is also getting new small patrol craft for basic seamanship and navigational training, many of the centres are finding it increasingly difficult to provide enough crews to meet all the many Nato and national exercise commitments each year.

'There is no lack of applicants to join the Reserve, but many have to be turned away because of the current limit on numbers.'

No one knows who this author might be, but he must have been in the RNR.

"Minesweeping is a science of vague assumptions,
Based on debatable figures taken from inconclusive experiments,
Performed with instruments of problematic accuracy,
By persons of doubtful reliability and of questionable mentality."

You really do not have to be mad to mine sweep ... but it might help.

The Sunday Telegraph followed the January 3rd statement with a splendid headline on January 8th 1984:

'Admiral Short of Ships for Nato Role.'

'A stern warning that the forces under his command are inadequate and that the politicians will have to stomach unpalatable decisions has been given by one of Nato's three top commanders.

'Admiral Sir William Staveley, the Commander-in-Chief, Allied Channel Command, says: "I can't do all the tasks laid upon me concurrently due to the fact that I do not have the forces, and balancing the risk is part of the business of establishing priorities." He added, "We are very short of mine countermeasures forces, sweepers and hunters".

The Liverpool Weekly News published an account of Lord Derby's annual outing to the Isle of Man in HMS Mersey (M1173) in August 1984. "Most years I come for a weekend. The first time was pre-1956. I think I was the only man on the ship that wasn't sick on that trip." In command was Lieutenant-Commander Rod Walker. On her way to 'Isle of tailless cats and three legs, Mersey met with fellow minesweepers Clyde and Kilmorey for dummy minesweeping communications and gunnery practice. Just another weekend with our Honorary Captain.

1984 was the year of Liverpool's International Garden Festival, the 40th Anniversary of the Battle of the Atlantic and the Tall Ships Parade of Sail. All this was in addition to a very busy 'routine' RNR year. Lieutenant-Commander Les Martindale, RNR, in January the following year, put some notes together for the RNR Newsletter. 'The Garden Festival was opened by Her Majesty the Queen and we all enjoyed on TV pictures of HMS Striker, our Tracker Class patrol boat, but there was more to it than that. The sail-past of local shipping included the famous Mersey Ferries, tugs in formation and the salvage vessel Vigilant with the fire-fighting monitors throwing impressive plumes of water. There was a lot of water. During the rehearsal, HMS Striker, at half standard distance, downwind, realised that they had solved the pre-wetting problem for that class of vessel. At least it was a learning curve going upwards and led to sensible avoiding action.

'The International Parade of Sail, which marked the end of the 1984 Tall Ships Race, created incredible interest on

Merseyside. The docks on both side of the river were thronged with visitors during the days that the ships were alongside. On the day of the Parade, in spite of it being overcast and raining, the numbers of people was assessed as 1,000,000 lining the river banks, peering from office windows and every conceivable, and some inconceivable, vantage points. On its completion, chaos ensued. The congestion was such that some people took five hours to travel five miles. Cars were abandoned and public transport overwhelmed. Anybody involved with war plans for the civil population, please note: When Joe Public decides to go somewhere, everything stops - and this was only for sailing ships.

'The Navy's participation was very much in evidence. HMS Britannia diverted into the Mersey with Her Majesty the Queen and HRH Prince Andrew embarked, on their way to Scotland. HMS Nottingham was escort to Britannia. The Division's ships were both 'on task' with HMS Brereton on the start line firing the starting gun for each group in the parade. To the more technically minded, who know that Ton class do not have starting guns please note the 'Junior Officer's Initiative Test, Mark 1 = Stuff a thunderflash in the ship's waste paper bin. HMS Striker was deployed as guardship to Britannia chivvying away the yachties, inflaties and canoeies! Our endeavours were effective, but, as always, open to criticism:
"Striker this is Britannia. PLEASE back off.
Your engine noise is annoying the Royal Party."
Fortunately the reply "Can you ask your Mum for some quieter ones?" was never sent. HMS Preserver and our RNX Loyal Watcher were also fully occupied. Commander Geoff Sample, RN, Retd., the much loved ex-NLO for Merseyside was 'back in the old routine' as a Senior Liaison Officer with the Sail Training Association.

'To continue the 'international ' theme, HMS Striker provided invaluable practical training for our twenty-five Junior Officers Under Training, going 'foreign' to the Western Isles for two fourteen day CTPs and innumerable weekends to the off-shore haven of the Isle of Man and the Principality of Wales. Good training, good fun, good craft, but a force seven in Liverpool Bay in a 20-metre hull is something else!'

There was one particular voyage that deserves comment. HMS Striker was on the way back home from the Western Isles with David Fearnley in command and Mike Tomkinson as Navigator. The craft was due to stop in Port Patrick overnight before the final dash to Liverpool. Mike had no fears. He had his entrance plan, saying to anyone who might be interested, "No problem, I have been in here before with my yacht." Confidence is all. But it was very dark. Striker was lined up for the final approach with anxious sailors (apart from the Navigator) observing rather nervously the rocks about them. Mike shouted "All clear, I have the leading lights in sight, keep on this course". At that moment the 'leading lights' changed from red to amber to green and every one realised (including the navigator) that the bearing was on traffic lights! The Commanding Officer got the ship safely alongside!

And 'don't forget the divers'! It was a cold January day in 1985 when eight of Eaglet's divers picked the wrong weekend to do some under water training. Regulations say that RNR divers must put in two hours practice every three months ... and Surgeon Lieutenant-Commander John O'Sullivan and his men choose the snowiest day on Merseyside for their pains.
But after the freezing sojourn in the icy water of Princes Dock, Lieutenant-Commander O'Sullivan's diagnosis was "It was

actually a bit warmer in the water than it was out." After 47 minutes in the water, the diving team, who are trained to make safety checks and repairs on ships, were grateful for mugs of hot soup.

We all trust that there was no brain damage!

They are all smiling . . . hysteria?

Under the headline: 'Hot Shots are the Pride of the Mersey RNR' was the following article. 'Mersey Division of the Royal Naval Reserve won the Cock-of-the-Fleet Trophy for the best all-round performance at the RNR National Rifle Meeting at Bisley last weekend (July 1985). They also won the Duke of Westminster Trophy scoring 673 to beat the Tyne Division by 83 points.

'Mersey Division won the Viscount Elvedon Cup in the pistol event, scoring 293 to beat Sussex Division by 11 points. 'They also took second place in the Target Rifle Match, won by Sussex, and finished second to Solent Division in the sub-machine gun event. Mersey Division Officers were winner and runner-up in the Champion at Arms competition for the best overall performance during the RNR meeting. Sub-Lieutenant L. Martindale won the Tyne Trophy, with 541 points and Lieutenant Commander D. Smith was runner-up with 511 points.'

For many years the Southern Divisions of Solent, Sussex and Wessex seemed to win all the prizes at Bisley. It was, after all, their 'home' range. The Eaglet team usually arrived late on the Friday evening after a long drive South, having had little practice to shoot on a strange range. At this time shooting was classified as a 'sport and recreation' that earned Green Drills towards your Bounty, but not pay for the day.

Mersey Division had a group of pretty good small-bore (.22) marksmen and women, who quickly adapted to shooting bigger bullets in the wind and rain. Consuming the unused bullets of the previous five years to train a team at Altcar Ranges, gaining the interest of the Permanent Staff Instructor (Gunnery Instructor), and asking the Royal Marines armourer to sort out some decent weapons, all helped to turn the tide.

After one trip to Bisley to learn the ropes, Mersey Division began to win prizes. The arrival of OUR Captain on the Sunday, to attend the prize giving, was unheard of. The Southern Divisions always saw their Commanding Officers ... until then Mersey never had. The team thought that Captain Frank Bennett and his wife Marjorie deserved something to take home. The 'Cock-of-the-Fleet' Trophy and the Individual Champion at Arms were a happy surprise for us all. The Duke of Westminster Trophy (Service Rifle Team) was a huge lump of silver that weighed over a stone, with a scrap value of around £10,000. This was promptly christened 'the baby's bath' with a bottle of rum that was enjoyed by all present.

Our GPMG (General Purpose Machine Gun) team consisted of two Medics, Surgeon Commander Don Smith, who became our Principal Medical Officer, and MT3 'Nobby Clarke', both of whom wore the Green Beret of the Royal Marines Reserve, but being Medics they carried RNR identity cards. This pair earned a reputation for being the best machine gunners in the RNR for a number of years. They became quite used to the comment, "Hello, the Scab Lifters are looking for business again!"

Over the next few years, Mersey Division reigned supreme in the RNR shooting world. Team and individual trophies; small bore .22 indoor (25 yards) and outdoor (50 and 100 yards); full bore, target and service rifle, general purpose and sub-machine gun, and service pistol, all found a home in HMS Eaglet's trophy cabinet. In one year Eaglet won 27 out of the 33 trophies available. Of the six we did not win, we were Runners-up.

Captain Frank Bennett, RD*, DL, RNR, commanded Eaglet from 1982 to 1985. He had joined the Division in 1954, and during his time in the Royal Navy he was commissioned as a Temporary Sub-Lieutenant (X) RNVR. Returning to Eaglet for a short time, he then transferred to the Tyne Division. There he attained his qualification for sea command and minehunting. He returned to Liverpool as Training Commander. Next he became the Commander and finally took over command and was promoted to be Captain of the Division. As President of the Admiralty Interview Board he was responsible for the entry of University Graduates into the RNR.

When Captain Bennett resigned from the RNR, he was to become closely involved with the Territorial, Auxiliary and Volunteer Reserves Association, holding the appointment of Vice-Chairman (Navy). He completed over five years as Chairman of the Greater Manchester County Liaison Committee and that post enabled him to promote the Royal Navy and the Reserves. In February 1992 Frank Bennett was appointed Deputy Lieutenant of the County of Greater Manchester.

Frank has recorded some memories.

'Lord Derby was our Honorary Captain and took great interest in our affairs. Above all he enjoyed the Irish Sea trips. He would arrive just before we sailed on a Friday evening with his personal valet and took over the Captain's cabin. Incidentally, his other titles included Earl of Sefton, King of Man. The port of Douglas in the Isle of Man was ever a winner. On one occasion we had safely berthed and His Lordship invited me together with several officers to have dinner in the then Douglas Head Hotel (long since demolished). We had a quiet table and a delightful meal and conversation. Then Lord Derby noticed that the Deemster of the Island was also dining there. The Deemster came across and Lord Derby had to explain that he really was not there and that he had merely dropped in on one of her Majesty's warships and was off in the morning at first light.

'The next problem was his desire to visit the Casino. We arrived by taxi and discovered that we had to complete a temporary membership form. The form asked for name and profession. His Lordship quickly completed his with 'Derby' and 'Peer of the Realm'. Then they asked for a temporary membership fee. It was ten shillings (a fair amount in those days) and, of course, he had no money on him! I paid, but did not linger.

'He was much respected by all in Eaglet and it was a privilege to know him. He helped us in many ways, including the provision of video equipment.'

Captain Bennett had other stories.

'Back in 1981 (I was Commander at the time) we had special guests at the Trafalgar Dinner ... Admiral of the Fleet Sir

Michael Pollock with Lady Pollock and Rear Admiral Hamm with Mrs. Hamm. The latter were paying a formal call to Liverpool in a United States Navy's aircraft carrier, in which he flew his Flag. With such distinguished overseas company, protocol had to be carefully checked and put in place. Most important was the Loyal Toast. That Toast by tradition in Royal Navy ships and establishments is made seated. That night with the Admirals present, the President (me) stood and invited those present to stand. The old and bold thought that Bennett had lost the plot! I then promptly proposed the Toast 'The President of the United States of America'. The band played their National Anthem and the glasses raised. Then Admiral Hamm was to propose our traditional Toast, special to Lancashire 'The Queen; Duke of Lancaster'. Then would follow Our National Anthem, raise glasses and all sit down. That was the proposed drill for the night.

'So in the Wardroom, just prior to going in to Dinner I did a check on proceedings. Rear Admiral Hamm was pleased to be involved, but just as we were about to proceed, he said to me that it seemed strange to call Her Majesty the Queen a 'Duke' (pronounced 'Dook) and that he would call her a 'Duchess'. My final words to him were 'Sir, would you please remember to call her a 'Dook'. He was word perfect!'

Then Frank went back a bit in time.

'Navigation is meant to be accurate and prior to sailing the Navigating Officer always produced a detailed Departure Plan. That is the theory. A junior officer, Trevor Jones, who was to become one of our distinguished Commanding Officers in time, had been excessively caught up in activities during a visit to a Norwegian port. Happily, the local Pilot gave advice to the Commanding Officer as we negotiated a meandering exit from the port.

'When clear water was in sight, the Captain called upon Trevor for a course to steer for a passage through the Pentland Firth, for a Northerly passage, before the return down the coast to Liverpool. With his chart of the North Sea on the chart table, he placed his parallel ruler on the chart with the Norwegian port at one end. With his eye at chart level, he 'sighted' along the ruler towards his pencil that he had placed at Pentland Firth. Then with the two points in line, ruler down to the compass rose, Trevor read off the course. It took only seconds! With total confidence he gave the appropriate course to the Captain. That

Farewell to Brereton.

was given to the Quartermaster and, once the Pilot left the ship, off we sailed.

'With no further alteration we made a dead centre passage through the Pentland Firth and Trevor received full praise. Trevor never tired of telling that story. But please remember that you can only be lucky once (maybe exceptionally twice) in a lifetime at sea. And that is a fact!'

On the 1st November 1985 HMS Brereton sailed out of Liverpool for the last time. A coastal mine hunter, she had been with us since 1981. She was built in 1954 and worked in the Irish Sea in many NATO and national sea exercises. Twenty-seven former commanding officers gathered at Pier Head to see her departure. Lieutenant-Commander Robert Barclay said: "It's a sad day for everyone connected with the old lady. Everyone regrets the passing of a ship that has served extremely well, but times change and we are getting a spanking new ship."

HMS Biter was commissioned on Saturday 25th January 1986. The Commissioning Warrant was read, the Ensign hoisted and the Masthead Pendant broken.

Lord, make us instruments of thy peace:
Where there is hatred, let us sow love:
Where there is injury, pardon:
Where there is doubt, faith:
Where there is despair, hope:
Where there is darkness, light:
Where there is sadness, joy.

In May 1986 HMS Ribble arrived on the Mersey scene. She was a new class of minesweeper built especially for the RNR and was the third ship to carry the name. Ribble was commissioned on June 28th.

It is a great temptation to produce the hundreds of Menu Cards that have been kept for over a century. They will rest in the archives, but here is one of particular interest to me. The date was 17th April 1986. The occasion needs some explanation. 'To commemorate The Sinking of UB82 in the NW Approaches by YOUNG FRED (1918) and The Award of the George Cross to Lieutenant E.O. Gidden, RNVR for mine disposal on Hungerford Bridge, London (1941).' However, all of that detail remains a mystery. The main guests were Commander James Weihage, USNR and Commander Peter Snow, RD, RNR. The entertainment was 'A funny hat routine by Mr. Ken Anders, and a Soft Shoe Shuffle by Commander Snow, if pie-eyed enough'. Please do not feel upset or confused by all this, as it truly is a little obscure, yet the menu should be studied.

WEE HAGGIS MELON
(American version of the famous Scottish Haggis
known locally as Elmer.)

METROPOLITAN SOUP A LA WILLIAMS
(Ancient recipe culled from the books of a secret society now
disbanded. Bluish tinge in normal form, but can turn pink if
(unlikely) overheated.)

TWO WAY FISH A LA WOOD
(Unusual pisceian form credited with phenomenal speed. Has
been sighted on both sides of the Irish Sea at the same time.)

ROMANOV STEAK
(Mysterious dish of reputed Russian ancestry.
Introduced to Britain via Ireland where dished out liberally at
parties. Also known as Smithski in a stew.)

POMME DE PHQ
(Battered collection of old spuds.)

SNOWY SWEETCORN
(Shy vegetable with orange tinge. Perks up when shown a
photo of Selina Scott.)

MUSHROOM MALAISE
(Has to be ingested carefully.)

KINGSTON TRIFLE
(Hodge podge collection of ingredients including old soaks,
lushes and mature women of dubious inclinations.)

SOO CHEESEBOARD
(No comment.)

WELCH COFFEE
(Unlike its Irish counterpart it is civilised and cultured. Also it
adds tone and presence to any occasion.)

The wines meandered from Sippers of Sherry via
Buckets of Vin Blanc through Beaucoup de Beaujolie to Plonkers
of Port.

This evening probably ruined our relationship with the
good old U S of A, but I included the menu because of the
obviously superb coffee. "There's lovely!"

Exercise Open Gate took place in the Mediterranean in
August 1987. Reservists were drawn from all eleven RNR
Divisions and seven River-class minesweepers were involved ...
HM ships Orwell, Spey, Arun, Itchen, Ribble, Humber and

Helford. During the first phase of the deployment, Captain Sea Training (Reserves), Captain F.K. Bennett, RNR, Mersey Division, paid a visit to the squadron, sailing from Gibraltar in HMS Itchen to observe minesweeping exercises.

The second phase was accompanied part of the way by Commodore Berry, RNR, Mersey Division, who visited several of the ships. At the Gibraltar exercise areas the ships carried out a live-surface-shoot as well as operating NBCD and mine counter-measures techniques. Then after a visit to Lisbon, the squadron sailed for UK in two groups. On the return passage more sea training was carried out before the vessels reached their respective base ports.

The new Chief of Naval Home Service Command, Admiral Sir 'Sandy' Woodward, paid his first official visit to Liverpool in September 1987. Flying his Flag in HMS Hermes in 1982, he had commanded the South Atlantic Task Groups in the Falklands War and was subsequently awarded the KCB.

Our Captain Ian Berry was to be appointed to the National RNR Staff as Captain Plans and Policy in 1982 and in 1988 became Commodore (List 3). At the end of his time in the Reserves, Ian was photographed signing the visitors' book in Nelson's cabin in Victory. We suspect that the quills were ornamental! It was the farewell end of an appointment call on the Commander in Chief, Admiral Sir Sandy Woodward of Falklands fame. On the right of the picture is Commodore Tony Barret (List 1). Ian writes, 'On a personal note, when I had been doing National Service (1955 - 57) for about a month as an Ordinary Seaman, I was a member of a Guard of Honour in Victory to mark the celebration of Trafalgar Day. Little did I think!'

There was much grief as so many of us watched on television on 15th April 1989 ... the Hillsborough Disaster. Ninety-six people died at Sheffield Wednesday's ground. It was decided to hold a memorial service at the Anglican Cathedral with some 1,000 relatives being bussed up from Albert Dock. Time was short. Arrangements for the service were made and the Dean (Derrick Walters) needed help to control such a large gathering ... getting them in, getting them seated and subsequently moving them to the Western Rooms to meet dignitaries after the service. So the Dean lifted the phone and called Eaglet. By various phone calls, the Battle of the Atlantic ushers and security teams were mobilised and duly arrived at the Cathedral on the day (rig suits) and ran the occasion.

I sat in my canon's stall and was deeply moved as a member (David Lockyer) of the Cross Guild placed a red book with the names inscribed inside on the altar. Then a small choirboy (Martin Polglaze) on his own and unaccompanied by music walked the whole length of the Cathedral and sang the Liverpool anthem.

> *When you walk through the storm*
> *Hold your head up high*
> *And don't be afraid of the dark*
> *At the end of the storm*
> *Is a golden sky*
> *And the sweet silver song of the lark*
> *Though your dreams be tossed and blown*
> *Walk on, walk on with hope in your heart*
> *And you'll never walk alone.*
> *You'll never walk alone.*

If you were there, it was a moment that you will never forget.

Spencer Atkinson, LMEA, tells a story that smacks of blistered feet, dehydration and bottled ale. The year was 1989. 'Madness became reality when it was decided that in two teams we would pull a gun-carriage for charity. We started outside Liverpool Parish Church with a blessing from the padre, Fr. John Williams, "God bless you, have a tot!" That was the easy bit. It was a long, hard day haul to Leyland. There we collapsed in the TA Barracks and we were wined and dined and de-blistered. Next stop was Clitheroe and in the Town Hall the Mayor 'fed and watered' us in good Lancashire style. I recall that it was followed by a nautical modicum of ale. So we set off for Preston, aiming for HMS Palatine for a 'bit of a do' in the Town Hall and that was followed by another modicum. At this stage blisters were totally unimportant and unfelt. Thence via Southport and Formby and Bootle Town Hall (you've probably guessed what happened there!) we staggered back to Albert Dock and probably should have sat in it. In truth it had been four days of hard but happy labour, often rather vaguely remembered. Cars had stopped and drivers had passed over notes, people had come out of their homes to help the cause, the generosity was tremendous. Well over one thousand pounds was handed to support N Ward in Alder Hey Childrens' Hospital. Well done everybody!"

In the Anglican Cathedral on the 2nd May 1993, the Freedom of Entry into the City of Liverpool was conferred upon HMS Eaglet, then commanded by Commander Philip Houghton RD*, RNR. It was over a hundred years since Boroughs were enabled to confer the Honorary Freedom of the Borough upon the persons whom they wished to honour. The first Honorary Freeman was created in Liverpool in 1886.

At a Special Meeting of the Council held in St. George's Hall, on Wednesday the 27th day of January 1993, in the presence of The Lord Mayor of Liverpool, Councillor Rosemary Cooper, and of a full Council it was resolved:

'That this Council, recognising the distinguished and loyal service rendered by the Royal Naval Reserve to Sovereign and Country, and noting that for over 100 years Liverpool Citizens have been recruited into the Reserve and its predecessors; wishing to declare the respect and friendship of the City and desiring this association to be fostered, do hereby confer on HMS Eaglet the Freedom of Entry into the said City and the right in perpetuity on all ceremonial occasions of honouring the City by exercising the privilege of marching through the City with colours flying, drums beating and bayonets fixed.'

The Anglican Cathedral Church of Christ was a wonderful setting for the Conferment of the Freedom of Entry into the City of Liverpool on May 2nd 1993. The address was given by the Ship's Chaplain, the Reverend John Williams, MBE, BA, RNR.

"Honour

Today's ceremony is a great honour for HMS Eaglet and is valued by all members of the Ship's Company. Here, in this Cathedral Church is represented to us all something of our lives and our hopes, our aspirations and our ideals, and the Spirit of this Great City to which we belong. On this historic day, we give thanks for the long and happy associations between the City and HMS Eaglet, the inter-twined story of the generations of officers, men and women of the Mersey Division and the citizens of this great port, the mutual support and concerns and the strengthening of one another by aiding and goodwill.

Ideals

Through good times and bad, through times of war and times of peace, it has been the steady maintenance of the ideals of seamanship, of patriotism and of civic pride and concern that has kept this remarkable association together, forming a bond and strength, and a flame of courage and pride.

We give thanks for all these achievements and opportunities over a period of ninety years; we give thanks for the mutual respect and affection, care and concern between the City and Mersey Division. Here is a true family relationship, at its best, of support and care; and of encouragement towards ever better and higher service.

Truth

But we should beware of making this an occasion for mutual backslapping! Why? This Conferment is taking place in a Church - a very grand and magnificent Church, but still a Church ... and a Church is a place of Truth. The truth is ... this world is a very dangerous place.

Bosnia is in the headlines ... but that is only one place of conflict. The dangers are immense.

Jesus did not say 'Blessed are the Peacelovers' ... he said, 'Blessed are the Peacemakers!'

And this is what we are called to be ... All of us, Peacemakers. Her Majesty's Ship Eaglet exists in order to promote peace; and peacemaking is a deadly serious business.

The Vision

That may seem a paradox ... after all do we not train for war? And is the Ship's Company not going to march through the City bearing arms? Yes, that is indeed so ... because this is an imperfect world. But we must always remember Christ's words, and hold them alongside the great vision of the Prophet Isaiah:

'They will beat their swords into ploughshares,
and their spears into pruning hooks;
nation will not lift up sword against nation,
nor ever again be trained for war.'

Isaiah 2.4

This can never be a safe or easy option!

Dedication

The Freedom of the City of Liverpool is a very gracious gesture, and is given as a sign of trust, of affection and of confidence, and we in Eaglet pray that we may be called worthy of it.

So here in God's House, let us rededicate ourselves to training and working for peace and justice throughout God's world, that the inhabitants of our Island and Commonwealth may in peace and quietness serve the Lord our God. This is our prayer this afternoon, and this must be our constant endeavour:

> *Lord, when thou givest to thy servants*
> *To endeavour in any great matter,*
> *Grant us also to know*
> *That it is not the beginning,*
> *But the continuing of the same,*
> *Until it be thoroughly finished,*
> *That yieldeth the true glory. Amen.*
> Sir Francis Drake."

Such an address not only expresses the reason for the existence today of the RNR and of HMS Eaglet, but also explains why we must be thankful that the organisation has survived into the present century. In common parlance, 'For evil to prevail, let good men do nothing!'

Padres have other tales, better told below the pulpit to selected people. Padre John Williams felt that this story might be of benefit to those who come after us. 'When the Division was still 'sea-going' it was a requirement that all such intrepid characters be 'in-date' with fire-fighting proficiency. A title for this cautionary tale might well be 'Fire Fighting with Fiery Jack'.

'Each year the ship's company were mustered at the Fire

Fighting School at Speke Airport. The time chosen was either mid-November or December when the Siberian winds guaranteed sub-zero temperatures. On completion of the necessary exercises, we were covered in gallons of diesel oil, drenched with icy water and then graciously allowed a cold shower in a disused air-raid shelter specially designated for use of matelots. All this was apparently essential in order to receive the required certification. Those friendly fire fighters stated that they had no intention of being unkind to us and we assumed that they were being just highly proficient fire fighting 'bastards'.

'Revenge was needed.

'We always had a 'friendly' game of rugby with those 'gentlemen' of the Fire Service and then entertained them in the Chiefs' Mess where they were introduced to the old maxim that 'you are not drunk if you are lying on the floor and can still hold on.' Revenge is sweet.

'There was one occasion when it all went wrong.

'A rugby fixture was arranged for the middle of January at the Mersey Road venue. There was a severe ground frost and a bitterly cold wind coming off the river. Incidentally I was the hooker ... at least vaguely sheltered in the scrum in spite of the physical danger. We were advised by the FFs to apply the time honoured 'fiery jack' to all our exposed parts as a protection from frost bite. That sounded good advice so we layered it on well with enthusiasm.

'Gentle and high-thinking readers should now skip a paragraph or two as this tale is about to go downhill ... metaphorically speaking.

'Two minutes before kick-off Eaglet's warriors decided that a visit to the heads was wisdom. Think about it! We ran on to the pitch and five minutes into the match asked that the game be abandoned with the urgent request that 'There's a fire down below' and we 'Need to cool it!' It was agony.

'The only pearl of wisdom that occurs is that, 'It might be better to wash before rather than after you kick off.' And if the message in this tale has escaped you, please don't worry about it.'

Tradition is not immutable and time moves on. One Saturday evening in 1993 shattered the past. Wrens were piped on board Eaglet for an historic dinner. After the Admiralty decided to allow Wrens on board Royal Navy ships, Wrens of all ranks hosted a formal mess dinner in the wardroom for the first time in the Division's history. The only male guest was the Commanding Officer Tom Cunningham. One assumes it was for the sake of propriety that the good Captain was accompanied by Eaglet's chaplain, the Reverend John Williams.

The farewell at Princess dock was happily not the end of the story.

THE LAST SUNSET   PRINCES DOCK
16th August 1998

Following Prayers by the Chaplain, the Band of SCC Ellesmere Port Beat Retreat.

At Sunset the ensign was lowered, folded and handed to the Commanding Officer, Commander Cedric J. Arthurs, RD, JP, RNR.

Commanding Officer: "Tonight we all have various memories of 27 years in Princes Dock. I would like to welcome in particular the former Commanding Officers beside me who have given support and continue to support Eaglet. The RNR and Eaglet have changed greatly since 1971. Admiral Commanding Reserves has gone, Flag Officer Plymouth has gone, we have seen hull sharing in the 70's, then the end of the Tons in the 80's, the MSFs and the P2000s came and went. The RNR is now a very professional force with over 7% of its members on Full Time Reserve Service. The recent SDR has been excellent for us, an extra 10% in numbers and a 40% increase in man training days.

The first Eagle at Brunswick Dock flew the Flag of the FOIC during World War 1.

The First Eaglet at Salthouse Dock flew the Flag of CINCWA during World War 2.

This Eaglet at Princes Dock flew the Flag of CinCNH during BOA93.

The new Eaglet at Brunswick Dock awaits a Flag Officer.

Tonight we are part of history. The Commissioning Pennant normally is struck only when a ship pays off. Well, we fought the cuts and won. A Pennant shift is rare."

Commanding Officer: "First Lieutenant, inform Brunswick Dock to standby to hoist Pennant."
First Lieutenant: "Aye, aye, Sir."
And a little later the First Lieutenant reported to the Commanding Officer that HMS Eaglet's Pennant was being flown at Brunswick Dock.

Another chapter of Eaglet's history was closed.

Final Sunset.

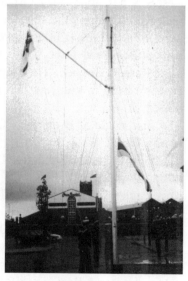

Brunswick Dock.

SODA WATER COCKTAIL

Chapter Nine

WOMEN'S ROYAL NAVAL SERVICE
THE WRENS AT WAR AND PEACE

Mention must be made of the formation of the WRNS. On the 26th November 1917, the First Lord of the Admiralty, Sir Eric Geddes, submitted a letter to his Sovereign, King George V, and it started with these words: 'Sir Eric Geddes, with his humble duty, begs to inform Your Majesty that the Board of Admiralty have under consideration the possibility of substituting women for men.' Those words marked the beginning of the Women's Royal Naval Service and two days later the King pencilled his approval to the document.

Dame Vera Laughton Matthews, DBE, Director of the WRNS from 1939 to 1946, tells how she became a Wren. Her civilian work was as a journalist, sub-editor of the 'Ladies' Field', and on November 29th 1917 she had presented herself at the first temporary WRNS office. Incidentally she had trekked to the Admiralty in 1914 and offered her services as a secretary/typist. She received the classical response, "We don't want any petticoats here." On this occasion she was seen by three ladies in mufti, one of whom was Katherine Furse, the first Director of the WRNS. Vera was called up for the first Officers' course in December and then quickly found herself with 10,000 sailors at the old Crystal Palace, HMS Victory VI, the main RNVR training centre. The Commanding Officer was no other than Commodore Sir Richard

Williams-Bulkeley, RNR ... the Commanding Officer of Liverpool's Eagle , 1911 - 14. That must suffice as the link between Liverpool and the formation of the WRNS.

The start of the Service in Liverpool was the appointment of a Director of Wrens and she received an instruction 'Appoint eight WRNS on attachment to Eaglet and secure accommodation.' That was the 8th January 1918. True to form she received a further cable on the 16th January, 'Cancel attachment'.

However, the Liverpool Wrens did get under way as the rather tired photograph of Eaglet's Division reveals. Liverpool was the last of the original Divisions and started in March 1918. The appearance of the first two WRNS Officers in uniform caused great excitement. The civilian women employed by the naval authority were initially reluctant to be enrolled. The work was mostly clerical with telephone operators and drivers. Two officers were seconded to Holyhead for de-coding duties. Others were employed at the Royal Naval Air Stations at Walney Island and Llangefni in Anglesey where they worked as cooks, stewards and in general duties.

Each Wren was given a pocket book with a paper to be considered as 'confidential'. It was signed by Katherine Furse. The content was surely pertinent to the times.

· 'You are being entrusted with the Honour of working for your Country and, as a member of the Women's Royal Naval Service, you must do your Duty in a serious and generous spirit.

'The Navy is the Senior Service, and we must proudly maintain its Reputation and prove worthy of its best Traditions as well as of the confidence now placed in us.

· 'Officers, Subordinate Officers and Women of the WRNS must unite in friendship, trust and kindness. Let us, by our courtesy, sincerity of purpose and understanding of mutual difficulties, bind our Service together with a bond of Loyalty to our King and Empire.

'Discipline is a necessity in a Service such as ours, but let it be obtained as 'in Honour bound' and not by penalties. If we can produce the Right Spirit we need have no fear of restrictions or punishments because each single one of us will be led to a greater effort for the good name of the 'Wrens'.

'No Work is menial or unworthy of any individual if it be undertaken with zeal and alacrity. We must share each other's toil and never hesitate to help where help is needed. We all know that it is merely our duty to carry through our individual task, and we shall need no reminder of this when we remember for ourselves what we are working for. Self-discipline leads to the greater discipline of the whole, so each one of us can contribute our mite to the Great Ideal.

'Let us always show Friendliness and Sympathy to our Sister Services of the Army and of the Air Force, only by kindly competition in Efficiency and games to obtain supremacy for the WRNS.

'As we all look for and depend on our Welcome from one another now, so let us extend it to all who join us in the future, putting aside all prejudice and remembering only that as women we are united in the WRNS to help our Country, the Navy and each other.

KATHERINE FURSE
Director,
WRNS.
1918

The following prayer was included with that citation.
'Consider NELSON'S Prayer
May the Great God whom I worship Grant to my Country and for the benefit of Europe in General a great and Glorious Victory, and may no misconduct in anyone Tarnish it; and may humanity after Victory be the predominant feature in the British Fleet. For myself individually I commit my life to Him, Who made me and may His Blessing light upon my endeavours for serving my Country faithfully. To Him I resign myself and the just cause which is entrusted me to Defend.   AMEN, AMEN, AMEN

'The last entry in Nelson's Diary, written on board HMS Victory on the morning of the Battle of Trafalgar, Monday, 21st October 1805:-
Remember the Empire expects that every woman will do her duty.
Fear God
Honour the King.'

On 18th September 1919, the Director of the WRNS received a letter from Their Lordships expressing appreciation for the Wrens' contribution to the war effort.

The branch was demobilised.

In October 1935, a Sub-Committee of the Imperial Defence considered the question of the creation of a Women's Reserve and in May 1936 reported: 'Women's Reserve deemed not desirable'. Dame Katherine Furse responded the following year by writing to the Board of Admiralty offering the Association of Wrens in the event of an emergency. This was not ignored and a Paper was submitted on 22nd November 1938 proposing the reformation of the WRNS.

The Government produced a booklet with two rather historic paragraphs:-
'WOMEN'S SERVICE IN THE ROYAL NAVY
'A number of women (initially about 1,500) will be wanted to take the place of Naval and Marine ranks and ratings in Naval Establishments upon secretarial, clerical, accounting, shorthand and typewriting duties; and domestic duties as cooks, stewardesses, waitresses and messengers.
'How to join. Further particulars will be announced in due course, and in the meantime anyone who is interested in this Service should send her name and address to the Secretary of the Admiralty (CE Branch), Whitehall, London, S.W.1, and particulars will then be forwarded to her as soon as possible.'

15,000 enthusiastic women of widely assorted ages, no age limits having been mentioned, wrote in to express their eagerness to serve the Navy!

In advance of formal approval until the outbreak of war on 3rd September 1939, 1,000 'immobile' Wrens had been trained in five different categories ... communications, including both signals and wireless, writer, motor transport driver, cook and steward. Training had been confined to weekly drills. Very soon special 'mobile' conditions were approved, self-contained units came into being and living quarters arranged.

Early in 1939, Mrs Vera Laughton Matthews was appointed Director of the WRNS and without any authority she made embryo plans for the start of recruiting. Approval for her plans was only given three days before the outbreak of war. By the end of that year the strength reached 3,000.

It was in January 1941 that the first Wrens sailed for overseas, a party of one Officer and 20 Chief Wren W/T operators was bound for Singapore. Wrens were in Washington and Gibraltar. Tragedy overtook the first WRNS draft to Gibraltar when SS Aguila was torpedoed and all were lost.

The peak number was reached in September 1944, when there were 74,635 officers and ratings in 90 categories and 50 branches. Towards the end of the conflict the Director used these remarkable words at the conclusion of a speech:

"Our lives are going to be wider and deeper because of all that we have learnt in the Service. And when peace comes you will take your place in civilian life to such good purpose that people will say, 'Well, you see, she was a Wren!'"

Eventually, all over the world, more than half of the total Communications Staff of the Royal Navy consisted of WRNS.

The reformation of the Wrens was celebrated on board Eaglet on 12th April 1939 with a Dinner. The Menu card is full of interest and puzzlement. It must speak for itself.

Toasts

Mr President: The President of the United States of America.
Captain USNR: The Queen, Duke of Lancaster.
Mr President: Services Wrendered.
First Officer Thomas: Bloody War and Sickly Season.

Menu

SOO Grapefruit
(Old sea dogs concoction)

SONCS Soup   (PHQ Sherry)
(Full bodied but thinning on top)

Poisson au Convoy   (Chateau Mersey)
(When consumed nothing to report)

Boarded Steak   (Chateau Princes Dock)
(Courtesy of GMC)

Movements Mushroom
(Grown on a special diet of signals)

MERZONE Onions
(Where's North on this damned map?)

American Potatoes
(Courtesy of Sir Walter Raleigh et al)

RNXS Mixed Vegetables
(If not available, due to tilly being missing)

CB Gateau
(Extremely rare specimen, found on skip)

MAY or MAY not be cheeseboard.
(Dark and mysterious with delicate feminine touch)
PERTWEE Coffee.
(Believed to be based on the recipe of the
monks of Winchester)

A chance meeting with Doreen Heward (nee Cresswell) brought back memories of sixty years ago. "I was based in Irwell (Birkenhead) from 1941 to 1943. I joined in 1941 and was sent to Scotland, Balloch, for training and then to the 'holding depot' at the Blundellsands Hotel. Assigned to Irwell, we were billeted at the Wrennery in Prenton, but as we did twenty-four hours on and twenty-four hours off, we slept on board. Most of us were in hammocks and the unlucky ones used the bunk beds ... first in were lucky! The minesweepers were all based with Irwell and as they left for patrol each vessel played its own signature tune. When they returned we listened to make sure that all were home safely. On one occasion Captain Johnny Walker arrived and the place was chaos. I was a steward in the Officers' mess and it was great to see Starling. I looked after them in the wardroom. My job was with the Captains and Commanders.

"Above our mess we could hear the defaulters being paraded ... much shouting and stamping of feet. The cells were quite near us and on one occasion I felt sorry for one man and took him a cup of tea. A chief went mad and I suppose it was what he would call a 'bollocking'. A lot of fuss about nothing!

"I remember in the early days that I served an Officer with a beer and then he came back to me and said, 'I'll have the other half now, please.' I replied, 'I'm terribly sorry, but I put it all in the one glass.' We had to learn!

"The trawlers also served as minesweepers ... I recall Northern Star, Northern Lights and Northern Gift. Life on the trawlers was less formal than the RN ships ... most of the Captains were the original men from the fishing days.

"We drilled in a shed alongside and there they held the

pay parades. In order to board Irwell we had to walk across the deck of a ship called Eastern Isles (also part of the Division). The Wren Officer had an office on the top deck, but did not pay much attention to us. Many Wrens lived at home and just came in to work ... we called them 'immobiles'. I was a 'mobile' Wren and was eventually sent to Northern Ireland to work in an officers' mess. Then, the big adventure ... Australia. I found myself looking after nursing sisters in New South Wales. By this time I was a Petty Officer. We were living and working well out in the bush in HMS Golden Hind (Herne Bay, Sydney) and at the end of the war, the POWs came to us from Japan. They were in a fearful state and we cared for them until they were strong enough to be re-patriated. Sadly some were so weak that they died. It was very sad.

. "What I do remember as I looked at those wrecks of men was calling out aloud, 'There should never be any more war!' "

It was a joy to have had such a conversation with an old friend.

Yet another friend from slightly 'way back' ... I tread very carefully about time and dates in this chapter ... is Lily Wilson (nee Hennesy). "I was one of the 'immobiles' and I lived in New Brighton. In May 1942 I was sent to work in the wardroom of Irwell. It was a smashing place to work and I made many wonderful friends. The initial training was in HMS Wellesly (the Royal Southern Hospital). Life was busy ... cleaning silver, pressing suits, serving food; it was all to do with people and minesweepers and trawlers. No day was the same and there were always new faces.

"I recall that Eleanor Roosevelt came to us once and inspected us. The King was in Birkenhead seeing all the bombing and he also popped in to have a look at us. It was really exciting. I recall once catching the ferry to Liverpool, but had to return because the debris from the bombing made it impossible to walk anywhere.

"I think that we immobiles were paid about one pound a week. Not a lot, but it was fine. Romance was ever in the air. There were dances in Wallasey with a band ... that was where I met 'my Mac', William Macdonald Wilson. He actually played in the bands in Newcastle and Victorious. We were married at the end of 1945.

"There were dances every night in Red Ensign House (Mersey Mission to Seamen). Many Wrens would go to the tunnel entrance and thumb lifts ... and that's how we came back.

It was completely safe.

"Discipline was no problem for us and I well recall that we had to 'march past' in single file because there was no room on the quay side."

At the beginning of 1941 the formation of the new Western Approaches Command with Headquarters in Liverpool meant a great increase in WRNS numbers. Dame Vera Laughton Matthews recalls a visit to Merseyside. "The Wrens in Liverpool at the height of the Battle of the Atlantic are a thrilling memory ... quiet, alert, tense with the supreme importance of their work and an inseparable part of that grand team."

In the W/T room at Derby House the first six Wrens made their appearance in January 1942. They gradually took over more and more responsibility until they became Heads of Watches, and by D Day the W/T room was entirely manned by Wrens. At the Tactical School in Eaglet WRNS Officers took a big part in training Naval Officers in the latest anti-submarine tactics.

Dinner recently in the Lord Nelson in Liverpool at the Annual Submariners 'do' found me sitting at table with Ian Fraser on one side and his beloved Melba on the other. It was a lively evening in spite of the fact that we had to 'sing for our suppers'. The end product was another story for 'the book'. It was a letter to me ... dictated by Melba and typed by Ian!

'Melba has put together the following report of odd experiences whilst stationed in Irwell during the war. Previous to joining Irwell she was stationed at Pwllheli in HMS Glendower.

'As she lived in Prescot Street at that time she caught an early morning bus from the Victoria Hotel in Seacombe Ferry where she met up with other Wrens and they all ran across the locks to HMS Irwell. Melba was in the Victualling Office where her main priority was to ascertain that the rum issue was always top of the list! In the general Wrennery gossip, word would occasionally get around that the Lotus shoe shop at the bottom of Bold Street in Liverpool had some Joyce shoes in stock, so that she and fellow Wrens would, during lunch hour, rush to the entrance of the Mersey Tunnel and hitch a lift to Liverpool on one of those quaint steam lorries that were used in those days. (I can just see them climbing up into the control cabin.) It was a great laugh; the drivers were most courteous. It is doubtful whether they would be allowed to help today. But then it was wartime. If they were able to get a pair of shoes they were made up!

Melba and Ian.

'On occasions they would go to Reeces for tea. There were always quite a number of American soldiers there and they were very friendly. One of them phoned Irwell and asked to speak to Wren Melba. Her Chief Petty Officer told him, 'Indeed not, she is married!' All in the office thought this was amusing.

'When Melba became pregnant, at three months Doctor Walker, her civilian doctor, confirmed it was so. But the rules of the RN declared that this had to be confirmed by a Naval Doctor before she could be discharged. Ian, who was on leave at that time, was furious and insisted on being there for the examination.

"I was, of course, discharged and was therefore able to travel to Rothsay to see Ian and HMS Bonadventure sail off to Australia. Very sad, but 'Operation Struggle' was a great success and he came home safely later to see his six month old daughter."

Lieutenant-Commander Ian Fraser won a DSC in the submarine Sahib when with the 10th S/M Squadron in the Mediterranean. In time he volunteered for X-craft and was shipped out in Bonadventure to the Far East. 'Operation Struggle' was to sink the 10,000 ton Japanese cruisers 'Takao' and 'Miyoko' in the Jahore Straits. It was a remarkable exploit ending with 'Takao' being taken out of the war. Both Lieutenant-Commander Fraser and his diver, Leading Seaman J.J. Magennis, were recommended for and awarded the Victoria Cross, which was gazetted on 13th November 1945 and presented by King George VI at Buckingham Palace on 11th December 1945.

At the end of the war the WRNS rapidly reduced in number, but many officers and ratings were still required to serve an extended Service. On 1st February 1949 the Service, first created to meet purely a wartime need, became an integral and permanent part of the Royal Navy. In September 1976 the WRNS Officers' Training Course moved from the Royal College Greenwich to the Britannia Royal Naval College, Dartmouth and in 1978, the Diamond Anniversary of its formation, the Women's Royal Naval Service became subject to the Naval Discipline Act for the first time, thereby accepting commitment with equal opportunity.

Whilst there is so much and so many people to remember, perhaps we will do well to recall the Reserve career of Cassandra Cornelius. Cass joined HMS Eaglet as a clothing

Wren in 1950. Ship's book number MD/W/16 ... the first New Entry Class WRNVR. At that time sixteen Wrens were taken into the Division ... eight had seen war service and eight were new entries (Cass was one of those having been in the Land Army). In 1952 she was commissioned as a Third Officer doing administration for Wrens and Seamen Ratings (she actually recruited Anne Boyle who was to marry the man we now know as Commodore Rod Walker!). It was in 1952 that the Wrens were enrolled in good numbers.

In 1954, Cass was promoted Second Officer and

Second Officer Cassandra Cornelius . . . communications.

specialised in communications and cryptography. There were numerous NATO exercises ... Malta, Fort Southwick, Pitrivie and Whitehall. She drove the steam pinnace Rosie on several occasions down the Mersey and in and out of Liverpool and Birkenhead Docks. She crewed in a Whaler Race in HMS Osprey at Portland.

1955 was the year that she trained a Wren crew and

turned Rosie into an Admiral's Barge with white and blue cushions, etc., and polished the ship's brass funnel top! Then they took the ACR across the river from outside Albert Dock to Morpeth Dock in Birkenhead for the ACR's Annual Inspection, passing HMS Theseus on the way and, 'As we had the Senior Admiral on board they piped the side for us!' She took Rosie from Liverpool Landing Stage into Canning Half Tide and Albert Dock at the request of the Staff Officer late one Sunday evening after a weekend exercise, the lads having to get home. 'I asked Ron Sutherland to lend a hand.' (That is the gentleman she was to marry!).

'Was organised in 1956 by the Staff Officer to play the part of the cow in Exercise Appointment with Venus with Ron as the 'other half', but Ma'am (Pat Stubbs) nearly had heart failure at the thought of one of her Officers doing such a thing! That was a fatal mistake. It hit the headlines across the world that I was banned. Dick Cattle took my place!!!

'In 1959 I dined in the Painted Hall at Greenwich at the Centenary of the old RNR. I led the Wren Platoon on several occasions at the Battle of Atlantic Service at the Cathedral.'

I'm not sure why she and Ron were covered with oil, but in this state he had proposed to her! Actually she and Ron were asked to move Rosie around the corner in Birkenhead docks and the harbour master insisted that she (Rosie) had lights. This involved cleaning and mastering two old fashioned oil lamps, just to move about one hundred yards! The official engagement was announced on the bridge of Amerton in Peel Harbour.

'Escorted H.M.S. Irwell out of Birkenhead Docks in HSL Rosie when they finally moved her.'

Ron and Cass got married in 1963 and had the reception on board HMS Eaglet.

'Was presented with the Reserve Decoration by Admiral

Place, VC, RN, on the 11th December 1968 at the same time and side by side with Ron.

Finally she finished in Eaglet, age and rank expired! And joined the RNXS as a rating. And here we go again!

Cassandra Sutherland worked her way back from a rating RNXS to a Mate with a Watch-Keepers's ticket and went to sea as First Lieutenant of an inshore sweeper. However she finally finished with the Navy in 1988 after 37 years experience.

But Cass was not quite finished with her sea career!

"My sailing activities then came to the fore and my final achievement was to become in the year 2000 the Commodore of the Royal Welsh Yacht Club ... the first Lady Commodore in its 154 years' life."

We all love Cass and Ron.

The Lawson Trophy, which was presented annually to the most efficient Wren Reserve Unit in the United Kingdom, was awarded on March 19th 1962 to the Mersey Division. The Director of the WRNS, Commandant Jean Davies, presented the Trophy to Chief Wrens Joyce Melsom and Florence Farrel.

Joyce Melsom jotted down a few memories. 'I went home from work on the tram and sat next to a girl who had been a wartime Wren (hostilies only) as I was. We chatted about our experiences and then she casually mentioned that there was to be a recruiting drive that evening on board HMS Eaglet to see if it was feasible to start an RNVR for ladies. A lot of people were there and I, with six others, was accepted on the spot. I was number four in the WRNVR.

'En passant I would say that the immediate difference between permanent service personnel and reservists is the jargon. Maybe the acid test is 'Blackouts'. If this is mentioned and recognised, the inference is that the person is permanent service. Why? Because the sailors called our navy-blue issue knickers from the clothing store 'Blackouts' ... or more familiarly CAKS - Closed At the Knees.

'We soon mustered a goodly number of recruits and training sessions were established with the ex-permanent service girls being very helpful with their RN experience. We also set up a social side and had many 'do's' on board. Then there were sporting activities. We had a WRNVR Netball team and played matches against local teams. There was also shooting and a number of girls were very successful at Bisley.

'HMS Mersey on some exercises carried Wrens. We all seemed to enjoy the man-over-board activity and the technicalities of lowering boats. On one of the Isle of Man trips we passed the Isle of Man Steam Packet ferry and were pleased to hear the remark 'We must be on course ... we've just passed the ferry.' On another occasion when we were returning from Llandudno, there was a national alarm and all defence establishments were closed down. By this time HMS Mersey was in the shore establishment at Trafalgar and we were not allowed into our normal berth and were disembarked at the stage. Eaglet was closed to us. This was a real disappointment as we were due to have a party that night and all that lovely food was wasted.

'Of course there was no sleeping on board in those days. We stayed at B and Bs if it was an overnight trip. Bounty night in the early days was payment by cash. It was a night of great hilarity when the paying out was completed. Some sailors never went home, slept under the tables, woke up still drunk and all the bounty spent! Cheque payment was a great improvement. Memories!'

Chief Petty Officer Sally Furlong (number 32) was grateful for the support of 'Blue Funnel' which enabled her to play a major role in the Division. An advertisement in the Liverpool Echo at the end of 1951 was all that was needed.

'I was interviewed early in 1952 with Pat Holbrook (number 3 ... she worked in the Pilot Office) and Marjorie Rotheram (she worked in the Dock Board). The drill deck was full of desks and we took an exam ... it was hard to get in! Started in Radar but there was no training until 1953. We went to Dale in Wales to Harrier ... remember the Griffin Pub and the cow pats? ... at least ten of us went from Eaglet. We lived in Nissen huts; you were allowed a little coal to start the fire and then top up with coke. We did fourteen days for four years and I became a chief in double quick time. Then Radar stopped and I became a Degausser and kept my rank. It was hard work with two exams each year. You had to learn to write backwards on the rear of the screen!

'1953 was the Bisley year. The presentations were made by the Duke of Gloucester and he looked so ill. The Duke of Westminster's Cup was huge and kept in a box 4ft. by 2ft. by 4ft. The box had rope handles. There were no trains but we got to London. It was 2 in the morning and the lads got into the Union Jack Club. We two Wrens were given that large box to guard! No taxis! One shilling a night including bunks and breakfast ... into Queen Anne's Wrennery.

'That year we pulled the whaler ... that was tough! Up to Dundee by coach on the Friday and slept on the Drill Deck. At the crack of dawn we were on the Tay ... Wrens, Officers and Ratings. Next it was Belfast via Heysham. Colin Pfeffers was there. We had to pull a mile in Belfast Loch. I was stroke. We wore square rig white shirts ... it was a lovely day. Then it was Weymouth for the Inter-Divisions Regatta. One Wren drove down in Commander Kershaw's Lagonda. All the Wrens stayed in the Sally Army Hostel. There was no sign of our Lagnda Wren! Just as we were about to hit the water, here she arrived ... furious! Apparently the good doctor stopped the car for catnaps on his rug on the side of the road ... it was endless that journey. She swore that a cyclist passed them on one hill! Apparently she refused to return home with him. Commander Kershaw was a hard taskmaster.

'Don't use that bailer like a powder puff!'

Then he would step in and show us how it should be done. Wonderful!

'I remember once that we took Rosie up the Manchester ship canal. Ann White produced a pan of stew made with Guinness. We all slept on the deck. Actually after that stew we probably all passed out on the deck! Memories. I almost forgot, but in the late 60's I was Wren of the Year and I was presented with a cup by Commandant D.M. Blundell, the Director of Wrens.'

There were eleven Wren Reserve Units in the United Kingdom. Commandant Davies, a native of Liverpool, came to visit us and presented a long-service medal to Chief Regulating Wren Florence Farrel. She served in the Wrens from 1942 to

1948 and had joined the Mersey division in 1952. In fact she was the first to sign on.

Our local Daily Post (8th September 1952) recorded what they claimed to be another 'first' for the WRNVR. 'For the first time in the history of the WRNVR a party of twenty-five attached to the Mersey Division took part in an exercise in Liverpool Bay. The girls embarked at Morpeth Dock soon after mid-day on Saturday. Wrens were at the wheel continuously from half-way down the Mersey Channel and Wren Patricia Carr was at the wheel as the ship entered Llandudno Bay at 6.30 p.m. Other members of the party undertook radar, signals, galley and other duties.

'Lieutenant-Commander N.P. Brown, Captain of the 250 tons-minesweeper, HMS Mersey, said "They were all thoroughly keen." Third Officer Pamela Rattray, in charge of the party, said that the exercise provided an excellent opportunity of putting theoretical training into practice. The planning for the adventure had been handled by Second Officer Barbara Hill, the Staff Officer attached to the Division.

'On arrival at Llandudno, the girls were welcomed by Councillor Hugh Owen, Chairman of the Council. They were entertained to dinner and a dance and after spending the night at two boarding houses, re-embarked yesterday morning. The exercise continued throughout the day until the ship docked at Liverpool in the evening.'

Vice-Admiral J.W. Cuthbert, the newly appointed Admiral Commanding Reserves, inspected the Division at Morpeth Dock. The parade was a thousand strong. The Admiral paid special tribute to the smartness of the women of the Division.

This was the second time the Admiral had admired the WRNVR efficiency. Earlier he had crossed the Mersey on board the Division's steam pinnace Rosie. The ship, manned by an all-Wren crew under the command of Third Officer Cassandra Cornelius, came alongside the dock wall 'in one' and with

Captain Turner and the ladies, 1955.

scarcely a tremor. (This was the chauvinstic comment of a Daily Post reporter!) Rosie was believed to be the largest naval ship to be crewed entirely by the WRNVR. The harbour steam launch, Rosie, just fifty feet long seemed even smaller compared with the ACR's 18,000-tons aircraft carrier, HMS Theseus. Both vessels were carrying the Vice-Admiral's flag.

Before the Admiral addressed the Parade, he took the salute when the entire company of HMS Irwell marched past in single file. This is the practice adopted on board ship where space is limited.

In the dinner at the end of that day in Eaglet, Lord Derby made his first appearance in naval uniform as Honorary Captain of the Division.

Tragedy hit the Division in September 1953 when Wren Elizabeth Joan Wright fell to her death from a cliff whilst carrying out fourteen days training at HMS Harrier in Kete, Pembrokeshire. Along with her old school friend, Wren Maria Isabella Dotto, they went for a swim at Marloes Beach and were cut off by the rising tide. The only escape was up the 200ft. cliff face and half way up Wren Wright slipped. Wren Dotto reached a narrow ledge ... she remained there for six hours. Fearing that she would not be rescued, she wrote a note telling the story and placed it in her handbag to be found. From time to time she struck a match in an effort to attract attention.

Search parties were scouring the cliff tops and at 1.30 that morning her light was seen. Able Seaman Milton went down the cliff by rope and Coastguard William Knight scrambled up from the beach. She was quickly taken to the RNAS to sick bay suffering severly from exposure and shock. There she asked that her 'last note' to her family be destroyed. Her ordeal was over.

The Wrens were truly versatile. Wren D.M. Hughes on 4th October 1953 was fourth in the Nursery Competition (.303) held at Altcar Range, only nine points behind Sergeant K.M. Dean, who had represented Great Britain in the Canadian Bisley the previous year as the finest cadet shot in the UK.

The announcement on 1st November 1958 that the RNVR and the RNR were to be unified under the title of Royal Naval Reserve also applied to the Wrens. The Women's Royal Naval Volunteer Reserve was renamed the Women's Royal Naval Reserve.

Second Officer Ann White, WRNVR, recalls joining the Division in 1955 under the 'T' Scheme. This was a method by which people in so-called 'reserved occupations' could volunteer and in the event of trouble would be called up, subject to Ministry of Labour approval. 'I served as a Radar Plot Wren for over two years until I was promoted. The New Entry training was somewhat like the curate's egg in those days and the bad parts were bad. The New Entry men and we were taught by fairly ancient Chiefs and POs whose ability to instruct was limited and whose discipline was lax to a degree. They had not grasped that volunteers or no, unless they cracked down on their classes it would be mayhem. It changed fairly soon as far as the Wrens were concerned.'

Ann continued.
'On promotion we were told we could be Degaussing Officers or, as an afterthought, Signallers. We chose the former. It was a new category and rather a half-baked scheme. It had all arisen because someone had found a new and very sensitive magnetic mine out East which was definitely Russian. Alarm bells rang all over ... 'start degaussing again, not enough bodies, no money' ... pause ... the answer ... The Reserves!' And so it was to be. There were no instructors, no instructions, no nothing. I was one of two Wren Officers to go on training and went to Stokes Bay, where a 'two and a half' RNVR, John Barret, was in charge. He'd been called back to cope! At one point in the war he had been the DG Officer in Morpeth Dock in Birkenhead.
'In a fortnight we were given enough notes to teach Wrens for two years. Other Divisions had a DG category eventually, but we were the first to go in 'boots and all'. '
Ann was to marry Lieutenant-Commander Alaistair White, RNR, an Engineering Officer in the Division who actually held a Watch-Keeping Certificate ... he chanced to be at University with me, a trusted friend.

The Liverpool Echo (7th February 1972) could not resist the headline 'Wren Flies off Today.' Basically it was quite true. An Eaglet Wren, Joyce Appleton, left her office desk in Aintree to join a warship in the Far Eastern Fleet for three weeks. She had been detailed to assist with the secretarial work on the staff of the Commodore Far East.

It was a tradition of the Division that whenever possible the Wrens would be taken to sea in the Minesweeper, sometimes to Douglas or Holyhead, where the Wrens would stay overnight on shore.

Commander Tom Cunningham recalls a 'Wrens Weekend'. 'In about 1974 the Squadron had been exercising for its 14-day continuous training in the Channel on a Vermex Exercise, this being a two-week stint of minesweeping out of HMS Vernon in Portsmouth under the guidance of the Vernon staff.

'At the end of the exercise we were to proceed to Cherbourg for our 'jolly' before returning to Liverpool. It was decided, by whom I know not, that our Mersey Division Wrens were to join at Portsmouth and be taken to Cherbourg where they would stay ashore before being brought back to Portsmouth to embus for home.

'As usual, as soon as the first heaving line went ashore, there came aboard the local Ships Chandler with all sorts of spirits and perfumes for sale. These were highly dutiable in the UK at the time and thus were a very attractive purchase, albeit that the quantities that could be landed were strictly limited. The Wrens duly made their various choices of perfumes and the chandler went away highly delighted, promising to deliver the goods to me the next day which he duly did. Payment was made from the Ship's cash. I do not know how I became involved in this transaction as I was the Engineer Officer and as such anything to do with cash and purchases was not in my bag. Something to do with being detailed off I think. It was nothing to do with democracy.

'The weather in Cherbourg was foul with high winds and rain and the First Lieutenant suggested that I take all the goodies ashore to the hotel, where the Wrens were staying and sort out the cash etc. in comparative calm, as it would be too rough once we sailed. 'Good idea,' said I. Laden with thousands of cigarettes, litres of perfume and umpteen bottles of spirits Phil Houghton and I proceeded ashore. Phil was the Pusser and had with him a suitcase containing about £5,000 out of which he was going to pay the Wrens and settle our account with our local suppliers of food etc.

'I should say here that the French Navy had made available to us a small car which we were free to use for the duration of our visit and it was into this that Phil and I loaded all the goods. Just as I was about to drive off, a rather seedy looking Frenchman in a shabby mac stopped me and enquired where I was going and what I was doing with the cigarettes etc. I told him, somewhat casually as I recollect, that I was taking them ashore to give to the Wrens and would he please get out of my way. It was at this moment that he drew himself up to his full 5ft. 2in. (clearly he suffered from the small man syndrome) and said he was the "Douanes Francaise" and that I had committed an offence already by landing the goods. "Nonsense", said I. That word sounds good in French!

'The situation deteriorated further and Phil and I were taken off in the car to the local Customs Office for further discussions. I was getting that sinking feeling. The Captain, Brian Parr, was called and pretty soon we were in the throes of a bit of an incident. Discussions took place with the Naval Attaché, who was by then in attendance, about whether to advise the British Consul. This was becoming a situation.

The Cherbourg Contingent.

'As time passed it became clear that the Douanes wanted to impose "un petit penalty" and had in mind the confiscation of the goods, the ship's money and the impounding of the car as an exchange for letting Phil and I go. That did not seem to be much of a deal and hardly a 'petit' penalty. I do not know the French for 'being taken to the cleaners,' but it looked inevitable.

'We were saved at that moment by the arrival of our French Navy liaison officer with whom we had happily passed some convivial hours in a restaurant the night before. There was much arm waving and Gallic remonstrations which concluded with him saying to the Douanerie that as the car belonged to the French Navy, there was no chance of them impounding it, unless Monsieur le Douanes wanted an interview without coffee and with the French Naval Commandant who was a pretty big wheel. Collapse of stout party.

'So it all ended happily, the Wrens got their duty free goods, the ship's money was restored and I got a fearsome dressing down from the British Naval Attaché! Vive la France!'

The work of the Wrens continued after the war and expanded. This was acknowledged on the 8th April, 1974, when the WRNS Regulations became obsolete and the Branch came under the Naval Discipline Act for the first time. Much more was to follow and the Geddes Statement of 1917 that there should be consideration of 'the possibility of substituting women for men' truly belongs to another century. But it actually happened! I received an e-mail as follows.

"Subject: Demise of WRNS.
The WRNS was subsumed into the RN on 1 November, 1993."

Ornithologists might know Troglodytidae as 'small, dull brown, shy birds who seldom venture far from cover'. Some of us will never believe it!

40th Anniversary Party, 1992.

PORT

Chapter Ten

THE NEW ROYAL NAVAL HEADQUARTERS
THE RESERVES TODAY

The new home for Eaglet is alongside Harry Ramsden's Fish and Chips emporium in the South Docks. As one wag put it ... 'At least they can save a dollar or two on the galley!' The new building, 'RN Headquarters, Merseyside,' for us will ever remain as HMS Eaglet. It was formally opened by the Admiral of the Fleet, The Prince Philip, Duke of Edinburgh, KG, Kt, on the 16th October 1998.

The Commanding Officer of Eaglet was Commander Cedric J. Arthurs, RD, JP, RNR. He joined the Division in 1973, served as New Entry Training Officer, Training Design Officer, serviced with Granada patrols and was promoted to Lieutenant in 1978. Other tasks followed ... Senior Instructing Officer, Intelligence Officer, Recruiting Officer (doubling the number of Officers and integrating the List 1 into the STC ... Sea Training

I'll use my own thank you!

Centre), the list continued. Appointed in command of HMS Palatine, the Communications Training Centre at Preston, he expanded the CTC to include NCS (Naval Control of Shipping) personnel. Cedric returned to Eaglet in 1990 and as Planning Officer oversaw the local implementation of Options for Change that saw Branch closures and transfers. Change was in the air. Appointed Executive Officer in 1994, he implemented the Way Ahead Measures for the RNR within Eaglet. This included the move of personnel to new Branches, the transfer of 40 reservists from the CTCs in Leeds and Manchester, which were closed, and overhauling the structure of HMS Eaglet to cope with the revised Branches and higher emphasis on Directed Training. Promoted

Commander in 1995, he was appointed Planning Commander. The STC was rebranded as an RTC. A greater task was ahead. He assumed command of Eaglet on 3rd September 1997 and oversaw the building of the RNHQ Merseyside where the RNR,

RMR and NORNE (Naval Regional Office Northern England) came together. He was the first Officer in Charge of the RNHQ when it started service on 10th August 1998 and organised the Opening Ceremony in the presence of the Duke of Edinburgh. Commander Arthurs retired in 2000 after a remarkable contribution to the life of the Division.

Cedric Arthurs put 'pen' to computer. "Joining the RNR was strange for a Sub-Lieutenant. There were just six of us, eight Lieutenants, eighty Lieutenant-Commanders, eight Commanders and four Captains. The mix was between war-served officers and National Service. We who were new really had no experience and were never likely to get it. But the Cold War was still on and that meant showing the Russians that the civilians in the UK were not going to let them win and were prepared to put the necessary time and effort in to achieve our goal.

"In the 1970's there were many Mechanical Engineers Marine (MEMs) who were very practically minded, but had got out of school as soon as possible. This became a barrier since they could not become Leading Hands or above without educational qualifications. Enter the Naval Mathematics and English Test (NAMET) which could be studied on board and exams taken. So with the assistance of the Instructor Officers (Ron Roby and I) quite a number PO MEMs gained advancement.

"By 1983 the end was nigh for ex-National Service officers and over a period of 18 months the number of Officers fell from 90 to 45. At this point there were only eight officers with Bridge Watching Certificates and five qualified Commanding Officers. However, with these Officers doing two weekends a month, the minesweeper went to sea each weekend.

"Between 1983 and 1986 with the help of Chief Wren Hogan the number of Officers in the Division was doubled and we stopped the outflow of Ratings."

Change was in the air ... not a wind, but a hurricane! In 1986 the RN decided to pay for Drill Nights at one quarter of a day's pay. This changed the manner of the RNR from a truly voluntary force to one of a second career, although it took ten years (and the Reserve Forces Act 1996) to complete the change.

Following the end of the Cold War, changes in the role and structure of the RNR began to appear. Commander Cedric Arthurs continued his appraisal.

Father John carries on! Another baptism in Eaglet!

"It was dramatic. The first move was called 'Options for Change' and saw the loss of the Dentists, Chaplains (incidentally Father John Williams just carries on!), Instructors and the task of Recruiting moved to the RN. Some of the CTCs were closed, including HMS Palatine. Then the main changes arrived in 1994. The RNR nationally was reduced from 5,600 to 3,500, although we found out later that the numbers had gone down to 2,900. Units were closed around the country, including HMS Salford. With the loss of the CTCs due to closure, the remaining STCs and

HQ Units were renamed Reserve Training Centres. The STCs, CTCs and HQ Unit descriptions were removed. Large numbers of Branches were closed ... Engineering, Electrical, Cooks, Diving, Port Defence, TSA and Regulating. Some Branches were reduced in size ... NCS and MW (Mine Warfare).

"Overall, Eaglet's numbers fell from 300 to 230. The RNR had little influence in the changes to be implemented and two lists were received by the Commanding Officer (Commander Phil Houghton) who had to inform individuals if they were in or out. In April 1994 some 17 Officers were dined out, whilst in June 1994 the last muster of the 70 leavers was poignant. Life was difficult. The next two years were very turbulent since there were no advancement courses and it was difficult to recruit since the RNR's role had not been defined.

"Finally, with the Reserve Forces Act 1996 the role was clearly stated and the RNR could work clearly with the Fleet. For the first time, Ratings could be mobilised 'if war-like operations were in force'. Previously, this only applied to Officers and to mobilise Ratings you needed either 'actual attack on the UK' or 'general war'. At the present moment all of this is in force because of the problem of Iraq. Mobilisation is under way."

Thank you Cedric.

Another change must be noted. The name Mersey Division was removed in 1996 and the result was that HMS Eaglet did not have a crest! The new crest has the colours of the Atlantic Star denoting the links with the Battle of the Atlantic. It shows a blue eagle holding the RM green anchor out of the water. Since the move to the new headquarters the redesigned Eaglet crest has received approval.

In March 2000 Commander Cedric Loughran, RD, RNR, was appointed Commanding Officer of HMS Eaglet. He recalls his memories. "I never felt prouder than serving in the ship's company as the Commanding Officer. I was to spend much time in raising the profile of Eaglet." Cedric Loughran was made Deputy Director of Amphibious Warfare and head of the General Service Seaman Ratings in September 2002. Little did he know that the Sub-Specialisation he was asked to refrain from exercising would be given him to head some fifteen years later.

Let's go back.

Cedric Loughran joined the RNR as a Seaman in 1975 at HMS President. At the Admiral Commanding Reserves inspection at the Temple in 1975 he was unfortunate in having his swallowtail flowing ribbons foreshortened by an enthusiastic GI. This was in the far off hazy days of seven horizontal creases in the bell bottom trouser. Sea time was undertaken in Fittleton and Crofton.

On joining the Merchant Navy as a Junior Engineer in 1976 he was informed that he would have to be discharged from the RNR. In time he was commissioned as an Engineering Officer and came home to Eaglet as a Probationary Acting Sub-Lieutenant. Under the guidance of that wonderful character Lieutenant-Commander Mike Barnes he was thrust into the Naval Control of Shipping Branch. The Engineering Branch was closed in 1984 and it was 'goodbye or transfer to NCS'.

His sea time was undertaken on Fisheries Protection Duties out of Rosyth in HMS Stubbington, fresh from refit, where on practising the deployment and operation of the magnetic loop, the winch failed. The Captain asked Loughran 'to attempt' to fix the winch. He was told that the task was impossible, beyond his capabilities and that of PO Greeny. By luck and a bit of judgement the job was done, Loughran was reincarnated as Isambard Kingdom Brunel and he offered thanks to God for the Merchant Navy.

A small excursion was made into the mysterious world of Amphibious Warfare during Exercise Purple Warrior. Shortly after it was explained in colour to Cedric that he was a NCS officer and should not stray into other realms. "Back in your box, boy!" He was not to be boxed for long.

The 1994 cut in the RNR saw a large transfer out of NCS, either to the retired list or other Branches. Cedric was fortunate in being transferred to Amphibious Warfare! Exercises were long and hard and he quickly progressed from Assistant Senior Naval Officer to SNO. He served on passenger ships, dock vessels and RO-RO ferries.

There are at present around three hundred reservists serving in Eaglet, 23 of them attend the Menai satellite unit in North Wales. The Menai Unit was established in 2001 and in Llandudno where ratings train as Communicators after completing their new Entry Training.

Commodore J.E.V. Madgewick, OBE, RN.

Here is a 'thumbnail' sketch of the work achieved in the establishment in Brunswick Dock.

This splendid new building is home to a number of units, including:

Naval Regional Officer Northern England, who is responsible for naval representation in the area bounded by the Dee-Humber line and the Scottish border, and including the Isle of Man. The

NRONE is appointed by the RN to handle 'Grey Ships' and he represents the Royal Navy in his area. He is not attached to Eaglet.

HMS Eaglet is the Royal Naval Reserve unit in the north west of England, together with its sub-unit at Llandudno (Menai Division).

RMR Merseyside, the Royal Marines Reserve unit on Merseyside, which also has sub-units in Manchester and Birmingham.

University RN Units for both Liverpool and Lancaster, and Manchester and Salford Universities, base their ships HMS Charger and HMS Biter at the RNHQ. The Liverpool URNU is also accommodated in RNHQ Merseyside.

Sea Cadets. The Headquarters of the 65 Sea Cadet Units in the north west of England is located in the RNHQ Merseyside.

The co-location of all these units in a new, purpose-built establishment has been highly successful. With appropriate Messes, galley, stores and a communications office, not to mention a well-equipped fitness centre, the building is well suited for its new role. It has also proven most flexible, able to provide accommodation and facilities for large numbers of Service fire-fighters during the national strike in 2002-03. And it does not simply deal with recruiting and training on a daily basis. There is very much a link with operations, as evinced by the recent requirement to mobilise many RNR and RMR personnel for a potential operational role in the Middle East. In short, RNHQ Merseyside has developed into a well-recognised and respected Liverpool landmark.

Eaglet's catchment area is large, with officers in particular travelling from Yorkshire, Wales and Cumbria as well as from the outer reaches of Cheshire and Lancashire. In September 2002 twelve of the ship's company were away serving on FTRS (Full time Reserve Service). Nowadays many of our young recruits, having sampled the naval life with the Reserve, go on to join the Royal Navy.

Junior Rates Mess.

A little must be said about the Naval Control of Shipping (NCS). Most of this information was provided by Lieutenant-Commander Peter Trevalion, RD*, RNR. Anyone with any knowledge of the last world war will have realised that this country depends upon trade to survive. Today 94% of our trade goes by sea ... this figure always surprises people! Over many centuries in all seafaring nations it has been acknowledged that merchant ships sailing in groups and escorted by warships have a better chance of survival. At the end of the 17th century the method was made compulsory for all British ocean-going vessels by Parliament. This was not enforced in the First World War until April 1917, but as the passenger liner Athenia was sunk on the first day of World War Two without warning, the convoy system was immediately put into operation. Initially control was centered on Plymouth and then transferred to Liverpool and HMS Eaglet. This control centre was established as the Western

Approaches Command and was based mainly in Derby House. The Command was responsible for assembling convoys, routeing, diverting and controlling all convoys and independently sailed merchant ships, and for directing escorts and anti-U-boat forces. Over 10,000 personnel were involved.

Liverpool became the major convoy port for the Atlantic trade, especially from America and Canada, receiving over 1,000 convoys during the war. Another shore base, called HMS Mersey, was established in 1940 near the docks in the David Lewis Northern Hospital. It was here that merchant seamen were transferred into the Royal Navy to train as gunnery crews on board Defensively Equipped Merchant Ships (DEMS). Towards the end of the war it was moved to Neston and the old building was quickly taken over by squatters ... mothers and children were desperate for a place to live as whole areas of the city had been totally bombed.

At the end of the war the control was passed to the Reserves, and NCS became a priority objective of HMS Eaglet. This activity has been maintained and every year there is a defence exercise including communication procedures, convoy assembly, routeing, diversions, convoy station keeping and signal publications. It is a major operation. Generally over 100 ships are visited and briefed, 'paper' convoys are assembled, Exercise Sailing Order Folios prepared for selected ships with details of communication instructions, times of sailing, convoy assembly points, station keeping orders, routes, convoy equipment, etc. Obviously links with Civil Authorities are another priority.

National Control of Shipping is now contained in two Branches.

The first Branch (AWNIS) is the Allied World-Wide Navigational Information System. The aim is 'To provide a complete navigational Safety Information Service for both Military Commands and Civil Shipping in an area of conflict'. This is ideally suited for the RNR.

The second Branch (NCAGS ... pronounced Enn-kags) is Naval Co-operation and Guidance for Shipping. In the 80's there was a closure of RNR Units, and there followed in 1994 the disbanding of the RNXS (Royal Naval Auxiliary Service) and a reduction in NCS Officer strength to less than one hundred. As a result of the Reserve Forces Act 1996 small teams can be utilised at points of conflict. A team went to Sierra Leone in 2001 and since October 2001 there is a permanent presence in the Gulf. The contribution of the Reserves has been significant and well-respected both by the RN and the merchant shipping community.

Handing over command.

Commander Christine Bradford was the first lady to assume command of the Division. The date was 29th November 2002. She writes: 'HMS Eaglet remains a vibrant unit with strong local links. Liverpool Reservists are still today as keen and as proud as were those who met on board in January 1904 to volunteer to join the Reserve for the first time. Eaglet is the Royal Navy in the North West of England.'

The RNR has altered dramatically over the years in response to the changing needs of defence. One factor has remained ... the proud tradition of training volunteer civilians from all walks of life as seafarers, serving alongside regular counterparts in peace and in war. These civilians must be brought to a common standard of fitness and knowledge and that is firmly achieved in the RTCs (Reserve Training Centres) such as Eaglet.

Recruiting is the responsibility of each unit and each New Entry person has to pass out at HMS Raleigh. The physical standards are those required by the RN ... a swimming test, a 2.4 km run and a variety of gym exercises. General training covers a wide range of naval skills and knowledge ... ship recognition, naval routine, branches and ranks are learnt, supplemented by practical training in drill, boat work, first aid and basic fire fighting.

Most RNR Officers will start as New Entries. The first hurdle is the Admiralty Interview Board ... the same Board as for regular RN selection! There follows a heavy programme of training and study that culminates in the examination of the Fleet Board. Time at sea is required as well as a course at Dartmouth, again in line with the regular RN Officer.

Ten small satellite units extend the recruiting range and create a Naval presence over a larger area. National Training Officers supplement the expertise of the RTCs and make better use of resources. The Officer Programme for Undergraduate Students (OPUS) provides a six-week concentrated course at Portsmouth during the summer vacations. This has proved to be highly successful. Today's RNR is probably more closely integrated with the Royal Navy than at any other time in the Naval Reserves' peacetime history.

At the time of writing, 'Eaglet has personnel on board Ark Royal, Merchant Ships and Royal Fleet Auxiliary vessels. Personnel are ashore at PJHQ (Permanent Joint Head Quarters) and at Andover. Medics are due to deploy to the 34 Field Hospital and the Primary Casualty Receiving Ship. Eaglet currently is providing the most personnel of the fourteen RTCs (approximately 11% of all mobilisees).' At present ten Officers, two Senior Rates and nineteen Junior Rates are involved in the Iraq emergency.

The final Battle of the Atlantic Commemorative Service, as we know it, will once again be arranged on behalf of the Royal Navy by Eaglet. It is the 60th Anniversary. It is expected that there will be a full Cathedral and 2,000 veterans in attendance. The programme is full ... a Royal Navy Ship will be moored off Albert Dock, visiting Navy Ships will be berthed in Canning Dock and open to the public, there will be a fly-past of the Royal Navy Historic Flight of a Fairey Swordfish and other aircraft

Today there are fourteen RNR Units all re-categorised as Reserve Training Centres.

Asford	HMS Ferret
Barry	HMS Cambria
Belfast	HMS Caroline
Birmingham	HMS Forward
Bristol	HMS Flying Fox
Devonport	HMS Vivid
Gateshead	HMS Calliope
Greenock	HMS Dalriada
Liverpool	HMS Eaglet

London   HMS President
Northwood   HMS Wildfire
Nottingham   HMS Sherwood
Rosyth   HMS Scotia
HMS Alfred established at Whale Island.

Prince Michael of Kent visited HMS Eaglet on 14th June 2000 and is seen looking at the signature in the Wardroom Mess visitors' book of his mother, Princess Marina, who visited Eaglet on 23rd April 1941. He is seen with Commander C.J. Arthurs, RD, JP, RNR, (Commanding Officer Eaglet 1997 - 2000) and Lieutenant-Commander CMP Bradford, RNR, First Lieutenant Eaglet 1999 - 2002, the present Captain.

HRH the Prince Michael of Kent, KCVO, is the honorary Commodore of the Royal Naval Reserve and sends this message to the Reservists.

"I am very proud of my connection with the Royal Naval Reserve and in the nine years I have been Honorary Commodore, I have always been impressed by the professionalism and good humour of all its people. I hope that they will enjoy celebrating the many achievements of our first centennium. May everyone in the Royal Naval Reserve continue to serve with pride and distinction for many years to come."

HMS EAGLET IS THE ROYAL NAVY IN THE NORTH WEST OF ENGLAND

Eaglet

Mersey Division RNR - HMS EAGLET

Commanding Officers

1904 - 1911   Comander the Earl of Lathom
1911 - 1914   Commander Sir Richard Williams
                Bulkeley, Bart

World War One - Base Ship for Liverpool

1914 - 1920   Commander Sir H Mainwairing, Bart
1920 - 1930   Captain W Maples, VD, ADC
1930 - 1939   Captain E Elgood, OBE, VD

World War Two - Flagship Western Approaches Command

1946 - 1954   Captain E N Wood, DSC, VRD
1954 - 1957   Captain A V Turner, DSC, VRD, DL
1957 - 1961   Captain B Smith, VRD
1961 - 1964   Captain A Letty, DSO,DSC, VRD, DL
1964 - 1966   Captain G N Sellers, VRD, ADC
1966 - 1969   Captain H T Duffy, MBE, VRD, DL
1969 - 1972   Captain R Humphreys Jones, VRD*
1972 - 1976   Captain J T Jones, VRD*, DL
1976 - 1979   Captain R M Eddleston, RD
1979 - 1982   Captain I A W Berry, RD*
1982 - 1985   Captain F K Bennett, RD*, ADC
1985 - 1988   Captain R H Walker, RD*
1988   Commander A R Williams, RD*
1989 - 1992   Commander T Cunningham, RD*

1992 - 1994	Commander P A Houghton, RD*
1994 - 1997	Commander F J C Bradshaw, LVO
1997 - 2000	Commander C J Arthurs, RD, JP
2000 - 2003	Commander C G Loughran, RD
2003	Commander C M P Bradford, RNR

Naval Regional Officers

Admiralty Regional Officers - North West Region

1945	Engineer Rear Admiral L Robins, OBE
1945 - 1948	Engineer Captain J Pattinson, RN
1948 - 1962	Captain I A P Macintyre, CB, CBE, DSO, RN
1962 - 1964	Captain H H R Moore, DSC, RN

Naval Regional Officers - Midland and North West Region

1965 - 1974	Captain H H R Moore, DSC, RN
1974 - 1979	Captain J Bishop, RN
1980	Captain D T McKeown, RN
1981 - 1986	Captain R D Franklin, CBE, RN
1986 - 1994	Captain H Mucklow, RN

Naval Regional Officers - Northern England

1994	Captain C M J Carson, RN
1994 - 1996	Captain P R Sutermeister, RN
1996 - 2000	Commodore P R Sutermeister, RN
2000	Commodore J E V Madgewick, OBE, RN

Naval Liaison Officers - Liverpool

1946 - 1949	Commander C A N Chatwin, DSO, RN
1949 - 1951	Commander E R Condor, DSO, DSC, RN
1951 - 1953	Commander A M MaKillop, DSC*, RN
1953 - 1956	Commander M Thornton, DSO, DSC*, RN
1956 - 1958	Commander W A Juniper, DSO, DSC, RN
1958 - 1961	Commander D J Beckley, DSO, DSC, RN
1961 - 1964	Commander J P Somervaille, RN
1964 - 1969	Commander B G O'Neill, OBE, DSC, RN
1969 - 1971	Commander J D Baker, RN
1971 - 1974	Commander R H Reynolds, DSC, AFC, AFRAeS, RN
1974 - 1977	Commander P F V Stigant, RN
1977 - 1982	Commander G D H Sample, OBE, DSC, RN

LIQUEUR BRANDY

Chapter Eleven

THE OLD AND BOLD
The Sea Urchins

What is a Sea Urchin? The dictionary helps a little. 'Any echinoderm of the class Echinoidea, such as Echinus esculentus, typically having a globular body enclosed in a rigid spiny test (shell) and occurring in shallow marine waters.' That interprets into 'Doing nothing very much, putting on weight and keeping one's feet on the ground for as long as possible'. With regret, in our brand of Sea Urchins there was a downward evolution of the species for some years, entitled 'sea slugs'. They tended to head for the nearest hostelry after the monthly 'do' and basically loitered with no intent. The least said about them the better as they have now disappeared from sight. Actually they really did nothing and, naturally, have left no trace of their nebulous lack of activities. If you are interested, a sea slug is 'a shell-less marine gastropod of the order of Nudibranchia.' You must surely have been educated by this paragraph!

There can be no better introduction to the Royal Naval Reserve Officers' Club (Sea Urchins) Liverpool than to reproduce the letter sent to the Private Secretary of HRH The Duke of Edinburgh inviting him to the 61st Anniversary of the foundation of the Club. The President that year was Lieutenant M.D. Wright, TD, RNR.

'The Club was founded in 1921 to promote contact between the Royal Naval Reserve Officers, and to foster their interests and traditions. Membership is confined to all RNR and RN Officers, Active or Retired, including those who have held temporary commissions in wartime. It also includes a small proportion (10%) of gentlemen who have a keen interest in the aims and objects of the Club and nearly always have a maritime interest.

'Last year was the 60th Anniversary of the foundation of the Club and we did ask the Duke of Edinburgh to be our guest speaker. He was, however, unable to accept our invitation because of his other commitments, and we would like to repeat the invitation this year which has been designated the Year of the Mariner, and in which it might be considered that a visit to Liverpool would be appropriate.'

The exceedingly courteous reply was 'I very much regret...'

However, the guest speaker in Eaglet at the Anniversary Annual Dinner on 3rd November 1982 was Captain N.J. Barker, CBE, RN. It was an inspired choice. Captain Barker's father was killed in 1940, whilst in command of HMS Ardent during an action against the German Battle Cruisers Scharnhorst and Gneisenau.

Here is exactly what happened that night ... more or less.

The passengers disembarking from the Euston to Lime Street Inter City Express gazed with interest and admiration at the gleaming open topped vintage, 1926, Blue Badge Bentley which awaited the arrival of a VIP at platform eight on a clear November afternoon, some five months after the Falklands War. Standing guard alongside this marvellous relic of a by-gone age were its owner, Lieutenant Matt Wright, TD, RNR, and Lieutenant-Commander Harry Harley, RN, a fellow Sea Urchin and Associate of the Awaited VIP. They are responsible for this particular tale.

A beaming smile above an immaculate Crombie overcoat heralded the arrival of Captain Nick Barker, RN, Commanding Officer of H.M.S. Endurance. With eagerness and an agility which belied his years, Captain Barker climbed into this unique 'staff car' and, sitting alongside Matt, he clearly enjoyed the sedate drive past many admiring onlookers as Matt navigated a circuitous route to the Atlantic Tower Hotel.

That evening after dinner at HMS Eaglet, Captain Barker delivered a truly remarkable speech to more than ninety enthralled Sea Urchins. After accepting the invitation, Captain Barker had asked Harry Harley if the 'venue was suitable for the use of a slide projector'. That evening the Drill Deck had been duly prepared.

In response to President Matt Wright's introduction, Captain Barker asked that any member of the 'media world' at the dinner treat his speech as being 'off the record'. Walking from the top table he took up station alongside the projector and proceeded to reveal his first hand experiences when commanding HMS Endurance, before, during and after the Falklands War.

Warming to his subject and clearly noting the vivid interest of the Sea Urchins, Barker ripped away the curtains of secrecy hiding political bungling, mismanaged diplomacy and extremely inept misreading of sound intelligence reports. A natural born mimic and raconteur, Nick Barker regaled the Sea Urchins with a series of colourful anecdotes, each one seemingly accompanied by an equally colourful slide. An example was Scott of the Antarctic ... an accident prone Able Seaman Scott who lost control of his motorised snow mobile and plunged from a great height into the Antarctic Ocean. Against all odds he escaped death by hypothermia! And another story. The Commanding Officer of the Argentine Submarine Sante Fe, when questioned after being taken prisoner after the action at Grytviken on South Georgia, was asked why he had not torpedoed HMS Endurance just one week earlier. He had replied, "How could I do such a thing when you had entertained us at such a wonderful party last March!"

Ministry officials, some 15,000 miles distant, had refused to accept Nick Barker's appreciation of the situation whilst Endurance held ASDIC contact on the Sant Fe.

There were many, many more such revelations.

Captain Barker addressed the Sea Urchins for some 45 minutes and it passed all too swiftly. As he walked back to regain his top table seat the Liverpool Sea Urchins arose as one and displayed their appreciation with an unprecedented standing ovation. It was great night in Sea Urchin history.

Captain Nicholas Barker, having severely and courageously shaken the British Establishment to its self-righteous, invincibility-riddled roots, had noted how his successful Royal Navy career had been side tracked accordingly, and he finally resigned from the Royal Navy in 1988.

Having survived the Falklands War, and the many bureaucratic battles that followed, he sadly lost his final fight with cancer and died in 1998.

There is much to remember.

The details of the birth of the Sea Urchins seem to be lost in time, but some memories remain. The president in 1927 was no light-weight. The lot fell upon Commodore Sir Bertram F. Hayes, KCMG, DSO, RD, RNR. At that time the Club met for weekly luncheons and boasted a membership of three hundred and nine. The outgoing president was Commander E.C. Roden and his parting words are recorded. "After the war, when I came ashore, I dug myself down on an office stool and forgot that I was a Royal Naval Reserve Officer, and it was the beginning of the Club that made me realise my responsibilities as an officer in the RNR. It is our duty to do all that we can to foster that brotherly feeling which had carried us through the war. That is the spirit that will carry this Club through to its high aims."

To this day we have a fascinating centre-piece on the dining table. It was presented to the Club in January 1932 by Captain S.S. Richardson, OBE, RD, our first President. The case and base were made from the timber of War Dame (then Delambre), the steps made of timber from HMS Conway and HMS Eagle. Small guns were made from the Eagle and are enclosed by stanchions and chains made from a metal bolt of HMS Clarence (the bolt was rescued from the river when Clarence was burned out in 1899). The trophy was made by John Scoberg, a carpenter from the Lamport and Holt Line.

The second presentation that night was the builder's brass name-plate of the Cunard liner Carmania from Commander J.C. Barr, on behalf of the company. Captain G. Davey, the President, said that Captain Barr had also offered to present a framed plan or chart of the action in which the Carmania under his command had fought the Cap Trafalgar. That action was the first between two merchantmen for over one hundred years.

Cap Trafalgar was sunk after a battle of one hour and forty-six minutes. Carmania had been hit by seventy-nine shells and her deck was in ruins. Escorted by Cornwall and Macedonia the stricken vessel reached Gibraltar for repairs, but eight weeks later she was back on patrol off Lisbon. Commander 'Smokey' Barr was given a CB and invalided home. He went on to command the troopships Mauretania, Saxonia and Carpathia. Captain Barr retired as Senior Commodore of the Cunard Line in 1916 and died in 1937.

In 1933 the Club held its luncheons in the Liverpool Constitutional Club. The president was Captain C. Edwards, DSO, RD, RNR. Weekly lunches continued and membership was two hundred and seventy-five. It had been a busy year in spite of troubled times in the shipping industry. Shooting, golf, visits to ships, a presentation by the Ship Model Society, Remembrance Ceremonies of Zeebrugge, Nelson Day and Armistice Day, the Annual Ball at the Adelphi, reciprocal visits to Southampton Master Mariners' Club (The Cachelots), the list was long. A Blue Ensign was presented to the Honorary Chaplain, Rev. S. Bradford, BA, RN, for his church during a ceremony and service held at Whiston Parish Church. The Sea Urchins were flourishing.

In the fifth year of the Second World War there was ample evidence of resilience. At the Club Annual Dinner, the loyal toast was followed by 'Absent members, particularly those in enemy hands'. The possessions were all intact and the Club was ready with funds, equipment and organisation for any expansion which members, present and future, might decide upon, when Germany was defeated and some, at least, of the members now absent on active service were demobilised. The past year had, not only been a victorious one for the Allies, but a successful one for the Club.

It would be possible to continue with these 'snap-shot' nostalgic memories down the years to the present time. My own thoughts go back to being elected Chaplain in 1962 and President in 1976, but such 'lamp swinging' is better behind closed doors and continued well into the small-hours.

Vice-Admiral Sir P.E.C. Berger, FO Plymouth,
Lieutenant-Commander David Knight, RN
Captain the Earl of Derby and Captain Bob Eddleston, RNR
Sea Urchins Dinner, 1979.

Today there are monthly Club Luncheons Meetings on board HMS Eaglet, an Annual Dinner in Eaglet, a Theatre Evening, a Ladies Dinner and a Golf Competition. Times have certainly changed, but the aims remain ... to foster the interests, prestige, status and traditions of the Royal Naval Reserves.

Much of the material in this book has been provided by the Sea Urchins and in most cases it has been as difficult as drawing teeth. The 'Silent Navy' is aptly named. However, I must record that with a little lubrication most lamps swing exceedingly well.

Royal Naval Reserve Officers Club (Sea Urchins)

Presidents

1921 - 1922	Captain S S Richardson, OBE, RD
1923	Captain J W Harris
1924	Commodore C A Bartlett, CB, CBE, RD
1925	Captain H J Temperley Grey, RD
1926	Commander E C Roden, RD
1927	Commodore Sir Bertram Hayes, KCMG, DSO, RD
1928	Lieutenant-Commander J Dobson
1929	Captain F E Storey, RD
1930	Commander M G Douglas, RD
1931	Commander G Davey, RD
1932	Captain C Edwards, DSO, RD
1933	Captain S S Fulford, RD
1934	Captain J W Williams, DSO, RD
1935	Commander M Creswell, DSO, RD
1936	Captain S S Richardson, OBE, RD
1937	Lieutenant-Commander J W Binks, RD
1938	Commander J L May
1939	Lieutenant-Commander C Douglas Lane
1940 - 1946	Engineer Captain W J Willett Bruce, OBE, RD
1947 - 1948	Captain H J Giles, OBE, RD
1949 - 1950	Commander F Tweedie, DSC, RD
1951	Lieutenant-Commander F C Hooper
1952	Captain A E Webster, DSO
1953 - 1954	Captain R V E Case, DSO, DSC, RD
1955	Commodore R P Galer, CBE, RD, RNR
1956	Lieutenant-Commander A H Smith, RD
1957	Commander L H Neal, OBE, RD

1958	Commander G P Billot, DSO, RD
1959	Lieutenant-Commander L C Hill, OBE, DSC. RD, RNR
1960	Captain E B Clark, RD, RNR
1961	Captain A Letty, DSO, DSC, RD, RNR
1962	Captain J H Wright, RD, RNR
1963	Captain J B Wright, OBE, RD, RNR
1964	Captain W R Colbeck, RNR
1965	Commander R B G Woolatt, RD, RNR
1966	Lieutenant-Commander F G Mugford, RNR
1967	Lieutenant-Commander R T Wilcox, RNR
1968	Lieutenant E Roberts, RNR
1969	Lieutenant-Commander J B Cox, RN
1970	Captain H T Duffy, MBE, VRD, DL, RNR
1971	Lieutenant-Commander R E Pickering, VRD, RNR
1972	Commander B G O'Neil, OBE, DSC, RN
1973	Captain E R Wildermuth
1974	Captain R Humphreys Jones, VRD*, RNR
1975	Lieutenant-Commander W A Taylor, DSC, RN
1976	Reverend R A Evans, BA, RNR
1977	Lieutenant-Commander R D Thomas, RD, RNR
1978	Captain F W Skutil, CBE, RNN
1979	Lieutenant-Commander D J Knight, RN
1980	Lieutenant-Commander B Parr, RD, RNR
1981	Lieutenant-Commander D H Campbell, RD, RNR
1982	Lieutenant M D Wright, TD, RNR
1983	Lieutenant-Commander P L Kemp, BA, RNR
1984	Commander R G Milles, VRD*, RNR
1985	Lieutenant-Commander T Abell, VRD, RNR
1986	Lieutenant-Commander A J Parks, RN
1987	Commander P R Watters, RD*, RNR

1988	Lieutenant C H Jeans, RNR
1989	Lieutenant-Commander E J Billington, RD*, DL, RNR
1990	Lieutenant Commander W J J Whetnall, RD, RNR
1991	Commander G D H Sample, OBE, DSC, RN
1992	Lieutenant-Commander M J Barnes,, RD, RNR
1993	Lieutenant-Commander D H Allen, RN
1994	Lieutenant R G Loram, RN
1995	Commodore R H Walker, RD**, RNR
1996	Major I R T Uzzell, RD, RMR
1997	Lieutenant P D Bird, RNR
1998	Commander M R Morgan, RN
1999	Lieutenant-Commander D F X Marks, RN
2000	Captain J Cosker, MN
2001	Commander H G Harley, RN
2002	First Officer L M F Peffers, RD, WRNR
2003	Lieutenant-Commander L G Martindale, RNR

CHAMPAGNE

Chapter Twelve

TODAY
2003

The first weekend in May marked the 60th Anniversary Celebration of the Battle of the Atlantic. The Northwest remembered its heritage and gave thanks for those whose endeavours so long ago ensured the final victory.

At a Dinner in the Merseyside Maritime Museum in aid of the King George's Fund for Sailors - the Seafarers Charity - Captain J. Colin Lee, OBE, C StJ, DL, proposed the toast to the Veterans of the Battle. Excerpts from his speech summed up the wonder of that long weekend.

'I am delighted to see so many Veterans here this evening ... so many medals, not only the coveted Atlantic Star, but the Russian Convoy Medals. It was the most complex naval battle in history, and one which, save for the heroism of the RN, MN, RAF and the Army, we could have lost. The Battle began on 3rd September 1939 with the sinking of the Donaldson Liner Athenia only nine hours after war had been declared and the conflict ended on the 7th May 1945.

'Winston Churchill used to read Rudyard Kipling's verse to keep his mind on the seriousness of the situation.

'For the bread that you eat and the biscuits you nibble,
The sweets that you suck and the joints that you carve,
They are brought to you daily by all us big steamers,
And if anyone hinders our coming - you'll starve.'
If it were not for you Veterans, we could easily have starved.'

Colin spoke for well over half and hour and we listened to every word.

'For those of us who did not take part it is impossible to imagine the fear and horror of it all. To see a tanker with high octane fuel torpedoed, with men, that is if they were not killed instantly, jumping into the water only to be burned to death when the water around the sinking ship became a raging inferno.

'To see a ship carrying iron ore disappear with all hands within seconds of being hit and that heart breaking agony of sailing through men in the water.

'And when not battling with U-boats, large surface ships, and mines sown around the major UK ports, there was the other enemy ... the cruel sea.

'The men of the Merchant Navy were learning to work with the men of the Royal Navy ... or was it the other way round? Station keeping had improved immensely, the MAC ships (Merchant Aircraft Carriers) had come on stream, these were grain ships with a 'lid on' or flight deck, grain in the holds and aircraft on deck. Ships flying the Red Ensign ... they had RN and MN crews with Fleet Air Arm pilots, and the Army as members of DEMS, the Maritime Royal Artillery (Churchill's 'sharpshooters').

'And then there were the people of Merseyside. They had stood up to the Blitz and the hardships it brought. But the worst fear was to see a telegram boy on his bike and praying that he would not stop at their house with that buff coloured envelope, marked OHMS, with its chilling message ... The Admiralty regrets to inform. These were terrifying years

'29,000 German submariners lost their lives, our Merchant Navy lost 30,000 and these figures are in the Battle of the Atlantic alone. The words of that lovely anthem that we will hear in the Cathedral on Sunday by Edward Elgar spring to mind ... "We will remember them."

'To those veterans of the Battle of the Atlantic with us this evening and to those unable to be with us, we owe a great debt of gratitude. Thank you.'

There was a moment of complete silence as Captain Colin Lee finished his speech. No more words were needed.

Commander Harry Harley, President of No. 10 Area RNA, wrote in the Area's magazine, Vanguard.

'As a seafaring nation we were ill prepared for the Battle of the Atlantic. Yet again, the so called 'great and the good' failed in their duty. Lord knows, they were warned enough. "... if our Fleet is overpowered and our ports blockaded, we would get no food and would have to surrender." Clear enough? Quite pithy really. Well, Shipmates, that wasn't Winston in the thirties ... it was Gladstone, speaking in Liverpool Town Hall in 1904!

'The lack of political will created fearful conditions for those in peril on the sea. The Battle of the Atlantic fighters, those who gave their lives and those who survived, are true heroes.'Commander Cedric Arthurs did much to organise the Service in the Anglican Cathedral. HMS Eaglet was at the heart of the task. Cedric writes: 'The past sixty years of the anniversary has had its effect on Eaglet, Liverpool and individuals.

'For Eaglet, the BOA Service has provided pride in a job well done, attempted to bridge the gap between the RN and the MN and honoured those who have gone before us.

'For the City, it had confirmed and helped continue our Maritime heritage whilst showing that it is not only St Paul's and the Abbey that can mastermind complex ceremonial events.

'For individuals, a time of remembrance with gratitude to those who ensured our freedom. For me, gratitude to my father who, as a 'non-combatant' MN Officer, sailed the Atlantic Convoys throughout WWII and survived several sinkings to enable me to be born. The Atlantic Star was hard earned indeed.'

The presence on Merseyside of all our armed forces, with HMS Invincible as the Flagship, was enhanced by ships from Belgium, France, Germany, the Netherlands, Norway, Poland and Russia. Probably, never again will there be such an assembly of vessels to mark the Battle of the Atlantic.

The greatest privilege was to sense the dignity of the Veterans as they marched past at the end of the remarkable service. There were memories of the many thousands who gave their lives for the survival of this country and a quiet pride in what was achieved at such a cost.

'These are mere mortals,
Just plain menfolk,
But at times their strength is supreme,
For they fight and they win their battle,
Nightmares to you if you dream.'
Dick Thomas wrote those lines during the conflict when as a teenager he left his Wirral home and joined the Merchant Navy. There is much to remember.

But what of Eaglet today?

2003 was a momentous year as the reservists were mobilised for the first time since the Korean War and the Suez Affair. This was made possible under the Reserve Forces Act 1996, which enabled reservists to be called up in situations other than direct threat to the homeland and which also gave reservists legal rights in terms of protected employment and pensions. Previously reservists could only be generally mobilised by a Queen's Order in Council.

Initially, 33 Eaglets were called up for the Iraq conflict. These comprised 4 Medical Support Assistants (MSAs) who served in 34 Field Hospital, (the most forward deployed in the Second Gulf War), 4 Communicators, 6 Logisticians, 2 Minewarfare specialists, 4 Amphibious Warfare Officers, (the former CO, Commander Cedric Loughran in HMS Ark Royal, 2 in merchant ships in the Gulf and one in Defence Transport and Movement Agency in Andover). Also 2 officers in the Naval Co-operation and Guidance to Shipping specialisation in the Gulf, 2 Headquarters Operation Officers and one Logistics Officer in the Permanent Joint Headquarters in Northwood and one Lieutenant QUARNNS (Queen Alexandra Royal Naval Nursing Service) in

Cyprus - who stayed until September 2003. The new s..b specialisation of General Service Seamen Reserves (GSSRs) provided seven ratings who acted as SPO teams (Ship's Protection Officers) on various ships. Two of these returned for a further period of mobilisation. In all, by the end of June 4 further ratings were mobilised and five of those who had returned volunteered to undertake a further period of duty. Eaglet's reservists served in Dubai, Bahrain, Iraq and Cyprus, at sea and at home.

RNR Trauma Team.

HMS Eaglet supplied the largest number of RNR personnel mobilised during the war. Thereafter   further personnel were mobilised in order to allow operations to continue during the post-war stabilisation and to relieve RN shortages in other parts of the world. For this to work efficiently a process called 'Intelligent Mobilisation' was employed. This meant that billets were identified and the most suitable candidates were asked about their availability. Where possible, those who most easily were able to take up the duty or those most willing to do so were mobilised. This was indeed an intelligent as well as successful approach to the task of mobilisation.

Leading Wren Medical Support Assistant Gina Ralph at 34 Field Hospital.

The experience for Eaglet mobilisees was a positive one in general terms. Reports received upon their return were fulsome in their praise for the competence, resolve and unfailing good humour with which they carried out their duties.

While reservists were mobilised it fell to those who remained behind to keep close contact with their families and friends and to pass on information as rapidly as possible. The strong family ethos, which is so much part of Eaglet's life, played a vital role in ensuring the families were given both moral support and constant encouragement. Newsletters, personal letters, telephone calls and invitations to events at Eaglet all contributed to this hearts and minds effort and the warmth and pride displayed by reservists towards the families of those mobilised was most impressive. For the CO, Commander Bradford, the most touching part of the

Don't ask!

whole period were those occasions when members of the ship's company phoned on Wednesday evenings from ships or shore bases to say hello, keeping her updated on their progress and sending their regards to the rest of the ship's company. She also received numerous e-mails, and airmail letters and was much impressed by the cheerfulness with which Eaglets described their experiences.

OP TELIC (Gulf War Operation) Families were invited to the sixtieth and final Battle of the Atlantic commemorative service on 4th May 2003. A reception, given by the CO in HMS Eaglet after the service took place in glorious sunshine on the Wardroom bridgewing.

The Families.

It is fitting that the last thoughts in this saga of HMS Eaglet are written by the present Commanding Officer, Christine Bradford, RNR.

"Having taken over command at the end of November 2002 I could not have imagined how different my reserve life would become almost overnight. We were in the throes of Operation FRESCO and the RNHQ was acting as the South Liverpool Fire Station! Each time the firemen came out on strike up to 100 men and women of the Queen's Lancashire Regiment, together with RN personnel, would man up one of the two Green Goddess fire engines and one Breathing Apparatus Response Team vehicle. Together with a police escort they would race off to the scene of the fire. Their accommodation was in classrooms. A catering contractor fed the fire fighters from the galley, the drill deck being used as a mess. With classrooms and drill deck out of use, we had to cancel our drill nights on two occasions.

"As we went into 2003 everyone anticipated mobilisation and indeed the former Commanding Officer, Commander Cedric Loughran, was the first to be mobilised, together with Lieutenant Stuart Wallace from our satellite unit in Llandudno. In the midst of this we were responsible for planning and executing the final Battle of the Atlantic Service, a major undertaking even in an ordinary year. In the event 2,600 people filled the Anglican Cathedral with another 2,000 veterans watching and listening to the service being relayed outside on Queen's Walk. 1,600 veterans took part in a very moving march past after the service. For Eaglet the huge success of this important service was a tremendous achievement.

"In February 2003, Lieutenant-Commander Phillip Russ, the Battle of the Atlantic Officer, had been mobilised. I had arranged for Lieutenant-Commander Simon Ryan (who had returned as an acting commander from Kosovo in the autumn of 2002) to take over as BOA officer in this event. However, almost simultaneously, Simon was also mobilised which left Eaglet with a major problem. I was the only other person with experience as BOA Officer. Several telephone calls to Director Naval Reserves secured permission to recall Commander Cedric Arthurs to active service in the role of Battle of the Atlantic Officer. His immediate response in our time of need is something for which I shall be ever grateful. It enabled me to keep an overview of the event without taking my attention completely away from other matters. These being, amongst others, the RNR 100 events to which we were committed during the first months of 2003.

Leading Seaman (LOGS) Gary Doke with other Eaglets at Wellington Barracks.

"The Centenary Service in Glasgow Cathedral on 8th March was a splendid affair with fifty Eaglets marching in the guard and in platoons from the Cathedral to the Assembly Rooms. Eaglet provided one hundred and fifty personnel for the RNR Centenary Parade and Presentation of the Queen's Colour on Horseguards Parade on Saturday 17th May 2003. Thirteen Eaglets were in the Royal Guard that day - again the greatest numbers from any single unit. Eaglet had many guests in London that day - all strong supporters of the unit. Two receptions were held. The first in Wellington Barracks, at which HRH the Prince of Wales met members of the ship's company that had returned from the Gulf. A second reception was given at the QE2 Conference Centre. The ship's company was accommodated overnight on the 16th May in Woolwich Arsenal after having taken part in the rehearsal on the Friday on Horseguards. The sight of 1,850 reservists marching on to the parade ground with two RM bands, even for the rehearsal and dressed in No. 3s was a sight that no-one who was there will ever forget. The day itself was even more splendid and the rain held off as an added bonus.

"On 18th June a ship's company BBQ was held to welcome back our mobilisees from the Gulf and to recognise the hard work that had gone into the first six months of 2003.

"By this time Liverpool had been successful in its bid to be European City of Culture for 2008 and our own plans for Eaglet's Centenary in 2004 had been finalised. As this book goes to print the provisional list of events for 2004 is printed.

"To take command of the ship for the years 2003 and 2004 was the most momentous experience for me and as the reader looks at this I hope that he can imagine the excitement of every member of the ship's company as we look forward to celebrating our own centenary."

The RDs arrived by post, so they presented each other with the medals.
Commander Christine Bradford and Lieutenant-Commander Nigel Bradford.
Well done, everyone!

*If you have enjoyed this
book turn over the page for other books
by Bob Evans*

DOG COLLAR IN THE DOCKS

Bob Evans £7.00

This book is much more than an autobiography. It is an encounter with almost thirty years of Ships and Seafarers in Liverpool at a time when this great port was adapting itself to the changes and challenges of the tail end of the Twentieth Century. The people are real, the pain and laughter compelling, the story is a good read. Bob Evans is part of that story. His ministry at the Mersey Mission to Seamen and the Royal Naval Reserve placed him at the forefront of waterfront life, as his 'dog collar' seems to open every door.

*Softback - 219pp - A5 -
ISBN: 0 907768 76 8*

MERSEY MARINERS

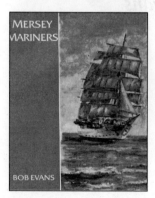

Bob Evans £7.00

The story of seafarers from the last two centuries. From sail to steam, boarding houses and crimps, extortion, poverty, the unforgiving sea; all these are vividly described. The courage of the men, the mix of nationalities and races and the cheapness of life all add colour to the scene. Against all this is the remarkable saga of the charities and welfare organisations that were set up to combat the problems. That story continues. Bob Evans is firmly part of that history and brings it alive for us in this compelling read.

*Softback - 285pp - A5 -
ISBN: 1 901231 05 4*

THE WAY TO LIVERPOOL

Bob Evans £5.00

This book is fun with laughter and tears, wit and wisdom, and tells the true story of life in the valleys of South Wales with magnolia mice and a colliery with no coal to be seen. From suburban Cardiff to an up-market Cathedral in Llandaff, we meet all sorts and conditions of humanity and another mouse. Then Bob Evans came to Liverpool and this autobiography is about that journey.

Soft back 159 pp - A5 - Illustrated.

ISBN 1 901231 14 3

THE TRAINING SHIPS OF LIVERPOOL

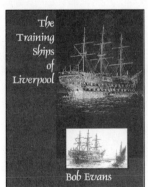

Bob Evans £7.00

The basic aim was the training of young lads. H.M.S. Conway was the officers' training ship and lay a little south of Rock Ferry Pier. The Akbar, a Protestant reformatory vessel, sat between Eastham and Rock Ferry. Next in line was Indefatigable, an old sailing frigate, housing orphaned sons of seamen of good standing. Life was really tough, but the great hardships of the reformatory ships were better than the streets of Liverpool. Bob Evans is again firmly part of this history. It is the story of Liverpool seafaring.

Softback - 205pp - A5 -
ISBN: 1 901231 31 3